Electric Rhetoric

Digital Communication
Edward Barrett, editor

The Nurnberg Funnel: Designing Minimalist Instruction for Practical Computer Skill, John M. Carroll, 1990

Hypermedia and Literary Studies, edited by Paul Delany and George P. Landow, 1991

Rhetoric, Innovation, Technology: Case Studies of Technical Communication in Technology Transfers, Stephen Doheny-Farina, 1992

Sociomedia: Multimedia, Hypermedia, and the Social Construction of Knowledge, edited by Edward Barrett, 1992

The Digital Word: Text-Based Computing in the Humanities, edited by George P. Landow and Paul Delany, 1993

Contextual Media: Multimedia and Interpretation, edited by Edward Barrett and Marie Redmond, 1995

High Noon on the Electronic Frontier, Peter Ludlow, 1996

Forward through the Rearview Mirror: Reflections on and by Marshall McLuhan, edited by Paul Benedetti and Nancy DeHart, 1997

From Web to Workplace: Designing Open Hypermedia Systems, Kaj Grønbæk and Randall H. Trigg, 1999

Electric Rhetoric: Classical Rhetoric, Oralism, and a New Literacy, Kathleen E. Welch, 1999

Electric Rhetoric

Classical Rhetoric, Oralism, and a New Literacy

Kathleen E. Welch

The MIT Press
Cambridge, Massachusetts
London, England

© 1999 Massachusetts Institute of Technology

All rights reserved. No part of this book may be reproduced in any form by any electronic or mechanical means (including photocopying, recording, and information storage and retrieval) without permission in writing from the publisher.

This book was set in Sabon by Asco Typesetters, Hong Kong, and was printed and bound in the United States of America.

First printing, 1999.

Library of Congress Cataloging-in-Publication Data

Welch, Kathleen E.
  Electric rhetoric : classical rhetoric, oralism, and a new literacy / Kathleen E. Welch.
      p.   cm. — (Digital communication)
  Includes bibliographical references and index.
  ISBN 0-262-23202-2 (hc : alk. paper)
  1. Rhetoric—Data processing. 2. Computers and literacy. 3. Rhetoric—Study and teaching—Audio-visual aids. 4. Literacy—Study and teaching—Audio-visual aids. I. Title. II. Series.
P301.5.D37W45   1999
302.2′244′01—dc21   98-43752
                                                                    CIP

It is time for the humanities disciplines to establish our cognitive jurisdiction over the communications revolution.

Gregory Ulmer, *Teletheory: Grammatology in the Age of Video*

For my husband, Howard Bluestein

mea gaudia narret …
non ego signatis quicquam mandare tabellis,
me legat ut nemo quam meus ante, velim

Sulpicia

Contents

Series Foreword   xi

Foreword   xiii

Acknowledgments   xv

I Classical Greek Literacy and the Spoken Word   1

1 Introduction: Screen Literacy in Rhetoric and Composition
   Studies   3

2 An Isocratic Literacy Theory: An Alternative Rhetoric of Oral/Aural
   Articulation   29

3 Disciplining Isocrates   75

II Logos Performers, Screen Sophism, and the Rhetorical Turn   99

4 Next Rhetoric   101

5 Technologies of Electric Rhetoric   137

6 Screen Rhetoric: Sophistic Logos Performers and Electric
   Rhetoric   191

Appendix: Excerpt from the *Origin Myth of Acoma and Other Records*,
recorded by Matthew W. Stirling   211

References   223

Index   247

Series Foreword

Digital communication is one of the most exciting, rapidly expanding fields of study and practice throughout the world, as witnessed by the increasing number of Web sites and users of the Internet, as well as publication and use of multimedia CD-ROM titles in schools, homes, and corporate environments. In addition, Web and multimedia publications have created a vast secondary literature of scholarly analysis in a range of subject areas. Professional societies and degree-granting programs devoted to digital communication have steadily increased. And the language and concepts of digital life have become central in popular culture. In cyberspace the roles of writer and audience are no longer static but dynamic; the concept of text is no longer fixed but fluid. Computational technology has delivered us a powerful tool for the creation, presentation, exchange, and annotation of a text (in words, images, video, and audio)—so powerful that we speak in terms of transparent and seamless information environments that integrate all media.

We are witnessing a profound revolution in communication and learning in a post-Gutenberg world. The MIT Press series on Digital Communication will present advanced research into all aspects of this revolutionary change in our forms of expression, thought, and being. This research will be published in traditional book format or as Web sites or multimedia CD-ROM titles, as demanded by content. Whether this series finds its expression in hardcopy or in digital format, it will seek to explore and define new genres of thought and expression offered by digital media.

Edward Barrett

Foreword

The electronic age is pulling together comprehensive areas of scholarship and understanding that had earlier been considered quite disparate. Previously opaque areas of study have acquired a new lucidity. One of these areas illuminated by Kathleen Welch's recent work has been that of pre-Platonic rhetoric and philosophy. Until recently, "real" philosophy and rhetoric had been presumed to be necessarily abstract and formal, as their main line of development had been since Plato. The holism of Isocrates' rhetoric, and indeed of pre-Platonic thinkers generally, has appeared (to lines of thought dominated by Plato and Aristotle) retrograde and inexorably confused.

Eric Havelock and others have shown the effect of the new technology of writing on Plato's patterns of thought. Drawing on the massive amount of work that has by now been done on preliterate, oral cultures, Professor Welch shows how Isocrates and other early Greek thinkers, by contrast, were not so textually dominated but were fundamentally oral in their thinking procedures. They were holistic rather than abstractly analytic. This makes them uncongenial to the analytic procedures that have marked the centuries leading to the now defunct modernism. More than Plato's linear chirographic procedures, the holistic thinking of Isocrates and other pre-Platonic Greek thinking was tooled to inner discourse rather than to linear thinking, to managing chaos rather than carefully packaging thought. For this reason, such thinking is particularly interesting in terms of the information chaos with which we must live today. Throughout history, oralism has been a means of managing chaos. In our present situation, the linear thinking that has dominated in the

West since Plato and Aristotle is not eliminated but is of only limited usefulness.

Professor Welch necessarily deals at length with women's issues. When we look at the long-term development of thought out of the pre-Platonic past, these issues enter into or form a background for almost everything, from philosophy and rhetoric to education, to medicine, to practical politics, and especially to early basic oralism. For centuries across the world—in Sanskrit and other Indo-European languages, Classical Chinese, Classical Arabic, Rabbinical Hebrew, and other writing systems— the use of writing was almost entirely a prerogative of males, and it was taken for granted to be a masculine activity. As computerization has situated writing in a new place in the human lifeworld, the relationship of women to writing has radically changed. This is a matter of great moment. For a while in some cultures in recent decades, women became writers largely as secretaries. This is no longer the case.

We are commonly not aware of the complex history of orality and literacy and of the effects of this history on the depths of human consciousness, where electronic communication is now having its deep and as yet not understood effects. Professor Welch's work can alert us to some of the in-depth understanding we need to be aware of where we really are.

Walter J. Ong
University Professor Emeritus of Humanities
Saint Louis University

Acknowledgments

I am very grateful to the readers who have read, and sometimes reread, *Electric Rhetoric* in part or in whole: Deborah Brandt, Richard Leo Enos, Cheryl Glenn, Catherine Hobbs, Geary Hobson, James L. Kinneavy, David Mair, Walter J. Ong, Jacqueline Jones Royster, J. Blake Scott, and Phillip Sipiora. Their written comments and dialogue have been very important to this project. My colleagues in the Composition/Rhetoric/Literacy Graduate Program in the English Department of the University of Oklahoma have provided an intellectual context, solidarity, and support for the merger of research and teaching that is the hallmark of U.S. composition and rhetoric studies: working with Michael C. Flanigan, Catherine Hobbs, Susan Kates, and David Mair has been central to my work, including this book. The ten-year construction of the M.A. and Ph.D. C/R/L Program with Michael Flanigan, David Mair, and our former colleague James Comas has provided important opportunities and challenges, and I am grateful to the University of Oklahoma for supporting our vision and letting us do our work.

I thank my collaborators in the formation of the Coalition of Women Scholars in the History of Rhetoric and Composition, who, beginning at a Chicago meeting in 1990, saw the importance of merging teaching and scholarship and worked hard to make the coalition the vibrant center of activity that it continues to be: Winifred Bryan Horner, Nan Johnson, C. Jan Swearingen, and Marjorie Curry Woods devoted many hours to the scholarly and political aims of the coalition, aims that have inspired me throughout the writing of this book.

Andrea A. Lunsford and Cheryl Glenn, with whom I undertook the experimental technology graduate course Histories of Feminist Rhetorics and Writing Practices, taught in the fall of 1997, are not only models of collegiality, feminist collaboration, and deep generosity; they also understand the particular political, intellectual, and spiritual issues that link women rhetor-writers with the technologies of written, spoken, and unspoken communication.

Special thanks go to the late Edward P. J. Corbett, Jody Enders, Winifred Bryan Horner, Janice M. Lauer, Steven Mailloux, Joyce I. Middleton, and Donovan J. Ochs, all of whose generosity helped me very much in the research and writing of the book. Walter J. Ong not only provided the foreword; he encouraged me consistently in emphasizing the centrality of women's and girl's rhetorics and writing practices and the inability of so many traditional scholars to see this centrality.

I also thank the National Endowment for the Humanities for a Summer Stipend that enabled me to draft chapter 2 and the American Council of Learned Societies for a travel grant to present portions of one chapter at a meeting of the International Society for the History of Rhetoric.

I am grateful to the Humanities Center of the University of Oklahoma, especially its director, Daniel C. Snell, for a course release that helped me to finish the book and to the University of Oklahoma Research Council, especially Vice President for Research and Graduate College Dean E. C. Smith, for a summer fellowship. I also thank my colleagues Geary Hobson for his advice on the *Origin Myth of Acoma*, David Mair for extensive help on the penultimate draft of chapter 1, and Catherine Hobbs for nearly daily discussions of composition, rhetoric, and literacy. I was not able to include any publications that appeared after April 1998, and any mistakes and infelicities are my own.

Howard B. Bluestein, my husband, has endlessly discussed electrical issues from various scientific and rhetorical perspectives, has listened to many drafts, and has supported the project wholeheartedly, including helping me to move hundreds of print books back and forth every year between Norman, Oklahoma, and Boulder, Colorado, the places where I wrote the book. I also thank the librarians of the University of Oklahoma Bizzell Library (especially Wilbur A. Stolt) and the University of Colorado Norlin Library (the latter named after the George Norlin who translated so much of Isocrates). The faculty office provided by the Bizzell Library smoothed the way for the research on the book. Also at the University of Oklahoma, I thank my current and former colleagues Keith R. Busby, Frederick H. Carr, John Catlin, Lee M. Colaw, J. Rufus Fears, Teree Foster, Gustav W. Friedrich, Penny M. Hopkins, James F. Kimpel, Roland E. Lehr, Judith S. Lewis, Sandra L. Ragan, and Stephen E. Tabachnick. At the University of Colorado I thank Elissa Guralnick, Paul Levitt, and Rolf Norgaard for their collegiality. I also wish to thank Rachel Fagan, J. Blake Scott, Christyne Berzseny, Jana Moring, Dianne Juby, and Karen Jobe for helping me to check out books and photocopy much material. I also wish to thank Dean Paul B. Bell: the support of the College of Arts and Sciences of the University of Oklahoma has been central to this book. I thank my parents, Mary Jane Hayden Welch and the late James K. Welch, for sustained inspiration and my sister Virginia Welch Moody for discussions of consciousness and language issues. My other two sisters, Mary Ann Welch Bendezu and Clarissa Welch Dare, and my brothers, James W. Welch and Mark H. Welch, have contributed as well.

My gratitude also goes out to Mary L. Coleman, David Racko, Don R. Nicholson, and Suzy Nicholson.

My students at the University of Oklahoma, from the freshman writing level to the Ph.D. level, have been central to my work. Their keen intelligence, insights, and hard work never cease to amaze me. They are a joy and a challenge to work with and have provided me with endless insight. These students possess phronesis. I also thank students I taught at the University of Colorado for one semester and, for short periods, at the University of Utah and Ohio State University.

I am deeply grateful to the MIT Press, especially the series editor Edward Barrett and Senior Editor Amy E. Brand, both of whom are unusual in understanding the radical implications of the new screen literacy. I also thank Alan Thwaits, my manuscript editor, for editing my work with keen insight and impressive knowledge.

I

Classical Greek Literacy and the Spoken Word

1

Introduction: Screen Literacy in Rhetoric and Composition Studies

Video Rules

Screens, in the form of computers, now dominate many workplaces, from the faculty office in the heart of a U.S. university to the McDonald's at the student union, from the New York Stock Exchange in Manhattan to the scheduling office of the Cleveland Symphony. Similarly, screens in the form of broadcast and cable television accompany us in our daily activities in many spaces, including some restaurants, car-repair waiting rooms, health clubs, general-merchandise stores, airport waiting rooms, book stores, automobiles, and even some U.S. Post Offices. In all these spaces, as well as many more, broadcast and cable reception appears to be regarded as a necessity. While intellectuals, business people, and other people who need long periods of relative quiet in order to work may find this proliferation of monitors to be irritating and distracting, many other people apparently tolerate it or even welcome it.

Video, yet another use of the screen, is deployed in highly beneficial ways. In electronic medicine, miniature video cameras now routinely provide, via fiber optic probes, representations of human interior spaces in medical procedures that enable physicians to screen bodily organs and functions. Many physicians and technicians spend much of their days watching video, as fiber optic probes, attached to tiny video cameras, are routinely inserted into every human orifice and into other bodily holes made by incision. The benefits of this kind of medical diagnosis and treatment are incalculable. The video representations of the organs and systems functioning in situ enable physicians to screen parts of the live body and to make diagnoses with electronic machines that are far less dangerous than, for example, the procedures of exploratory surgery, in which the body must be opened for direct viewing by the surgeon. We cannot escape video screens, nor would we altogether want to. Computer screens and video screens have gradually so infiltrated our habits of being that their presence has become normal for many citizens at work and play.

Yet screens accompany us in an even more profound way. They have come to constitute, in part, our intersubjectivities, our language inter-actions with others and within ourselves, including identity formation. Powerful explications of computers, rhetoric, and composition have been provided by Cynthia L. Selfe, Gail Hawisher, Laura J. Gurak, Stephen Doheny-Farina, Myron Tuman, Richard A. Lanham, and Jay David Bolter, to name some scholars whose work I draw on here and whose deployment of rhetoric and composition history is evident, but very few theorists in the humanities have attempted to theorize video or its insti-tutionalized form, television, by deploying historicized rhetoric. This serious avoidance of historicized rhetoric exists in spite of the important efforts of many video theorists, social scientists, and scholars in cultural studies. Video remains untheorized across the curriculum, across the academy, and across North America. Our students, living their lives in the hegemony of the television screen and speaker and the computer screen and speaker, are now literate in ways never imagined two gen-erations ago. When we in the humanities ignore or, worse, jeer at the acoustic/spoken/visual/written bases of their new literacy, their special knowledge/ability, their new routes to the achievement of arete (the classical Greek concept of a person's or thing's own unique excellence), we fail them as their teachers and exemplars of language. We also fail the larger national community that remains in dire need of what we have to offer and that pays our salaries.

The screens of television appear nearly everywhere in the United States, in locations of power as well as of powerlessness. In contrast, the screens of computers mostly appear in locations of power. As a result, representation (mimesis), including fluctuating representation within the mind (which is never fully within a discrete, individual mind) and written and spoken language habits, has changed drastically. These changes have not been adequately taken into account by the humanities, all of which disciplines tend to marginalize screen study, if it exists at all.[1]

Many scholars in the humanities have actively resisted the theorizing of video. In spite of protestations about the importance of student writing (for rhetoric and composition studies), of pantextualism and Saussurean sign systems (for poststructuralism), many scholars in the discipline of English seem loathe to theorize video. In fact, the strength of their responses makes it appear that many intellectuals are reviled by it. This resistance must be interrogated if the humanities are to reassume effectiveness and to reverse their long march into ineffectuality. While rich empirical research on television proliferates among social scientists, showing us trends and providing us with invaluable quantitative analyses, nonnumerical/rhetorical research on the televisual phenomenon has remained remarkably small, inappropriately disseminated, and practically hidden.[2] In fact, of central concern in this book are the twin erasures of video and of the gendered history of rhetoric and writing.

Video rules because its monitors have been emitting signals in mostly private locations, on a mass scale, since the late 1940s. The humanities disciplines, so definitively enamored of the printed word (more than of the spoken word or of the language of graphics), have not taken account of this ubiquitous symbol system and its definitive dependence on writing. Video needs to be theorized by rhetoric and composition studies, as well as by almost all the other branches of the humanities; this book contributes to this need. Western rhetoric has existed continuously (that is, has been constructed) for at least 2,400 years. It has risen and fallen with and through waves of politics, governmental forms, school and university curricula, gendered divisions of labor (usually unac-

1. Of course, important research and teaching on television have taken place for decades in various academic venues, usually as part of communication departments or journalism and mass communication programs and colleges, or film and video departments. Since most of the communication departments have designated themselves as part of the social sciences, they do not fall into the particular interpretive move I make here. Rhetoric and composition studies have been working on computer theorizing, new pedagogies, and their societal impact for a very long time, as I will elaborate on below.

2. See, for example, the standard *Reading Television* by John Fiske and John Hartley.

knowledged), constructions of race (also unacknowledged), changes in communication technology, and other power relations. Video joined rhetorical history when it was developed as a technology in 1928. It is past time for the humanities disciplines to theorize, analyze, and deploy the new communication technologies, including video. Both video and its cousin the computer are now hegemonic. Rhetoric is now electric. Writing is now electric. Nevertheless, video exists in the academy as another kind of madwoman in the attic.[3]

Regendered/Reraced Classical Greek Rhetoric and Current Screen Literacy

To understand the ubiquitous screens of video and the less widespread screens of computers, this book appropriates a new version of classical Greek rhetoric and literacy before Aristotle as one system for intellectually engaging the future of literacy in the United States. It seeks to understand electric rhetoric by deploying some historical correspondents and then offering new kinds of language performance. While many of these historical correspondents may be utterly useless, they may also be helpful as we chart our way in the world of electronic communication technology. Historically, in the traditional versions of the West that continue to constitute the public imagination, particular deployments of Aristotle have provided ways of understanding an agreed-upon reality, ways readily understood by people whose identities are apparently stable. The Enlightenment subject remains entrenched. Nevertheless, this reality has now been so thoroughly challenged by rhetoric and composition theory, cultural studies, and postmodernism that its limitations have been fully exposed. One result of this unveiling is that theorists across a number of fields are renaming the humanities the "posthumanities." In place of an Aristotelian paradigm, I ask my readers to consider an Isocratic Sophistic construction of written and spoken articulation that will partly account for the electronic forms of discourse that have achieved so much power in the last two generations and that daily acquire even more power. Throughout the book I contend that current literacy cannot be

3. See Sandra Gilbert and Susan Gubar's classic *The Madwoman in the Attic*.

adequately theorized unless one takes account of writing as a definitive aspect of oralism/auralism, or the oral structures of articulation. These oral/aural structures possess inevitable connections to writing that must be better understood, taught, and deployed by the citizens of the larger public. A retheorized pre-Aristotelian theory of rhetoric offers crucial strategies to help us do that more productively, by which I mean democratically and on a widespread scale. Rehistoricized classical rhetoric that has been worked through some strands of composition and rhetoric theories provides powerful strategies to help us explain the pervasive seductiveness of the current electronic forms of discourse, all of which are embedded in a merger of written, oral, aural, and visual structures of articulation. The fluctuating features of this merger are now not adequately understood. If we do come to understand them, then we can lead the way to new social action, including a new pedagogy that more meaningfully interacts with cultures outside the academy.

Isocratic Sophism, Oralism/Auralism, and Video

Part I of *Electric Rhetoric* applies a newly theorized classical rhetoric (Isocratic Sophism that is raced and gendered) to explain literate oralism/auralism as the consciousness of the pre-Aristotelian period (specifically, in the generation before Aristotle). Part II adapts these Isocratic Sophistic theories to the literate, visual, electronic oralism/auralism that inhabits us now. The problem of the book centers on three of the many issues that constitute relationships among writer-subjects, reader-subjects, cultures/ideologies, and the material texts that circulate in these three:

• Literacy issues (both ancient and modern)[4] arise from the fact that forms of communication technology condition (although they of course do not fully determine) how people articulate within and around their ideas, their cultures, and themselves, including their subject positions.[5]

4. Any period of Western historicized rhetoric could be examined here, not just the classical Greek period. For rhetoric and the western European Renaissance, see Wayne A. Rebhorn, *The Emperor of Men's Minds: Literature and the Renaissance Discourse of Rhetoric*, especially pp. 1–22. See also William J. Kennedy, *Rhetorical Norms in Renaissance Literature*.

5. See Susan Miller, *Rescuing the Subject*, esp. pp. 11–20, for an explication of the subject and rhetoric/composition studies.

• Any current definition of literacy must account for changes in consciousness or *mentalité*, including the subject, brought about by electronic forms of communication and their inherent mingling with writing.
• Literacy (in any historical period) depends on social constructions (including gender and racial constructions) that give value to some writing and speaking activities and that devalue others.[6] Versions of oralism/auralism exist in all historical periods (and prehistorical ones), mingle with different technologies, and partly determine who is allowed to speak, who is silenced, and how subjectivity is constructed.

These three issues coalesce around the thesis that literacy in the United States in the twenty-first century must account not only for the new configuration of intersubjectivities brought about by the merger of consciousness/mentalité and electronic articulation but must also account for the social constructions in which writing takes place (what I call an Isocratic Sophistic performance, as I posit it in chapters 2 and 3).

Electric Rhetoric attempts to argue persistently against the still-powerful idea that knowledge is a retrievable reality "out there in the world," to be owned and stored as necessary, and that literacy is a skill in the sense of an external tool that one can own and apply as necessary.

This book defines literacy as an activity of minds/bodies/intersubjectivities that are conditioned within specific cultures/ideologies, all of which have oral/aural features of discourse such as the reliance on repetition, spoken ritual (religious activities, for example), and first-language acquisition that are, in turn, merged with other features, almost all of which are embedded in writing as a way of knowing.[7] A person in, say, Kansas City, who does not speak is nevertheless strongly conditioned intersubjectively by writing because her culture, her interactions, and her everyday behavior are enveloped in and defined by language. The United States at the turn of the millennium is thoroughly immersed in the written word, even though many of our citizens have been damaged by an absence of training in functional literacy. In our time there is no speaking without writing.

6. Brian V. Street makes this point in *Literacy in Theory and Practice*.

7. See Walter J. Ong, *Orality and Literacy: The Technologizing of the Word*, pp. 37–57, and Roger Chartier, *Forms and Meanings: Texts, Performances, and Audiences from Codex to Computer*, pp. 12–14.

One specific location for the study of a previous, strong change in the dynamics of writing/speaking and the accompanying change in consciousness/mentalité is Isocratic classical Greek rhetoric and writing performance. Many other locations exist as well, both inside and outside the West. Isocrates, of course, dynamized one center of classical rhetoric and provided a pedagogical/cultural/citizenship model that emphasized his version of logos performance. In the all-encompassing universe of discourse that Isocrates constructed from his own historical situation, writing as a cultural practice achieved unusual power in his Athens.[8] In similar as well as dissimilar ways, electrified communication technologies have brought about new ways of articulating, or a different rhetoric. One of the biggest differences is that Isocrates was screenless; he was not, however, textless. In addition, he operated within one of the most oppressively misogynistic and racist cultures that has ever existed, as I explore in chapters 3 and 4.

I emphasize that I am on an avenue of exploration and that I aim not so much to answer questions as to redirect inquiry into historicized Western rhetoric and writing practices, current literacy, and electronic screens, all of which are central to our culture. Our citizenry remains in great need of new theorizing and historicizing to account for the differently written, oral, aural, and visual era in which we now live. This accounting would then enable us more effectively to determine future action in the academy and its rapidly changing relationship to culture. In addition, I hope to contribute to a repositioning of the humanities/ posthumanities from the wizened, dull, uncommunicative, elitist studies that it has been for much of this century to a set of interrelated Sophistic logos studies that are performative, democratic, and open to all kinds of symbol systems as well as to all racial and ethnic groups and both genders.

Part II of this book, "Logos Performers, Screen Sophism, and the Rhetorical Turn," focuses on the oral/aural/visual literacy of television of the last forty years (a technology that is, of course, undergoing radical economic/technological change as I write and as you read) and its theoretical relationship to classical Greek rhetoric as it has been richly

---

8. For universes of discourse, see Moffett, *Teaching the Universe of Discourse*.

retheorized since the second half of the 1980s. While I treat the equally important electronic forms of word processor and computer, I make more particular statements about video and how it has changed articulation, and therefore literacy, rhetoric, and writing.

Classical Communication Technologies and Rhetorical Change

In this book, pre-Aristotelian Greek rhetoric is represented by Isocrates, the fourth-century B.C.E. rhetorician, writer, and, I contend, Sophist, who embraced writing, experimented with and empowered prose genres, and maintained ownership of a remarkably powerful and long-influential educational institution, one that preceded and then competed directly and fiercely with Plato's Academy.[9] To discuss Sophistic rhetoric, I deploy Isocrates as a definitive Sophist, and not as the peripheral and enfeebled "thinker" he is characterized as in dominant histories.

I reinterpret Isocrates through the only stances we have, our inter-subjective, cultural, fluctuating positionings as interpreter-subjects, positionings that conflict in many ways. My proposal for action based on some aspects of Isocrates' Sophistic theories is for more inclusive, citizen-based agendas for literacy today as it is conditioned by oralism, that is, the oral/aural/written structures of consciousness/mentalité, or electric rhetoric.

What does an ancient Greek rhetorician, little heard of outside the academy, have to do with the current rapid change in communication technologies? One answer resides in his deployment of writing, his school, his *paideia*. Isocrates' own general education/rhetoric/program of informed action fits into this current agenda as part of a larger rewriting of the history of rhetoric and writing. In this work on recognizing the inherent rhetoricity of literacy, I position Isocrates as a pivotal Sophist, a writer/teacher/scholar, and the owner of an advanced school (an economic privilege that enabled him to control the entire curriculum and, of course, much of the students' behavior) whose writings transcended their breathless generic crossovers and intertextual movements. Isocrates relied on, and helped to provoke, the energy available from the emerging,

---

9. Isocrates' prevarication at being called a Sophist is itself a very Sophistic move. See *Against the Sophists*, sections 1–8.

uncharted power of prose as it sought to move power away from the hegemony of poetry. Isocrates worked diligently, in what we would call his teaching and research, to wrest power from this language form.[10] The power struggle against the hegemony of poetry has been briefly acknowledged but has not been normalized in the historicizing of classical rhetoric and writing practices.[11]

I realign Isocrates' rhetoric/writing against that of Plato. In their heated competition (completely entwined with pedagogy) Plato "won" in the sense that his *philosophia* dominated what came to be named Western metaphysics. I offer Isocratic rhetoric as an alternative. This move follows a repositioning of the Sophists as primary performers of rhetoric and a rejection of the familiar Western "tradition."[12] I realign Isocrates as a pivotal theorist for our own times as we continue to critique the strong belief in stable meanings, including beginnings.[13] To position Isocrates in this way, I apply a Diotimic reading in chapter 3, where I

10. It is difficult in our time to understand the centrality that poetry held in schools in particular and in cultural transmission in general. For some discussions of this phenomenon, see H. I. Marrou, *A History of Education in Antiquity*, pp. 9–10, 41–43, 71, 153–154, 169–170; Werner Jaeger, *Paideia*, vols. 1, 2, and 3; Eric A. Havelock, *Preface to Plato*, passim. There is a tendency in the historicizing of ancient Greek schools to apply a familiar three-part system: grammar school, high school, and college. See Welch, "Writing Instruction in Ancient Athens after 450 B.C." See also Kenneth J. Freeman, *Schools of Hellas*, and Frederick A.G. Beck, *Album of Greek Education: The Greeks at School and Play*. This construction is understandable from the point of view of ontogeny and individual development. However, it is not in accord with the gender constructions, educational modes, and other constitutive aspects of fourth century B.C.E. formal education and its radical change from older, more sporting models.

11. See, for example, George A. Kennedy, *The Art of Persuasion in Greece*, pp. 33–35 and 67–68 (partially reprinted in *A New History of Classical Rhetoric*), and *Classical Rhetoric and Its Christian and Secular Tradition from Ancient to Modern Times*, p. 78. For an example of a subversion of the dominant historical stance presented in these three books, see Takis Poulakos's "Towards a Cultural Understanding of Classical Epideictic Oratory."

12. This move is related to, but different from, the repositioning of Derrida's Plato in "Plato's Pharmacy" and the deconstructionist critique of Western metaphysics.

13. For discussions of logocentrism and other Derridean ideas as they exist for rhetoric/composition studies, see Sharon Crowley, *A Teacher's Guide to Deconstruction* and Jasper Neel, *Plato, Derrida, and Writing*.

reposition Isocrates' rhetoric with that of Diotima, who, of course, was cast as Socrates' teacher in the *Symposium*.

I also contend that Isocrates' linguistic/cultural/rhetorical power positioned him to enact a cultural/ideological/pedagogical agenda, an *enkyklios paideia*, that can help us in this era of profound change in literacy, education, rhetoric, and the nature of writing practices.[14] In other words, Isocratic rhetoric and writing can contribute directly to current rhetoric, composition, and literacy studies.[15] It provides new theoretical material for devising advanced, inclusive theories of literacy for the present day, a day suffused with the electrified word and its attendant postmodern leanings. In claiming Isocrates' positioning and agenda, his rhetoric and his *paideia*, as a powerful version of classical Greek rhetoric for the postmodern and after-postmodern world, I aim to fortify the newly recognized establishment of a Sophistic (anti-Aristotelian) classical rhetoric. This move goes against the twentieth-century grain of Aristotle's dominance—a frequently unrecognized hegemony in various disciplines, including those of English, Anglo-American philosophy, and communication studies, to name three.[16] In *Electric Rhetoric*, classical Greek rhetoric and writing practices are Isocratic, which is to say Sophistic, intersubjective, performative, and a merger of oralism and literacy. The last feature, it needs to be immediately emphasized, refers not to the acts

14. Marrou, *A History of Education in Antiquity*, translates the Greek term as *éducation générale*; Lamb then translates it into English as general education. See pp. 176, 183, 211, and 281.

15. As I will discuss below, many of Isocrates' theories are already thoroughly in place and are unconsciously used in many writing programs, as well as in the wider discipline of English and in fact in the "general education" changes that have preoccupied almost all colleges and universities in the United States.

16. In traditional literary studies, Aristotle's *Poetics*, of course, has found remarkable dominance; in rhetoric and composition studies (not in the untheorized and unhistoricized car-repair versions of the teaching of writing that continue to exist in various institutions but in the theorized and historicized programs) Aristotle's *Rhetoric* has been the text of reverential choice. On untheorized writing pedagogy, see Theresa Enos, "A Brand New World." She writes, "We need to keep in mind that only about thirty-five hundred college writing teachers out of over thirty-five thousand have professionalized themselves by learning the history, theory, and praxis of rhetoric, by participating in our national conferences, and by contributing to journals and professional books in rhetoric and composition" (p. 7).

of speaking and writing, as I discuss later in this chapter, but to kinds of consciousness/mentalité.

In this book, I work with three related strands (frequently conceived of as fields of study):

• *The redeployment of Sophistic classical rhetoric.* This revisionary move has taken place actively since the appearance in the 1980s and 1990s of books by Cheryl Glenn, C. Jan Swearingen, Susan C. Jarratt, Richard Leo Enos, Edward Schiappa, Takis Poulakos, Victor Vitanza, John Poulakos and of essays by many others.[17] I hope to persuade my audience that productive action can derive from this move, a site of intense research.[18]

• *Current literacy theories within the field of rhetoric and composition studies.* This important work, which of course covers an enormous area, has not yet fully investigated the historical correspondences that would strengthen their already strong cases about the changing state of literacy in our time.

• *The inherently rhetorical nature of television and computers and their inevitable relationship to writing and the histories of communication technologies.* The rhetoricity of television—its persuasion, communication, identification, disembodiedness, and basis in the written word— makes it amenable to the complicated rhetorical theories (including regendering) that have been reworked in recent theories.

In arranging and rearranging these strands (and watching two of them frequently merge), this book aims not only to contribute to the cultural conversation, or the Burkean parlor of ideas, but to contribute to a movement that changes the actions people take in their daily writing and speaking lives. The ordinary, raced, gendered, technologized world that all social classes in the United States inhabit and negotiate forms the ultimate center of concern in this book. This change would be brought

17. See Glenn, *Rhetoric Retold*; Swearingen, *Rhetoric and Irony*; Jarratt, *Rereading the Sophists*; R. Enos, *Greek Rhetoric before Aristotle*; Vitanza, *Negation, Subjectivity, and the History of Rhetoric*; J. Poulakos, *Sophistical Rhetoric in Classical Greece*; T. Poulakos, *Speaking for the Polis*; and Schiappa, *Protagoras and Logos*.

18. Classical rhetoric, in fact, suffuses rhetoric/composition studies to an extraordinary degree. Frequently its appearance is as a devil term, a site of evil in writing studies. See, for example, Knoblauch and Brannon, *The Rhetorical Tradition and the Teaching of Writing*.

about largely through critical pedagogy, a primary location for cultural change.[19] In weaving these strands, I violate the twentieth-century academic standard of occupying a single, delimited area. This transgression is, in my view, necessary if humanists are to help direct the future of technology and not just tag along complaining about Philistines or ignoring the digital world that now exists.[20]

"Literacy," obviously and happily, has acquired a proliferation of meanings in the last twenty years or so, but as a keyword it has always had complex signification. By "literacy" here I mean not just the functional ability to write and read (although, of course, these basic actions are and always have been crucial[21]—more crucial than frequently they are said to be [a distinction I explore in chapter 4]). I also mean an activity of inherently verbal minds conditioned within and sometimes against specific cultures, all of which have oral/aural structures of articulation—especially in writing and speaking—and most of which have merged these structures with structures based on literacy in the sense of consciousness/mentalité. Our own structures of discourse are now propelled by the electronic forms of discourse, particularly on the screens of computers and the screens and speakers of television.[22] Visuality has

19. Of all the disciplines and subdisciplines of the humanities, only rhetoric and composition studies identifies itself as thoroughly imbricated in pedagogy, which has (sometimes for good as with Isocrates and sometimes for ill as with Ramus) always constituted a definitive aspect of rhetoric, as quickly revealed by a glimpse at Sappho, Gorgias, Isocrates, Plato and Plato's "Socrates," Aspasia, Quintilian (to ponder only the classical period). While pedagogy has been of marginal interest in poststructuralist theory (and this so-far limited interest should be applauded) and of no interest in most humanities disciplines, rhetoric/composition studies located at the site of English have from their beginnings identified pedagogy as a definitive element, not as a do-good afterthought. Schools and colleges of education are not, in my view, in the humanities; they are, rather, in the social sciences.

20. Many of the current, rich controversies in Anglo–North American literacy studies can be advanced by the study of historical rhetoric, or historicized rhetoric and writing studies.

21. Deborah Brandt makes this point in *Literacy as Social Involvement: The Acts of Writers, Readers, and Texts*, pp. 9–10.

22. See especially chapter 6 of my *Contemporary Reception of Classical Rhetoric*, "Classical Rhetoric and Contemporary Rhetoric and Composition Studies: Electrifying Classical Rhetoric."

changed dramatically with these screens. Literacy as consciousness/ mentalité has changed even more.

In the second strand emphasized in this book, literacy (within rhetoric/ composition studies) continues to be impeded by the current-traditional paradigm, that quintessentially modernist construction.[23] It continues to poison the well of the teaching of writing. As has been amply documented in a tidal wave of extraordinary research in rhetoric and composition studies,[24] and as just as amply has not been adopted in many curricula, the current-traditional paradigm assumes a universalized reader who does not change from era to era or even moment to moment; in fact, crucially and even more damagingly, the interior dialectical struggles of a reader ideologically embedded in a community are not even

---

23. The current-traditional paradigm of writing pedagogy relies on drill-based instruction typified by the five-part theme. In the first section (frequently a paragraph), there is an introduction and announcement of three parts. The second, third, and fourth sections or paragraphs are elaborations of the issues announced in the first section. The fifth part is a summary. In the 1970s, the expressivist-process movement interrogated and rejected the five-part theme, which represented all "expository writing" in many North American schools and universities. The current-traditional paradigm consists of a universal, reliable, stable, third-person narrator who reports from a position outside history to a universal audience. The current-traditional paradigm seems to be highly teachable because its rigidity enables correctness officers, as it were, to enforce the rules that construct it. In fact, as rhetoric/composition research since the early 1960s has shown, it kills written invention. Its major achievement is the inculcation of fear and loathing in writers, particularly student writers (but also other writers who might turn to a current-traditional textbook for help). Reading the themes tends to produce pain in the teacher/reader and so is delegated to marginalized teachers of writing who work part-time. Crowley, in *Methodical Memory*, deconstructs this dangerous form and practice by historicizing its development from Lockean empiricism. Its transmission occurred through George Campbell, Hugh Blair, Alexander Bain, and the writers of hundreds of writing textbooks down to the current day. See also Daniel Fogarty, *Roots for a New Rhetoric*. The current-traditional paradigm is alive and well in hundreds of writing programs in the United States and elsewhere, as well as in most of the writing textbooks that continue to infect the culture and to maintain the current uselessness of the humanities.

24. See, for example, the journals *College Composition and Communication, Rhetoric Review, Written Communication, Research in the Teaching of English, Journal of Basic Writing, Rhetoric Society Quarterly, College English*, and many others.

recognized by the conscious and unconscious adherents of the current-traditional paradigm. Instead, this damning ideology blindly trains students to cling to the deeply held habit of being that regards knowledge as static and therefore consumable. In addition, the current-traditional paradigm bores the writing teacher, whose mind goes numb from the militaristic enforcement of the unacknowledged and unidentified subject, not to mention the obsessive error correction and other features of the universal-audience classroom. This habit is normalized in United States cultures, where the lure of whatness is not recognized, even as general and unexamined dependence on it numbs us to alternative ideas. Andrea Lunsford and Lisa Ede, Sharon Crowley, Susan Miller, Kenneth Burke, Roland Barthes, Julia Kristeva, Luce Irigaray, Michel Foucault, and, in a different line, Susanne Langer have led the way on this radical change, and in the United States and western Europe, at least, the battle has been intensely fought. However, the change in the dominant culture, or even in the academy, has not yet been made. The resistance—the cry of (functional or Cultural) illiteracy among the masses, back-to-basics nostalgia, elitism, and right-wing attacks on the humanities—remains as fascinating as it is dangerous.[25]

One of the aims of this book is to understand and take action against the still-dominant idea that writing is a secondary activity that, to one extent or another, represents the more important material already stably located in the mind. This unconscious depriviledging of writing has contributed to the radical disempowerment of large groups of people who give up on the defining activity of writing because they have been so well taught to do so in our schools, colleges, and universities, that is to say, in our institutions that reinforce the status quo of social and other privileges, even as they also contain rich veins of subversion.

As I worked through the issues in *The Contemporary Reception of Classical Rhetoric: Appropriations of Ancient Discourse*, classical rhetoric and writing should not be resuscitated as a merely enriching homage to antiquity or as an ossified, taken-for-granted Tradition of Great Books and Great Writers (who, in our current historical moment, are almost inevitably dominated by Male Masters with token women and/or

25. See John Trimbur, "Literacy and the Discourse of Crisis" for an example of the so-called literacy crisis and its manufacture.

minorities dotting the verbal landscape to enable its promoters to claim that they are committed to diversity).[26] As the energized debate about literary canonicity has taught us, no objective canon of Great Books exists as any kind of palpable, objective reality. The fact that particular writers have been appropriated in various versions of the so-called Western tradition is not a sufficient reason to go on studying them (although the texts deemed important by particular groups in a culture can offer powerful insight into that culture).

In *The Contemporary Reception of Classical Rhetoric*, I interrogated the Heritage School, those receptors of a classical rhetoric that is monolithic, monocultural, monolinguistic (it presents the Greek and Latin languages as the same), prescriptively formalistic, and, most important, dull in the way in which the functionless makes vivid material boring. Proponents of the Heritage School work from the tacit and usually unexamined premise that there is an objective reality of language, a static world that can be analyzed according to the formalist principles on which this stance relies.[27] The unrecognized formalistic constructions in rhetoric/composition studies and literary studies—much of it traceable to unexamined deployments of Aristotle—lead these writers to dismiss quickly or erase altogether the formative issues of situation, subject position, culture, and ideological embeddedness, including gender. In another common historicizing move writers erase Diotima, for example, from rhetoric and philosophy and other fields altogether. In a different move, they equate Cicero and Aristotle as two classical rhetoricians in the same category, with the same ideological constraints, with the same motives and agendas, and even with the same language. The equation of Attic Greek and Latin, the idea that they are the same, even though they do not use the same alphabet, illustrates this problem. This still numbingly familiar stance is reinforced by a reliance on static translations that depend on one-to-one substitution of words and, perhaps most significant, a relentless emphasis on the assumption that thought is prior to and

26. See the list of Great Books, now featuring token women. The Great Books Foundation and their reading groups are still in operation. The readers in these groups have a hunger, a legitimate intellectual hunger, that is not being fed by this elitist, sexist, racist list.

27. See "The Heritage School of Classical Rhetoric" in my *Contemporary Reception of Classical Rhetoric*, pp. 3–33.

superior to articulation, an Aristotelian rhetorical stance that they impose not only on the ancient writers who enacted their agendas in particular ideologies but unwittingly on themselves as interpreters, and so, of course, on their students.[28]

In Part I, I connect strands one and two: a redeployed Sophistic classical rhetoric and current literacy studies within the field of rhetoric and composition studies. I reinterpret and reposition Isocrates for rhetorical action in another way as well. By deuniversalizing readers of Isocrates and other relevant pre-Aristotelian Greek theorists of rhetoric and writing and by examining the still-dominant formalist assumptions that interpreters in U.S. culture tacitly maintain (largely because of outmoded literacy assumptions made in our schools), we can establish new action for writing theory and for the production of discourse, which is now inevitably suffused with the oralism/auralism and visuality of the electronic forms of discourse in many ways. Isocratic classical rhetoric can be reinterpreted and reactivated by juxtaposing it with current literacy studies, including gender construction.

A Glance at the Rhetorical Canon of Great Books[29]

The heated disputes about Great Books need to continue and to be energetically incorporated into all our rhetoric/writing and literature classrooms. We must continue to search for alternative ways to examine all the bases we can find for the investigation of particular writers, groups of writers, and cultures/ideologies that enabled them to produce the work that constitutes classical rhetoric. This project includes continuing to unmask supposedly neutral forms of historicizing that assume without analysis a privileged, middle-class, white, male subject who is thought to be universal and to represent marginalized Others, such as women and/ or people of color.[30] This is Aristotle's Greek man. If a canon of classical

28. Crowley, in *The Methodical Memory* and "Modern Rhetoric and Memory," explicates this issue in more detail.

29. As opposed to the five traditional canons (*erga*) of rhetoric.

30. I do not place all white, middle-class men in this category of privilege. While the availability of power is much greater for this group, many of these men are in fact oppressed in ways as serious as those fought by women, African Americans,

rhetoric (or any other field) does emerge, contesting it should be studied as well. There is no self-evident reason to study classical rhetoric, classical literary texts, or any other group of books. The reasons for studying them should be made new and explicit on a regular basis, and those reasons should be worked through with our students in all the classes we teach.[31] A classical rhetoric canon revivified partly on the basis of new theories of canon formation will occupy part of this book. I also propose to offer reasons for the study of some ancient rhetoricians (particularly what they did, or their performances) and some rhetorical theories as they unfolded within shifting ideological constraints. I then look at how they apply to particular current controversies in literacy and, crucially, look for encoding activities that need to derive from the study. Here I share the stance of John Schilb, who argues against canonomania in *Between the Lines*, and of Jane Tompkins, Henry Louis Gates Jr., and many literary theorists that a canon of any nation or period is not static but remains in flux and that it is by its nature a construction that arises from ideologies and human beings. I reject the idea that a classical rhetoric canon of great texts is self-evident, retrievable, and out there to be studied by so-called objective or obvious criteria—a stance that has not been interrogated as fully in rhetoric/composition studies as it has been in literary studies.

Issues of canon in rhetoric and composition studies share some of the attributes of work in literary studies; however, great differences divide them. The fields, while frequently housed in departments of English, remain quite different, as I demonstrate in chapter 3. This is so partly because inaugurating a curriculum of study is not the same as revising a curriculum that is entrenched. In other words, English literary studies have been strongly embedded in U.S. education and culture for about one

---

native North Americans, and other groups. For example, mental disruptions, the undue pressures of Western ideas of masculinity, and other problems do much to undo the privilege they might exert. Class barriers may provide the biggest challenge for this multifaceted group.

31. It should, but does not, go without saying that in every classroom in every college, university, and school, the teacher should teach the students why they are studying as they are. In English studies, teachers should be able to state why the government and other entities compel them to sit in their chairs. The standard response that this is good for you is not sufficient now and never has been.

hundred years, ever since the modern languages usurped the hegemony of Greek and Latin (with the vital assistance, of course, of classics as a discipline). In contrast, rhetoric and composition studies do not possess this established/rigidified/institutionalized position from which to work. We have, from one point of view, 2,400-year-old sophisticated, elaborate, and potentially enormously useful lines of theories/curricula in the form of so-called rhetorical traditions. The primary existence has been in freshman writing, an array of advanced writing courses, and Writing across the Curriculum programs. With these programs and courses (regarded as central by administrators and by faculty members in other fields but usually for instrumentalist reasons), graduate programs in rhetoric/composition studies have proliferated, enabling current scholar/ teachers to devise their own curricula.[32]

So we see two very different histories and agendas for change available in rhetoric/composition studies and literary studies. To revise literary studies requires one to resist strongly held values and institutional inertia. The struggle against the deep commitment and institutional placement of unexamined Great Books, literary chronology, and a desiccated, racist philology continues as a central location for the Culture wars that continue to take place as we struggle to leave the worst of modernism behind.[33] This change cannot be made by those who continue to believe in a unitary, stable subject.

The institutional/ideological resistance to allowing rhetoric and composition studies to flourish within the literary hegemony of English departments has a very different history and agenda. The tenacity of current-traditional rhetoric and the continuing placement of writing as

32. It is important to recognize the centrality of strong rhetoric/composition graduate programs in changing departmental culture and student attitudes toward encoding. Strong graduate programs promote literacy culture, showing teaching assistants, for example, how to theorize, and to take seriously, freshman writing courses.

33. One of these difficulties is the strategy of "teaching the conflicts," usually associated with Gerald Graff. This popular strategy, however, poses severe limits on the cultures of many English departments, where students are shown (even if they are not told) that competing ideologies are bad. See Patricia Bizzell, "Praising Folly: Constructing a Postmodern Rhetorical Authority as a Woman," for a useful critique of Graff on this issue. One might add that Graff's warmed-over pluralism does nothing to help students become more effective writers.

Other (in the attic with the madwoman, in the basement with the sad women, or segregated in a separate and less beautiful building) provides the big resistance for rhetoric/composition studies. In spite of all these different histories, agendas, and institutional placements, traditional English literary studies and traditional writing studies share a strong bond: They are both in the grip of a desiccated formalism. Each resides in a faraway, enfeebled land where gender construction does not exist and where the tenacious legacy of race-based slavery continues to pollute every aspect of lived life. Each of these bankrupt formalisms is highly teachable. Unfortunately, each is just as frequently highly useless and, in fact, dangerous. It is dangerous because when students learn to hate their native tongue, to believe that art belongs on the margins as a matter of *physis* and not as *nomos*, and to view rhetoric as inconsequential decoration, then the cultural status quo remains intact.[34]

A central tenet of this book is that historical rhetoric and writing practices must now be reperformed (rewritten and reenacted) in our scholarly, teaching, and everyday lives. This move acknowledges the inherent rhetoricity of all symbol systems, including the electronic forms of discourse. It acknowledges that our immersion in written/aural/visual oralism and the continuing denial of oral consciousness/mentalité has contributed to the silencing of Others whose oral/aural power has provided them enormous intracultural power but has been used against them in many of the received, traditional ideas of print literacy.[35] As I demonstrate in chapter 5, the literary writings and other central symbolic constructs of some groups, such as some African-Americans and some

---

34. At this point, I must mention one glaring issue that lies at the heart of this story. A commonplace of English language holds that "rhetoric" is like the icing of a cake, a pretty application without substance. This trope of rhetoric as decoration derives from a number of places, but its most powerful base lies with Petrus Ramus and his partitioning *the classical* five canons of rhetoric (*erga* in Greek; *officii* in Latin; offices, functions, or canons in English) before he was murdered in the St. Bartholomew's Day massacre of 1572, partly for his academic politics. In *Aristotelicae animadversiones* (Observations on Aristotle) and *Dialecticae partitiones* (The divisions of dialectic), he removed from rhetoric the canons of invention (*heuresis*; *inventio*), arrangement (*taxis*; *dispositio*; form), and memory (*mneme, memoria*), leaving behind the now very familiar style and delivery (*lexis, elocutio* and *hypokrisis, pronuntiatio*), the canons that have characterized English studies and some communication studies.

35. See, for example, Shirley Brice Heath, *Ways with Words*.

Native North American Nations (for example, the Acoma Pueblo Nation and the so-called Five Civilized Tribes located in Oklahoma), have been and continue to be erased (in spite of rich, ample research now available) or, when acknowledged, marginalized, because of the oral/aural structures of articulation privileged by many of these groups for strong and important cultural reasons.[36]

I intend to move away from the standard notion of thinking and its Cartesian splitting to focus on articulation, or language production. Part of what I intend to signify by the term "articulation" is action: language behavior regarded as active *because it is active* in the sense or *actio*, the fifth canon of rhetoric (usually translated into English as delivery). I explore this issue in chapter 4, where I discuss Lev Vygotsky's "Genetic Roots of Thought and Speech" and other essays. Vygotsky sets forth a theory of language that is inherently interactive and that demonstrates how thought and speech depend on each other and that they do not remain separate.[37] One source of this idea is Vygotsky's conceptualization of the relationship between what has been translated into English from Russian as "language" and "thought."[38] One of the greatest obstacles to

36. I emphasize here that there is no such entity as "the Black community" or a "Native North American" community. There are communities of people who have been designated Black or Indian (through a construct, not through some version of reality). The plurality in these cases and in the cases of other groups must be maintained. The everyday use of, for example, the phrase "the Black community" erases differences that proliferate among African Americans, who, it *should* go without saying, form as many and varied communities as do so-called Whites but who remain particularly affected by difference. The habitual use of this racial monolith reveals volumes about the hegemony of White people who articulate race in this convenient but finally very racist way. Most White U.S. citizens appear not to know of the historical, sometimes antagonistic, sometimes cooperative differences (with, of course, important similarities) among Native North American nations. If one does not educate oneself to understand these differences among groups that the dominant culture continues to merge into a false oneness, then one will be participating in the perpetuation of racism and other exclusions.

37. See Vygotsky, *Thought and Language*, pp. 33–51. I develop this idea in chapter 4.

38. As with all translation, the one-for-one substitution of terms is inadequate, as Saussure and others have noted. The Russian words for "language" and "thought" come in a Russian context. And so our appropriation of them into the language of English is especially problematic, and we have to be cautious.

the advancement of active literacy is the dualism that leads to the split of thought and articulation (whether in writing, speaking, videotaping, filming, dancing, painting, sculpting, or other actions) and the privileging of thought, which is assumed to be prior and superior. I will argue that this is partly an issue of understanding how consciousness/mentalité operates.

I hope to demonstrate that rhetoric and composition studies need to approach this issue without the (frequently tacit) split and to place articulation, or performance, in the category of concern. I believe that Sophistic performance in particular offers us powerful bases from which to enact this change. Rhetoric/composition studies would then lead the way for English and the rest of the humanities to reassert their centrality not only in education but in everyday life as well. This move would work against the powerful inertia that maintains the humanities' current marginality as frivolous diversions that are vaguely good for people and that are segregated into pablumized "arts weekends," "arts fairs," and other largely consumptive—in all senses of the word—activities. This movement must, however, lead outside the academy into other areas. The primacy of encoding must be reargued and reenacted more strongly; the staging for this enactment occurs pivotally in the classroom (in all classrooms, not just writing ones or literary ones or scientific ones). The electric rhetoric of the computer offers us the opportunity to increase student and citizen language action, although the hype that surrounds the computer as liberator or democratizer is overstated.[39] One of the ways to do this is to reposition the liberal arts as activity-based educational actions and habits and to remove them from their frequently moribund state, where they are now often entombed. In chapter 6, I discuss the ideological center that promotes passivity and resignation first and most powerfully in versions of school literacy and then on other cultural stages as they relate to the liberal arts and their nearly terminal problems.

39. There is no liberation by computer if the student does not attend a wired school. There is no liberation by computer if the student is hungry. Since 25 percent of U.S. children now live in poverty, it is reasonable to assume that these children are too hungry to learn to work on computers or any other technology, including that of pencil and paper. See Freire, *Pedagogy of the Oppressed*; Shor, *Critical Teaching and Everyday Life*; and Trimbur, "Literacy and the Discourse of Crisis."

A Next Wave of classical Greek rhetoric and writing practices emerges here, an Isocratic classical rhetoric, a Sophistic, alternative classical rhetoric that not only accounts for the *writing* brilliance of Isocrates, Plato, Aristotle, Sappho, and others but also enabled the nongolden age of Greece to colonize Others, including women, slaves, and selected *barbars*.[40] By reworking this account, we are able to help tear down the facade of the Heritage School, whose sexism, racism, and dependence on slavery make it unacceptable as a model of behavior, even as much of the rhetoric and writing of this period offers us some rich possibilities.

Historicizing Communication Technology

I rely on the adjective "historicized" because it acknowledges the subjectivity of the writer and distances the writer and her writing from the still-dominant history writing produced by a purportedly neutral historian who is unimplicated in the constructions of the issues being written about but instead reports on a tacitly presumed reality. My encoding position as a white, middle-class female U.S. academic inevitably infuses this book. I assume that every book, every graffito, every mark, every text of any symbol system derives from a multiply constructed writer who can tell a story but cannot tell it by escaping her or his gender, class, race, and other constructions. While I hope that this book is read by and influences people who believe in the objective nature of reality and who believe that history writing consists of representing that reality in various complex, traditional ways, I am compelled to assume the rhetorical stance that the writing of any history inevitably remains ideological and unstable. I announce my race (a construction), my gender (a construction, as opposed to sex), my social class, and my citizenship so that decoders will know some basic issues that inevitably construct this book.

A historicist stance, of course, differs from the foundationalist stance that historical reconstruction is assumed to be more or less neutral or the related stance that posits one, universalized reader. Such stances disregard the ears, lenses, and ideology of a given interpreter and place him or her in very different ideological, historical, and technological cir-

---

40. A *barbar* is a non-Greek and as such helped to construct Greek identity through the establishment of otherness.

cumstances. My case for new rhetorical action based on some (not all) aspects of Isocrates' theories enables me to propose more inclusive, action-based issues for literacy today as it is conditioned by literate, visual oralism/auralism, that is, not merely the act of speaking but the intersubjective, voiced activities of minds undulating within a specific dominant culture and usually interacting subjectively with other cultures. A primary site for this literacy is television. I aim not merely to make a case for Isocrates as a central component of a particular textual canon of classical Greek rhetoric. For many readers, he is already there in a second tier, at a level that is persistently inferior to that of Plato and Aristotle, a replication of the anti-Sophistic agenda put forth by Plato and Aristotle themselves (in different ways and with different motives) and that was so well explicated by writers whom I will discuss in chapters 2 and 3. Such a reading would simply perpetuate the idea of decrepit and, in fact, moldy Great Books of Rhetoric.

Instead, I aim to suggest ways to integrate recent North American theoretical material into what we have received as classical rhetoric, so that we can reconstruct Isocrates' writings with different values in mind and, crucially, with new performance. It is of central importance to make Isocratic Sophistic classical Greek rhetoric and writing part of the cultural conversation and agenda for action in the current pedagogical scene and in other scenes, including, of course, interior dialectics, or how people articulate within themselves (constitute themselves) and with other people in everyday ways.

Isocrates remains crucial in de-Heritaged Sophistic classical rhetoric and writing practices because of the unique infusion of oral/aural articulation (meant here as oral/aural structures of thought/language action) that he lived and at which he made a living. I will connect his historical, Sophistical moment with the current massive transition into electronic forms of discourse, or what Walter J. Ong has named secondary orality.[41]

41. See Ong, *Orality and Literacy*, particularly pp. 11, 135–138, and 158–164. Ong provides important material on electronic forms of consciousness; he has not yet (as he points out) explored its implications. Nevertheless, his references to secondary orality in *Orality and Literacy*, as well as in other texts, indicate his recognition of this enormous change. I have not used the phrase "secondary orality" for reasons I explain in chapter 2.

Issues in ancient literacy resemble our own. This is so because ancient literate oralism/auralism occupied a central position in fourth-century-B.C.E. dominant culture, a position that the inhabitants themselves were aware of only partially, if at all.[42] While William V. Harris, an ancient historian, approaches literacy as the ability to read and write, emphasizing functional literacy,[43] I approach the issue differently. In this book, I study oralism/auralism as a system of consciousness/mentalité that has been as vaguely understood in our own time as it was in Isocrates' and Diotima's, and for many of the same reasons. Just as many of their issues in literacy resemble our own, so many more are utterly different.

It should go without saying (but, of course, it does not) that various epochs of historical rhetoric and writing provide valuable locations for the study of difference. The correspondences between Isocrates' Sophism and video performance are in fact dwarfed by their differences. While the Greek aristocrats and the barbars provide important lessons in cultural difference and how it is constituted, their rhetorical/cultural situations remain dramatically different.

Literacy studies in rhetoric/composition, already a rich location of productive research that opens the borders between research and pedagogy, need to be more fully informed by historicized rhetoric and writing practices. Traditional historical rhetoric studies remain in dire need of theorizing. At the same time, postmodern literary studies on electronic media are in dire need of literacy studies, a retheorized historical rhetoric, and a theorized pedagogy. Postmodern studies in particular need to follow the lead of rhetoric/composition in centralizing pedagogy and not marginalizing it. While the contradictions among Sophistic classical rhetoric, rhetoric and composition studies, and television and computers are vast, the similarities remain striking.[44] Attention to the three areas—especially to how they have been constructed and how they might be

---

42. I adapt this idea of a central position from Walter J. Ong, *Orality and Literacy* and *The Presence of the Word*; and Eric A. Havelock, *Preface to Plato* and *The Greek Concept of Justice*. In chapter 2, however, I split Ong from Havelock and show Havelock's severe limitations.

43. See "Levels of Greek and Roman Literacy," in Harris's *Ancient Literacy*, pp. 3–24, for example.

44. The strands I set out above are constructed from these three fields.

constructed—can strengthen the humanities as they now reunfold. We stand at a powerful historical moment, at a time when we are able to make substantial changes in how language is deployed (and understood) particularly by the general population, most of whom believe, partly as a result of school literacy, that thought and articulation are separate activities, connected only by the idea that articulation is a secondhand representation of the real and prior phenomenon of thought. If we grasp this opportunity—what I will discuss later as the kairic moment, the classical concept, central to rhetoric, of the timely, opportune moment for persuasion and belief to occur—then we will be able to accomplish many things, one of which is a revivification of the humanities as a series of connected activities and intersubjective performances for mass groups, rather than the commodified, unsatisfied desires of the midcultists who think of themselves as more "literate," more "cultured," than their mass-cult cousins.[45]

We have arrived at a crucial historical moment when the humanities need to reassert leadership over radical changes in technology, gender construction, racial categories, and ethics. Rhetorical studies across many fields and rhetoric/composition studies in English provide powerful intellectual, historical, and, most of all, ethical bases for the advancement of the electronic revolution and the new literacy that it has brought us.[46]

45. See Dwight Macdonald's essay "Masscult and Midcult," in *Against the American Grain*, pp. 3–75. Macdonald's sexism (for example, his consistent exclusion of women writers) and elitism (for example, "Masscult is bad in a new way: it doesn't even have the theoretical possibility of being good," p. 4) can make the study of this essay difficult. His categories of "High Culture," "masscult" and "midcult" retain usefulness , however, and help to move away from the still common binary of high art versus low art or high culture versus low culture. Van Wyck Brooks's "brows" remain useful as well, even as many of us may reject his ideological positioning as well. For other, more-probing examples of cultural criticism, see Raymond Williams, E. P. Thompson, and Tania Modleski.

46. The story of the resurgence of rhetoric since 1963 or so has been told many times. See, for example, Robert J. Connors, Lisa S. Ede, and Andrea A. Lunsford, "The Revival of Rhetoric in America;" Berlin, *Rhetoric and Reality*; Welch, *The Contemporary Reception of Classical Rhetoric*; and others. Certainly central in this resurgence are the Dartmouth Anglo-American Conference on the Teaching of Writing, Edward P. J. Corbett's *Classical Rhetoric for the Modern Student*, and the cultural upheavals of the 1960s, including the Civil Rights movement, the anti–Vietnam War movement, and the Second Wave of U.S. feminism.

The general U.S. public, including many students, now have been conditioned by three generations of desiccated formalisms: the current-traditional paradigm in writing instruction and New Critical formalism in literary studies. Both branches of English studies have been tacitly committed to the pseudo-Romantic idea of artistic genius. This ideology severs students from their writing and other kinds of encoding by singling out the "geniuses," who are seen as having special power not available to student and other writers. The power of European Romanticism of the late eighteenth and early nineteenth centuries, so transformative for writing, has now been vitiated. We now live in a state of romantic devolution in which the clichés of a great intellectual movement prevent student and other writers from participating fully in literacy. The pseudo-Romantic residue in U.S. English instruction makes the task large; the agenda for continuing change must proceed in a number of steps.

2

An Isocratic Literacy Theory: An Alternative Rhetoric of Oral/Aural Articulation

Posed against rhetorical torture and the scourging of the opponent in philosophical combat lie the practices of the Sophists and the procedures of the radical democracy of fifth-century Athens. Ancient democracy must, of course, be mapped as an absence. We have only hostile, aristocratic representations of it, from thinkers like Plato, appalled by mob rule, resolutely opposed to sophistic teachings; we have only the most pitiful shreds of the words of the Sophists. The *demos*, the people themselves, have no voice in history; they exist only as figured by these others. The democracy is a present absence, something difficult to capture, since our vision of it is presented by the countertradition, the antidemocrats, the anti-Sophists. But democracy was meant to be rule by the people, an ongoing process of dialogue and debate in the city's assembly. Although aristocrats often ruled the ancient city through powers of eloquence and traditional authority, although slaves, women, and foreigners were excluded from the democratic process, although corruption and bribery often tainted the process and its forms of dialectic, there is nonetheless something extraordinary in the practices of the Sophists and in the Athenian assembly. Their history is one of particularity, or rooted historicity and limited, nontheoretical, absolute temporality.

Page duBois, "Violence and the Rhetoric of Philosophy"[1]

Diachronic study of orality and literacy and of the various stages in the evolution from one to the other sets up a frame of reference in which it is possible to understand better not only pristine oral culture and subsequent writing culture, but also the print culture that brings writing to a new peak and the electronic culture which builds on both writing and print. In this diachronic framework, past and present, Homer and television, can illuminate one another.

Walter J. Ong, *Orality and Literacy*[2]

1. In T. Poulakos, ed., *Rethinking the History of Rhetoric*, pp. 132–133.
2. P. 2.

The "traditional," historicized U.S. rhetoric that has been in place since the nineteenth century does not work anymore.[3] It is out of date and out of touch with rapidly changing communication technologies, gender constructions, and the racial constructions of America. Literacy in the twenty-first century needs to be better understood within the newly historicized rhetoric exemplified by duBois's and Ong's reconstructions above. Traditional literacy does not work because intersubjective and intrasubjective communication has changed drastically, for many reasons, one of which is the change in communication technology that has permeated the last one hundred years, allowing electronic forms of communication to reshape literacy. Another central change is the restructuring of subjectivities. The rehistoricizing has been taking place since the mid 1980s with great energy and debate. As the newly historicized accounts of classical rhetoric proliferate, a rich renewal of Sophism has emerged within English studies as well as within communication studies.[4] As Susan C. Jarratt points out with her epigraph from Friedrich

3. After-modernist versions of eighteenth and nineteenth-century rhetorics have enabled rhetoric and composition studies to appropriate these important eras in ways that indicate rhetoric's most recent "death" is now over (compare Jane Sutton's "The Death of Rhetoric and Its Rebirth in Philosophy" for a useful version of the birthing and dying of rhetoric in ancient Greece). The birthing and dying of rhetoric have characterized its 2,400 years of existence in the West. For eighteenth-century rhetoric in English, see, for example, H. Lewis Ulman, *Things, Thoughts, Words, and Actions: The Problem of Language in Late Eighteenth-Century British Rhetorical Theory*; Catherine Hobbs, "Eighteenth-Century Language and Rhetoric: The Death of Rhetoric and the Birth of Rhetoricality"; Thomas Miller, *The Formation of College English: Rhetoric and Belles Lettres in the British Cultural Provinces*. For the nineteenth century, see Winifred Bryan Horner, *Nineteenth-Century Scottish Rhetoric*; Nan Johnson, *Nineteenth-Century Rhetoric in North America*; James Berlin, *Writing Instruction in Nineteenth-Century American Colleges*; Robert Connors, "Personal Writing Assignments"; Gregory Clark and S. Michael Halloran, eds., *Oratorical Culture in Nineteenth-Century America: Transformations in the Theory and Practice of Rhetoric*; Catherine Hobbs, ed., *Nineteenth-Century Women Learn to Write*; and Susan Miller, *Assuming the Positions*.

4. Sophism has been a center of interest in classics as well and in philology in Europe. See, for example, Jacqueline de Romilly's *Rhetoric and Magic in Ancient Greece* and her more recent book *The Great Sophists in Periclean Athens*. Philosophy as well has shown renewed interest in Sophism, and all these disciplines have shown an intermingling. However, as I will argue throughout this book,

Nietzsche, Sophism tends to be historically revived in periods of great social change.[5]

In this chapter, I will present Isocrates as a Sophist whose writing and teaching life offers us a vision of Sophism that we can adapt to our scholarly and teaching lives.[6] Isocrates is a literate Sophist, in more ways than one, but in many ways he is an anti-Sophist: he would not speak publicly—a decision that had the effect, whatever his intentions, of privileging writing. His negative attitude toward spoken performance in fact changed Sophism. The energy of the spoken word, its evanescence, as Ong describes speaking, was transmuted by Isocrates. Pamphlets replaced the spoken performance. With this change came a turn; that is, with this change we can detect movement in the patterns of thought and action in Isocrates' written performances. While the noetic of his Greek world remains primary for him, a new noetic begins to take shape, and it is based partly on a different kind of performance that includes the disembodied acts of writing and reading and interpreting and acting. For Isocrates, the production of discourse, not just the passive consumption of it by a hearer/reader/interpreter, remains central to his concept of *philosophia*, a concept quite different from the Platonic concept of philosophy now taken for granted. For Isocrates, *logos* lies at the center of learning, the center of the curriculum, and the center of social action. His *paideia*, more than Plato's, empowers people and culture.

---

disciplines construct knowledge to a large extent. The deployment of Gorgias in, say, the discipline of classics, differs substantially from his deployment in rhetoric/composition studies in English.

5. *Rereading the Sophists: Classical Rhetoric Refigured*, p. xv. The epigraph reads, "Every advance in epistemology and moral knowledge has reinstated the Sophists" (from Nietzsche's *Will to Power*).

6. For traditional treatments of the older Sophists, see George A. Kennedy, *Classical Rhetoric and Its Christian and Secular Tradition from Ancient to Modern Times*, pp. 25–40; G. B. Kerferd, *The Sophistic Movement*; Mario Untersteiner, *The Sophists*; W. K. C. Guthrie, *The Sophists*; Jacqueline de Romilly, *The Great Sophists in Periclean Athens*; and Edward Schiappa, "Sophistic Rhetoric: Oasis or Mirage." For newly theorized work on the Sophists, see Susan C. Jarratt, *Rereading the Sophists: Classical Rhetoric Refigured*; John Poulakos, *Sophistical Rhetoric in Classical Greece*; and Barbara Biesecker, "Coming to Terms with Recent Attempts to Write Women into the History of Rhetoric."

Isocrates' broadly based development of judgment, a quality that transcends knowledge and includes ethics, enables the individual to act within a culture. Life issues that cannot be predicted are met by a mind and sensibility trained in *philosophia*. Isocrates' *paideia* and how an individual can best interact with it provides one challenge to the still hegemonic Platonic agenda of knowledge and a very different kind of philosophy. In addition, the Isocratic theory of culture as critical response is central to current appropriations of Isocrates in rhetorical theory and in educational systems.

As I discussed in chapter 1, the general U.S. public, including many students, now have been conditioned by three generations of rigorous training in desiccated formalisms in writing instruction and in literary chronology. Both branches of English studies have been tacitly committed to the pseudo-Romantic idea of artistic genius, an ideology that severs students from their writing and other kinds of encoding and from "geniuses" who are seen as having special powers not available to students and other writers. The power of European and U.S. Romanticism of the late eighteenth and early nineteenth centuries, so transformative for writing, has been vitiated. We live now, in fact, in a state of Romantic devolution in which the clichés of an important intellectual movement prevent students and other writers from participating fully in literacy as consciousness. The pseudo-Romantic residue in U.S. English instruction makes the task large; the agenda for continuing change must proceed in a number of steps. One of these steps is the reconstruction of historical rhetoric.

Isocrates' *logos* is rhetorical, theoretical, and not rigidly logical; rather, *logos* operates in Isocrates in ways that differ from the dominance of logic (in the sense of the rational) associated with receptions of Plato and Aristotle in traditional lines of inquiry. Isocratic *logos* is more associative than linear, more concerned with belief and "right" action. We can make this move because of Isocrates' historical moment, his particular positioning as an oral/aural-dominant and literate-dominant Sophist. He is a writing Sophist and a formulator of one version of early classical Greek rhetoric, a version that evolved from his appropriation of writing as a primary way of articulating, from his interpretation of culture, and from how rhetoric operates within individuals and within the culture that the individual inhabits and negotiates. Isocrates' rhetoric and writing enable us to construct versions of classical rhetoric that are more powerful (partly because they are more useful) than the familiar classical rhetoric exemplified by Aristotle and his positive appropriators (for example, James J. Murphy) and his detractors (for example, James Berlin.)[7] As I discussed in *The Contemporary Reception of Classical Rhetoric*, the dominant twentieth-century versions of classical rhetoric begin seriously with Aristotle, thus creating a strand of classical rhetoric that is, not surprisingly, categorical and highly ordered. I, in a continuing project, reconstruct classical rhetoric for the twenty-first century in an after-postmodern world, a world where a shifting episteme is taking place. This world attends to Isocrates' theories about the production of discourse and its relationship to the training of the mind and sensibilities in and out of school. What happens to classical rhetoric when Isocrates' rhetorical theories are interpreted as a central, and not merely a decorative, part of the ideology that incorporates a traditionally received body of material?[8] I contend that we do not now know Isocrates' rhetorical theories well enough, because we have not understood classical Greek rhetoric and writing practices for our electrified time. After I rehearse traditional lines of response to Isocrates, I position his work/activity differently, that is, according to an electrified rhetoric/writing version, a version that takes account of some postmodernist moves and then looks beyond that ism to the new discursive situation in which we find ourselves because of electric rhetoric. I then demonstrate the limitations of an Isocratic theory of rhetoric, particularly as it is interpreted with attention to the category of woman in classical rhetoric and Isocrates' explicit imperialist agenda, stances that are, of course, mutually reinforcing. However, according to this interpretive move, Isocratic rhetoric and

7. See Murphy, *A Synoptic History of Classical Rhetoric*, and Berlin, *Writing Instruction in Nineteenth-Century American Colleges*.

8. I use "ideology" throughout this book in the sense that Terry Eagleton develops it in *Ideology* and other places. Obviously this keyword is problematic and is undergoing important new conceptualizations. See, for example, Lynnette Hunter's "Ideology and Ethos in the Nation State." See also Christine Oravec and Michael Salvador's "The Duality of Rhetoric: Theory as Discursive Practice," in Poulakos, *Rethinking the History of Rhetoric*, pp. 173–192, where "ideology" is positioned in helpful ways.

writing practices can be deployed in a way that adapts his oralism/auralism and that at the same time acknowledges, understands, and eventually condemns Isocrates' imperialism toward women of all social classes and *barbars* in carrying out his all-Greek vision (that is to say, the panhellenism to which he was so committed).

Isocrates and indeed all classical rhetorics offer us alternatives to the hegemony of modern rhetoric, which has, until very recently, dominated not only the scholarship in rhetoric and composition (think only of the current traditional paradigm) but also the pedagogical practices that are inevitably theorized, whether the writing teacher knows it or not.[9] As Sharon Crowley writes,

Rethinking modern rhetoric is hard to do in the absence of postmodern rhetorical theories. However, ancient and medieval accounts of composing do present us with dramatic alternatives to modernist accounts, and hence they can serve as sources for understanding the workings of human communication in nonmodern ways.... The existence of alternative models of composing demonstrates the ahistoricity of modern attempts to prescribe a universalized composing process based on literate skills.[10]

For Isocrates, rhetoric consists of language as it constitutes part of thought (that is, interior discourse) and language as it constitutes one's negotiations with the world (that is, exterior discourse). Writing, speaking, and thinking are mutually dependent for him and, I contend, heavily conditioned by the technology of writing. In *Antidosis*, Isocrates writes,

The same arguments which we use in persuading others when we speak in public, we employ also when we deliberate in our own thoughts; and while we call articulate those who are able to speak before a crowd, we regard as wise those who most effectively deliberate their problems in their own minds.... None of the things which are done with intelligence take place without the help of *logos*.... In all our actions as well as in all our thoughts language is our guide, and is most employed by those who have the most wisdom."[11]

9. On this point, see Welch, "Ideology and Freshman Textbook Production: The Place of Theory in Writing Pedagogy." Obviously, this material applies to other fields of teaching as well. My focus here is rhetoric/composition studies in English.

10. "Modern Rhetoric and Memory," p. 34.

11. Sec. 256. The translations are George Norlin's, *Isocrates*, vol. 2, Elaine Fantham's unpublished translation, and, to a limited extent, my own. I have maintained Greek keywords that I have found to be pivotal in redeploying Isocrates.

Isocrates refers in this passage, and throughout *Antidosis*, to the relationship between thought and articulation that formed a center of his *logos*-dominant rhetorical theory. The work is in the genre of an apology, commonly written, of course, at that time (Plato's *Apology* for Socrates is perhaps the best known now), and functions as an explanation of Isocrates' attitude toward language and culture.[12] The nature of this inner deliberation and how it can be trained through education and ethics lies at the center of my inquiry in the Isocrates portion of this book. Isocrates claims that rhetorical study can produce wise interior discourse, or deliberation with oneself across a range of subject areas. He did not confine himself to the public, the external, or the material, as positivist interpretations so frequently suggest—a claim that has been made repeatedly about classical rhetoric in general, by such scholars as Lil Brannon and C. H. Knoblauch and as Douglas Ehninger, as well as many others.[13] Isocrates preoccupied himself with advancing a rhetorical theory that develops inner speech, and particular kinds of inner speech, that enable the person studying to develop advanced, complex thinking, part of which stems from the act of writing (for example, abstraction, the disembodied construction of audience, and the ability to hold competing

---

For example, *philosophia*, as I argue later, must be maintained as a Greek keyword so that we can separate Isocratic *philosophia* from normalized Platonic philosophy, as I do below.

12. Plato's *Apology* is frequently linked to *Euthyphro* and *Crito* and presented as the "beginnings" or "origins" of genuine Western philosophy (or just philosophy). This linkage and presentation and disciplinary lineage construct, of course, the nature of philosophy for many readers. See, for example, *Euthyphro, Crito, and Apology*, all in *Opera*, vol. 1, ed. E. A. Duke et al. These presentations—taken for granted as they have been—need to be reconceptualized so that we teach our students more effectively. For example, the historical situation in which these three works were written, including the situation of subjectivity, is central to an inclusive study of Plato. When they are presented for their content, in a mode that pretends that disciplinary presentation makes no difference, then receptions of Plato lead to strange constructions of rhetoric/writing. For more on this issue, see my "Appropriating Plato's Rhetoric and Writing into Contemporary Rhetoric and Composition Studies," *The Contemporary Reception of Classical Rhetoric: Appropriations of Ancient Discourse* (pp. 93–111).

13. See Brannon and Kaoblanch, *Rhetorical Tradition and the Teaching of Writing*, and Ehninger, "On Systems of Rhetoric."

concepts simultaneously in a written text). From this base the individual negotiates a relationship with the public world. The critical commonplace that holds that Isocrates and other classical rhetoricians split public discourse from private discourse is not in accord with the ideologies/texts of classical rhetoric and writing. That split has been constructed for various reasons that do not work now.[14] One of the reasons is that our conceptions of the public and the private are, of course, not those of fourth-century-B.C.E. Athens. The century of electronic discourse from the 1890s to the 1990s has further rearranged the interrelationship, the changing mixture, of public and private. The repetition of these splits reinforces the myth chain that makes any ancient culture interesting but irrelevant.[15]

Isocrates' innovative theories of rhetoric synthesized material from the Older Sophists and refuted material from the hucksterish Sophists—particularly the Eristics—who converted language into a series of skills that discounted *logos*, for example, Alcidamus.[16] Isocrates' rhetoric was very much a part of the new ways of thinking that made the fourth century

14. See, for example, Robert Connors's adaptation of this presumed split in "Personal Writing Assignments," an essay that has the virtue of historicizing (although Connors does not use that word) classical rhetoric and writing practices. His reliance on a modern, romantic conception of the "personal" is not in accord with the epistemologies of the two periods. For a helpful analysis of expressive writing and its recent hegemony in many institutional writing practices, see Lester Faigley, "Ideologies of the Self in Writing Evaluation," in *Fragments of Rationality: Postmodernism and the Subject of Composition*, pp. 111–131. For an alternative view but one that also questions the cult of individualism, see Bleich, *The Double Perspective*, especially pp. 187–218. Public-private constructions as they relate to gender are here treated in chapter 3.

15. See Roland Barthes, "The Rhetoric of the Image." See also standard works on semiotics for further analysis of myth chains.

16. The designation "Older Sophists" refers to one of the earliest known groups of Western language performers such as Protagoras, Gorgias, and Alcidamus. Mostly itinerant teachers, they tended to be outsiders to Athens and caused some dismay for charging fees for their teaching. Their otherness disturbed many people. We do not have their writings extant, but we do have fragments of their writing embedded in the writing of other writers. The standard text in English for these embedded fragments is *The Older Sophists: A Complete Translation by Several Hands of the Fragments in "Die Fragmente der Vorsokratiker," Edited by Diels-Kranz, with a New Edition of Antiphon and of Euthydemus*, ed. Rosamond Kent Sprague. The writings of the Older Sophists represented in Sprague (Protagoras, Xeniades, Gorgias, Lycophron, Prodicus, Thrasymachus, Hippias,

B.C.E. intellectually so different from the fifth, particularly in the realm of *paideia*.[17] Isocrates' writing (in his encomia, letters, and apology) depends partly on a new kind of abstraction: it is heavily subordinated, as his periodic sentences reveal. At the same time, it displays oral features: his writing is partially additive, with phrases strung together with "and" (Greek *kai*); his writing is both formulaic and repetitive; and frequently it is woven. His writing fluctuates between eye dominance and ear dominance.[18] He relies, in fact, on what we now regard as sampling,

---

Antiphon, Critias, Anonymus Iamblichi), in addition to the *Dissoi Logoi*, constitute a canonization by Diels and Kranz; this canon was disseminated through various other modern languages. Obviously, however, the list has the traits of other textual canons: exclusivity, hardening of the categories, and even whim. For a useful recent account of Alcidamus, see Tony Lentz's "The Unlettered Author: Alcidamus' Written Attack on Isocrates' Writing," in *Orality and Literacy in Hellenic Greece*, pp. 136–144. See also Phillip Sipiora, "Kairos in the Discourse of Isocrates."

17. For vivid analyses of these contrasts, see Werner Jaeger, *Paideia*, vols. 1, 2, and 3; George A. Kennedy, *Classical Rhetoric and Its Christian and Secular Tradition from Ancient to Modern Times*; Samuel Ijsseling, *Rhetoric and Philosophy in Conflict*; and Jean-Pierre Vernant, *Myth and Society in Ancient Greece*. See also H. I. Marrou's *History of Education in Antiquity* ("We know in fact that each new advance made by the Greek genius was soon followed by a corresponding endeavour to create an educational system that would disseminate it," p. 46).

18. See Ong, *Orality and Literacy*, pp. 36–50, for an important discussion of oral features of written and spoken discourse. For background on the reorganization of the sensorium, or the relationships among the five senses, see Marshall McLuhan, *The Gutenberg Galaxy* and *Understanding Media*. For an important theoretical extension of McLuhan for rhetoric and composition studies, see Patrick Mahony's "Marshall McLuhan in the Light of Classical Rhetoric." McLuhan's rereading of historical rhetoric remains central, even though in the United States he frequently is dismissed by scholars in the humanities; his reception in Europe remains very strong and widely recognized. See, for example, Lynette Hunter, "Ideology and Ethos in the Nation State." See also the critical biography *Marshall McLuhan: The Medium and the Messenger* by Philip Marchand, a text that reveals a number of troubling issues about McLuhan. Neither Marchand nor McLuhan saw McLuhan's deployment of a unified, modernist, white-male historical rhetoric that defined so much of McLuhan's innovative work. As Marchand points out (see, for example, pp. vii–viii, 54–56, and 91–100) McLuhan was deeply influenced by the New Critics in the United States. This deep connection partly accounts for McLuhan's misogyny, illustrated in virtually all his titles (see, for example, his first book, *The Mechanical Bride*).

a musical construction defined by recording one musical text onto another.[19] Isocrates samples extensively in *Antidosis*, where he quotes previous writing he had circulated (see, for example, section 59, the "extract" from *Panegyricus*, secs. 51–99; section 66, "extracts" from the oration *On the Peace*; and section 73, "extracts" from *To Nicocles*). This genre of verbal repetition is a primary location for understanding Isocrates' particular merger of writing and speaking. He achieves repeatability in writing, in striking contrast to Plato, who appears to have redrafted extensively. Isocrates' ability to write with this kind of abstraction, to maintain the resonance of his oral features, and to incorporate that ability into his theory of rhetoric puts him in a crucial place intellectually. The drive toward one kind of abstraction, toward the disembodied communication between writer and reader (and between writer as writer and writer as reader) that largely constitutes writing and the different epistemology required by writing, is central to understanding the range and adaptability of classical rhetoric, from Sappho, to the Sophists, to Quintilian.[20] Isocrates preoccupies himself with language as it constitutes part of thought and with public discourse.

In rudimentary form in the early *Against the Sophists* (written about 390 B.C.E.), and later developed with more complexity (for example, in the late *Antidosis*, written in 354–353 B.C.E.), Isocrates returns repeatedly to the development of judgment through the development of language ability. Writing constitutes a central role in this agenda. Crucially, Isocrates uses the word "philosophia" to signify the development of judgment, not just the gathering of knowledge, so that everyday issues as well as more momentous ones can be negotiated as they develop. Isocrates' use of the word "philosophia" is very different from our conception of the word philosophy. Our construction of philosophy is largely the Platonic and Cartesian construction and indicates the foundational principles that underlie Western knowledge and being (or reality). In the fourth century B.C.E., Isocrates and Plato promoted competing notions of

19. For a longer discussion of musical sampling, see David Sanjek, "Don't Have to DJ No More: Sampling and the 'Autonomous' Creator," especially pp. 610–611.

20. "Abstraction" in oralism is a complicated issue that I investigate below, along with the many genres of abstraction that exist.

"philosophia." For Isocrates, it involved the development of active judgment to enable one to interact within a culture. For Plato, it was understanding knowledge and being (reality) through the process of dialectic (one version of abstraction) and an understanding of how the soul recollects knowledge. So Isocrates and Plato deployed the word "philosophia" in radically different ways, finding in the keyword waves of meanings that led each one in a particular direction.[21] The English translation we now use so effortlessly, so normally, does not signify in even similar ways what the two writers were doing in their rhetorical/political/educational agendas, so much at odds with each other.[22]

Whenever the word "philosophia" appears in Isocrates (as it does, for example, throughout *Against the Sophists*), Norlin and Van Hook provide the wrong connotation when they translate it as "philosophy." It should be translated as "judgment" or the "development of judgment," and it should be carefully distinguished from our normalized sense of "philosophy." This distinction has not been made thoroughly enough. R. C. Jebb, in the standard *The Attic Orators from Antiphon to Isaeos*, describes "philosophia" as a "theory of culture," and Norlin in footnotes

21. For an explication of keywords and classical rhetorics, see Welch, *The Contemporary Reception of Classical Rhetoric*, pp. 12–28, 45–54, and 73–79.

22. The continuing dialogue on the nature of translation has everything to do with this issue. Translation experts of various schools reject the idea that Saussure complains about, that the general public believes that translation is a one-to-one substitution (see Welch, *The Contemporary Reception of Classical Rhetoric*, pp. 10–12, 16–17, and 28). Translation of keywords is, of course, complicated by the fact that readers collaborate in constructing texts and interpret from partly tacit ideologies. We cannot get back to an originary meaning of "philosophia," and I do not advocate that move here, even though so many philologically minded critics do. At the same time, the hardening of the categories of, say, English translations of standard Greek rhetorical and other texts has reinforced receptions of Greek rhetoric that have so damaged the historicizing of Western rhetorics and the historicizing of ideas. For an example of a radical improvement in the reception of an important rhetorical text, see George A. Kennedy's return to nonsexist language in his translation of Aristotle's *Rhetoric*. The generations of readers who absorbed sexist usage repeated as "truth" were damaged by these serious mistranslations of sexist material. Kennedy's improvement does not, of course, absolve Aristotle of his own baseline misogyny, which is, of course, considerable even when further sexism is not translated in.

to *Isocrates* glosses "philosophia" as judgment.[23] (Nevertheless, Norlin consistently translates the word as "philosophy.") The broadly based development of judgment (a quality that transcends knowledge) enables the individual to act within cultures. Issues in life that cannot be predicted are met by a mind and sensibility that have been critically trained and can determine how to respond to a variety of situations.

Modern Isocrates

Isocrates' modern reception has relied on a binary opposition of content and form in which the content has been acknowledged and dismissed and the form decontextualized from the supposed meaning and culture. The Isocrates portrayed in standard twentieth-century rhetorical histories for the most part has been appropriated in one of two ways: (1) he has been erased, as the Murphy and Berlin examples illustrate, or (2) he has been presented as the quaint "father" of a reputed liberal-arts tradition, segregated in the field of education specialists, or pablumized in a visionette of so-called general education.[24] He appears as an afterthought or is summarized in many twentieth-century works in ways that exclude his rhetorical theories, his version of *logos*, and that refuse to see his work on interior rhetoric and its relationship to culture. Kennedy, for example, in *The Art of Persuasion in Greece* (1963), marginalizes Isocrates' theories by declaring, with little evidence, that Isocrates was an "opportunist" (p. 175), that he was "tiresome," "long-winded," "superficial" (p. 203), and that he works through "decoration and obfuscation" (p. 203).[25] In

23. Although Jebb is philologically "standard," the fact that *The Attic Orators* is out of print presents a problem for the teaching of rhetoric and writing as an ancient cultural practice. This situation, of course, obtains in many burgeoning fields, where inordinate numbers of photocopies must be relied on. For other views of *philosophia*, see Edward Schiappa, "Isocrates' *Philosophia* and Contemporary Pragmatism," especially pp. 41–48, in Mailloux, *Rhetoric, Sophistry, Pragmatism.*

24. For a useful example of the devolution of the trivium portion of the liberal arts, see Grafton and Jardine's *From Humanism to the Humanities.* See also Martin Camargo's "Rhetoric."

25. Part of his book has reappeared in *A New History of Classical Rhetoric: An Extensive Revision and Abridgment of The Art of Persuasion in Greece, The Art*

Classical Rhetoric and Its Christian and Secular Tradition from Ancient to Modern Times (1980), Kennedy moves away from this dismissive stance.[26] Nevertheless, he refrains from treating Isocrates' work on interior and exterior discourse and Isocrates' persistent desire to help people think in more complicated ways. Kennedy assumes what can be called the sophisticated, conventional twentieth-century view that writing for Isocrates consisted of thought decorated with periodic sentences or that he merely applied Gorgias's figures to his own prose. This is the approach of formalism, a hallmark of twentieth-century teaching of writing and reading from the middle-school level through higher education. In each kind of formalism, language is viewed as a tangible, secondary object overlaid on the substance of thought. Articulation and thought are thus divorced, and so, of course, Isocrates' writing seems to be deficient. It is important to note that Kennedy in these texts interprets Isocrates as all scholars and indeed all readers interpret texts or construct texts: by relying on the training one has received. U.S. classics scholars, like scholars in all the disciplines of the trivium, have a particular kind of training deeply conditioned by formalist reading theories that privilege writing issues such as "clarity," "grace," and the deployment of figures. Kennedy, of course, transcends formalism and deploys current theory with a depth of scope that has helped to drive rhetoric and composition studies, as well as work in classics.[27]

In *Antidosis* and elsewhere, Isocrates rejects the idea that language is a container that holds meaning, a ubiquitous attitude toward language in U.S. culture and an attitude that poses one of the most pressing challenges for people who work with theories of discourse. The positivistic

---

of Rhetoric in the Roman World, and Greek Rhetoric under Christian Emperors. While Kennedy has revised his earlier texts for the 1993 volume, the scholarly apparatus remains in these earlier books.

26. See, for example, pp. 31–36, where Kennedy reexplicates Isocrates, a reading I will further treat below.

27. See his four essays in Kennedy, ed., *The Cambridge History of Literary Criticism*, vol. 1, for example. See also his trenchant essay in *The Politics of Liberal Education*, edited by Gless and Smith, an unusual volume in that, aside from Kennedy and perhaps two other writers, the contributors appear to believe that the liberal arts are equivalent to the humanities, and thus not only erase the quadrivium but also historicize ideas in a bizarre way (see pp. 114 ff.).

attitude that language is a thing out there, retrievable, tangible, and de-terminant, plagues not only our own scholarly endeavors; it persisted as an issue in ancient Greek rhetoric, which relied frequently on rule-bound handbooks, rote leaning, and the imposition of static models of dis-course, all of which are depressingly familiar in the late twentieth cen-tury. Both Isocrates and Plato fought fiercely against this instrumentalist attitude toward language. A number of the Sophists, for example, Alcidamus, had relied on this use of language. The premise that language is a container that holds meaning (usually unmentioned because it is assumed) converts not only discourse into a mechanical object but human beings as well into mechanical objects. Isocrates' rhetorical theory consistently works against this premise in his analysis of Helen in the *Encomium* for Helen, in *Panegyricus*, in *Antidosis*, and in other places. Nevertheless, numerous commentators interpret Isocrates as a manipu-lator of language regarded as decoration, including Samuel Ijsseling, whose reception of Isocrates has been representative.[28] In this and other ways, modern reception of Isocrates resembles that of his teacher Gor-gias, the magical *logos*-user.[29]

A second dominant twentieth-century appropriation of Isocrates occurs in his designation as the "father" of the liberal arts, a paternity that exists in some histories as a form of hermaphroditism, since one cannot locate a mother of the liberal arts with whom the father Isocrates would have collaborated.[30] This designation of paternity constitutes a

---

28. See *Rhetoric and Philosophy in Conflict: An Historical Survey*, pp. 18–25.

29. For the important area of rhetoric and magic, see William A. Covino, *The Art of Wondering: A Revisionist Return to the Art of Rhetoric*. See also Jacque-line de Romilly, *Rhetoric and Magic in Ancient Greece*, and Kenneth Burke, *A Grammar of Motives*.

30. Some schools of feminist theories teach us, of course, that the erasure of a maternal source in metaphorizing men into "fathers" is dictated by an ideology of male dominance in which women are to be forgotten, a debilitating relation-ship to culture that enervates as it erases (see Judith Butler, *Gender Trouble*). The counterpart linguistic move of, say, making nature, nations, and ships maternal does not, of course, equalize the "father of" motif. Rather, the feminine desig-nators further ghettoize women primarily as nurturers, gestators (see Shulamith Firestone), and angels of the household (see, for example, Smith-Rosenberg, *Disorderly Conduct: Visions of Gender in Victorian America*) in a way that characterizes nineteenth- and twentieth-century Western culture.

dismissal of his rhetorical theory that treats relationships between thought and language and makes central the development of critical judgment among individuals and the development of healthy cultures. The dismissal of Isocrates as a clever deviser of a nice curriculum bypasses not only Isocrates' complex rhetorical and cultural agendas; it bypasses the changes in writing that Isocrates and his students brought about.

Postmodern Isocratic Rhetoric

What happens to classical rhetoric, we may ask, when Isocrates' rhetorical theories are interpreted as central to or definitive of a rehistoricized classical rhetoric and not as decorative pieces that are remarkable for being linguistically clever? What happens to classical rhetoric when Isocrates is not erased, marginalized, or ridiculed? Does the Isocratic theory of culture as critical language performance offer a way out of the binary opposition of content and form that continues to enervate all areas of the trivium and maintain their triviality?[31]

If we redeploy Isocrates in the ways I have suggested, then we see a number of important issues for rehistoricized rhetoric and writing practices: that the dependence of thought and language on each other is definitive in Isocrates' far-from-modern rhetorical theories; that neither Isocrates nor other Greek rhetoricians maintained the idea of language as a container; that deliberation with oneself across a wide variety of subjects (interior discourse) is a central part of Isocrates' rhetorical theories; that rhetoric works toward more complex thinking, part of which derives from the act of writing, which brings with it the ability to construct a disembodied audience. Further, a redeployed Isocrates would reveal strategies that strengthen exterior rhetoric, discourse as communication with the world. The rhetorician is strengthened because he or she develops the ability to make sound judgments about many kinds of issues and actions. This accords with Isocrates' use of the word "philosophia,"

31. I refer here to culture with a small "c," not to the more common, elitist appropriation of Culture with capital "C," a stance based on the consumption of artifacts that have been made inert and in which therefore the acts of consuming and unidirectional transfer dominate, a process that grows out of the pipe-transfer mode of learning in many schools, ancient and modern. This modernist stance is antidemocratic.

which signifies something more akin to judgment, not philosophy as an underlying set of principles or as an area of study.

If we integrate reconstructions of Isocrates' rhetorical theories into the standard modern array of theories of classical rhetoric, then we find material or strategies we had not known. By reconstructing Isocrates, we are able to reconstruct classical rhetoric from a series of inert pre-scriptions (for example, that classical rhetoric is dominantly oral/aural and that writing is peripheral, not influential, or just another convenient tool) and from lists (for example, that classical rhetoric consists of three kinds of speeches, six parts of an oration, and so on)[32] into a comprehensive system that depends on weaving articulation and thought, places an emphasis on the production of discourse, and is not confined to the analysis of discourse. Of course, interpretation was crucial, but interpretation as it arises from discourse production remains the key issue for Isocrates from the early fragment *Against Euthynus* (403 B.C.E.) to the late piece *Panathenaicus* (342 B.C.E.), written when he was 98. Isocrates is useful as an historical correspondent: he is a rhetorical theorist who can offer us an alternative to the modern current-traditional paradigm (which is a reduced Platonism) and the attendant tenacious belief in language as a container that holds meaning. By placing Isocrates on the same level with the (often tacitly) revered Plato and Aristotle, we make a radical move.

It is imperative to step back and announce that even this reconstruction is inadequate until recent theorizing is used (1) to interrogate the ideology of the individual that I have set up in this analysis and (2) to persuade my audience that traditional classical Greek rhetoric and reconstructed classical Greek rhetoric are going to (and should) remain only of antiquarian interest unless the inherent nature of politics and the tenacity of gender obliviousness and race construction are addressed.

Classical rhetoric as a comprehensive system of discourse theory remains unique among the rhetorical theories available to us because it depends on the relationships among rhetoric, history, politics, educational institutions, and, perhaps most important, the everyday uses of languages that arise from ideological positioning. It treats not only public

32. Although, see an alternative stance on the issue of these formulas in my *Contemporary Reception of Classical Rhetoric*, pp. 101, 108.

and private discourse but also the intricate and interdependent relationships between articulation and thought. And it does so in a way that offers powerful alternatives to the normalized way of viewing knowledge in the modern period.[33]

Isocrates' rhetorical theories competed in the fourth-century-B.C.E. flux of language, thought, and action, all three of which were embedded in the keyword *logos*.[34] *Logos* forms a center of Isocrates' rhetoric. The

33. Lest I read or sound like a cheerleader for classical rhetoric, an old-books fan of a New Humanist kind, let me refer you to two literary theorists who are energized proponents of classical rhetoric. In "A Small History of Rhetoric" (in *Walter Benjamin, or Towards a Revolutionary Criticism*), Terry Eagleton claims, "A political literary criticism is not the invention of Marxists. On the contrary, it is one of the oldest, most venerable forms of literary criticism we know. The most widespread early criticism on historical record was not, in our sense, 'aesthetic,' it was a mode of what we would now call 'discourse theory,' devoted to analysing the material effects of particular uses of language in particular social conjunctures. It was a highly elaborate theory of specific signifying practices—above all, of the discursive practices of the judicial, political and religious apparatuses of the state. Its intention, quite consciously, was systematically to theorize the articulations of discourse and power, and to do so in the name of political practice: to enrich the political effectivity of signification. The name of the form of criticism was rhetoric. From its earliest formulations by Corax of Syracuse in fifth-century Greece B.C.E., rhetoric came in Roman schools to be practically equivalent to higher education as such" (p. 101). (See Welch, "Interpreting the Silent 'Aryan Model' of Classical Histories: Martin Bernal, Terry Eagleton, and the Politics of Rhetoric and 'Western Civilization.'") The second energized proponent from the realm of literary theory is Jane P. Tompkins, who concludes "An Introduction to Reader-Response Criticism" with, "The view of language as the ultimate form of power is not unlike that of the Greek rhetoricians who believed that speech was a 'great prince' able to transform human experience. Both views of language restore to literature what literary theorists since the middle of the eighteenth century, in the interests of literature itself, had been denying that it possesses—the ability to influence human behavior in a direct and practical manner. In order for literature to perform its function as a civilizing agent, it was thought necessary to set it apart from the merely mechanical and practical spheres of life" (p. xxv).

34. I use "keyword" as a term that resonates with related Greek concepts that cannot be effectively translated into English, and so, that work more effectively as loan words or loan phrases. (See my *Contemporary Reception of Classical Rhetoric*, pp. 12–14, 16–19, 21, 27–28, 45, 49, 54, 64, 73–79, and 169. See also Raymond Williams, *Keywords: A Vocabulary of Culture and Society*, particularly pp. 11–27; W. K. C. Guthrie, *The Sophists*, p. 55; Trevor Montroy, "An Appropriation of Five Keywords in Contemporary Rhetoric.")

Thesaurus Linguae Graecae demonstrates the rich variations of context of *logos*. In addition, Liddell and Scott's *Greek-English Lexicon* provides evidence that *logos* signifies not simply speech but rather can signify thought, reflection, deliberation with oneself, deliberation with others, an account, a rendering, a story, history, or reasoning. The locations of *logos* provided by *Thesaurus Linguae Graecae* enable us to see in Isocrates' writing a complex system of *logos* that is remarkably abstract and complex, as an investigation of the undulation of his periodic sentences reveals.[35]

The persistent reductionism of twentieth-century English translations of Isocrates' pivotal theory of *logos* as speech derives in part from George Norlin's and Larue Van Hook's translations from the late 1920s and the 1930s and the repetition of them by the commentators who acknowledge Isocrates' powerful theories just to erase them. Norlin's and Van Hook's English translations remain important sites for the twentieth-century marginalization of Isocrates' rhetorical theory. Norlin translates *logos* as "speech," bypassing the many other connotations demanded by the contexts in which Isocrates uses this word. Norlin in particular repeats and helps to sustain the unreflective use of *logos* as uttered speech (usually an oration) and so bypasses or understates the centrality of inner speech, or self deliberation, a concept that Isocrates worked on consistently. In my own translations of Isocrates' work, I make fuller use of the many connotations of *logos* in Isocrates, concentrating on the relationship between inner speech and thought and the centrality of rhetoric in this relationship. Isocrates' development of judgment through interaction of various kinds of language—in writing, in speaking, and in self deliberation—make his rhetorical theory highly useful for today's postmodernized rhetorics and writing practices.

35. See Kennedy's explication of one of Isocrates' periods in *Classical Rhetoric and Its Christian and Secular Tradition from Ancient to Modern Times*. Kennedy writes, "The translation [Kennedy's] attempts to show how some of the Gorgianic figures are utilized. There is a pervasive antithesis or balancing of concepts, two or more clauses or phrases are often given approximately the same shape and length, and in the original there is a considerable amount of similarity of sound at the beginning or end of sense units. In the translation some of these sound effects are identified by italics. The rhythm of the concluding words in Greek is that of the end of a line of heroic verse: dactyl plus spondee" (p. 35).

A second keyword bypassed or unreflectively rendered by Norlin and Van Hook is *paideia*, a kind of culture promoted or reinforced by various kinds of education. Norlin renders *paideia* as "education," a translation that discounts Isocrates' work as a cultural critic and promotes Isocrates as a mere pedagogue rather than as an abstract thinker.[36]

To absorb Isocratic performance into new theories for current rhetoric and composition studies, it is necessary to reconstruct his deployment of Attic Greek as a Sophist: as a premier member of this amorphous and nonmonolithic group, he needs to be constructed as central to the Sophistic turn.[37]

Isocrates' work does not conform to many of the truisms of Sophism, those constructions promulgated by Plato's agenda and then by Aristotle's different agenda and then appropriated in various ways by subsequent receptors (neoplatonists, for example). In many ways he is an anti-Sophist: he would not speak publicly—a decision that had the effect, whether intended or not, of privileging writing and its disembodiedness. His attitude toward performance changed Sophism. The energy of the spoken word, its evanescence,[38] was transmuted by Isocrates. Pamphlets replaced performance. The separation (potential or realized) of writers from readers (including even the writer) solidified writing. With this change came a turn. Whereas John Poulakos locates the Sophistic turn at an earlier time, one could as easily locate it at this later time. The turn is completed with Isocrates. Havelock's literate revolution was advanced substantially by Isocrates,[39] but, as John Poulakos has pointed out,[40] Havelock ignores Isocrates almost completely. With

36. Of course, the standard treatment of the concept of *paideia* is Werner Jaeger's *Paideia* in 3 vols.

37. See John Poulakos, *Sophistical Rhetoric in Classical Greece.*

38. The metaphor is Ong's. See, for example, *Orality and Literacy*, passim, and *The Presence of the Word: Some Prolegomena for Cultural and Religious History*, pp. 77–87.

39. See, for example, Havelock's collection of essays *The Literate Revolution in Greece and Its Cultural Consequences.*

40. Poulakos made this audience comment at a joint meeting of the American Branch of the International Society for the History of Rhetoric and the Speech Communication Association, New Orleans, November 1988.

the Sophistic turn, we can see changes in the pattern of rhetoric in Isocrates' writing. While the noetic of the oral/aural world remains primary for him, a new noetic begins to take shape, and it is based on the activity, the performance, the disembodiedness, of writing. In chapter 3, I study his sentences that are subordinated, not additive, as Kennedy's explication indicates, and that are abstract in a different way, not situational, as long passages from *Antidosis* reveal. I then compare them to his additive, or strung-together, sentences, to sentences in the *Odyssey* and the *Origin Myth of Acoma*, and to the situation-specific aspects of some of his prose. The analysis shows the growing power of prose and the issues that surround the hegemony of poetry. When Isocrates' prose languishes in the formulaic, a primary feature of oral Greek language, he moves over to the subordination and one version of abstraction that characterizes written language. Interpreters now are frequently put off by the agonistic tone characteristic of oral cultures. Isocrates' agonistic use of epideictic rhetoric is related to his being part of an oral culture. His long condemnations of Persians, his apparently never ending praise of Timotheus in *Antidosis* (secs. 101–140), and his commitment to what we would call digressions are all symptoms of oral structures of articulation. But Isocrates was primarily a writer.

The fascinating oral features coexist with features of writing and can be made to arouse interest in Isocrates' writing rather than diminish it, a diminishment so many commentators have claimed and that have formed the dominant receptions of Isocrates. The deriding or mere dismissal of oralism of this kind remains a key issue in current misunderstandings of the nature of literacy, misunderstandings that drive attitudes toward student *logos* performance and that, in the U.S. certainly and in other places probably, fuels racist assumptions. For example, against Black English Vernacular, a dialectic long recognized as rich and important, and more recently viewed as central in numerous indigenous U.S. art forms (jazz and rap, for example) and other forms such as the novel (*The Color Purple*, for example) the slurs continue unabated, including in the academy. The rejection of the oral, whether in the form of speaking/performance or in the form of consciousness, remains entrenched. The deep commitment, particularly by many humanists, to the printed text continues unabated because the psychological and social connections in the academy to this kind of text are so deeply entrenched that they are not even seen as constructions.

For Isocrates, the production of discourse, not just the passive consumption of it as a hearer or a reader, is central. In fact, production of discourse dominates all the most important epochs of rhetoric. For Isocrates, rhetoric is the center of learning, the center of the curriculum, and, perhaps most important, the center of social action, which Isocrates merges with public behavior. Nonetheless, he performed his *logos* in writing, not in person. Through writing he enacted his public agenda. This action resembles some of our own conceptions of citizenship. The historical correspondences strikingly resemble our own cultural deprivations in that those people who are voiced through publication tend not to be women or other marginalized Others.

Isocratic Rhetoric and the Category Woman

And so Isocrates reveals for us strikingly one of the hideous aspects of classical rhetoric; it appears to erase women or to victimize us. This erasure works hand in hand with Isocrates' agenda of imperialism, an intolerance, a dehumanizing of Others, for which he must be held accountable. In addition to Isocrates' participation in and promotion of the backward institutions of slavery, woman erasure, and imperialism, we have to untangle, or begin to untangle, the receptions of this behavior among all the ancient Greeks and then, most important, to revise the little histories that we have right now in our minds' articulations and in our expressed articulations as part of our habits of being. In chapter 4, I offer a version of Lev Vygotsky to explain the little histories that U.S. citizens in particular tend to walk around with. These little histories—for example, snippets of ideas about the "greatness of ancient Greece" unconditioned by an awareness of slavery, woman erasure, or imperialism, or a paradigm that dismisses history altogether as irrelevant—work powerfully all the time among our own citizenry and are endlessly reinforced by the repetition provided by the new communication technologies. Obviously, different discourse communities have different little histories, little stories that condition and help to bring about behaviors, including racist and sexist behaviors. Oralism/auralism as an intersubjective activity plays a major part in this issue. It is for rhetoric and composition studies to show the way in accounting for the little interior histories that construct to a large extent the dominant culture we live in, that is changing so radically right now, and that requires a radically new *paideia*.

Isocrates' *Paideia*

Isocrates' agenda stands before us in the early, fragmentary *Against the Sophists*, where the unfolding of Isocrates' rhetorical project can be seen in outline. In this piece he positions himself as a writer and a teacher. At sections 17 and 18, Isocrates writes that five issues are required for discourse training and a broadly based education to produce a person, that is, a privileged young man, with effective judgment. These five requirements include (1) aptitude, (2) knowledge of different kinds of discourse, (3) practice, (4) a teacher who provides instruction in the principles of discourse, and (5) a teacher who displays a mastery of discourse. While the first three of these requirements are well known, the last two tend to be erased (as in R. C. Jebb's *Attic Orators*[41] and in the rapid summaries of Isocrates' "philosophy" that have substituted for theoretical treatment in much of the twentieth century). The crucial, definitive interaction of student with teacher is left out.[42]

The five aspects of discourse training in this early piece rely on the development of judgment in addition to knowledge. Isocrates' construction of "philosophy," or what Jebb translates a "theory of culture" and Norlin translates judgment, can be compared to versions of critical

41. P. 9.

42. Even Kennedy, in his thoughtful 1980 discussion of Isocrates, enacts this erasure: "There are in fact three successful elements in oratory—and these remain permanent features of classical rhetorical theory—nature, training, and practice" (*Classical Rhetoric*, p. 32). Here Kennedy makes the standard move. However, he corrects himself in the next sentence: "It is the function of the teacher to explain the principles of rhetoric and also to set an example of oratory on which the students can pattern themselves" (p. 32). The second sentence is crucial, but the magic number "three" remains in the "three successful elements in oratory." The number is five, and the second two aspects reside in the teacher. The three-part presentation is made in order to cascade into "the history of rhetoric." Kennedy makes that crucial move here, even though he presents the fuller version.

thinking that surface periodically in U.S. education.[43] The broadly based development of judgment (a quality that transcends knowledge, *episteme*) enables the individual to act within cultures. Issues in life that cannot be predicted are met by a mind and sensibility that have been trained in critical thinking. Isocrates' education in culture and how the individual can best interact with it provides one challenge to the then still hegemonic Platonic agenda for knowledge and his very different kind of philosophy. In addition, Isocrates' theory of culture as critical thinking is central to a twenty-first-century appropriation of Isocrates in discourse theory and in educational systems. In this section I will discuss two cultural issues for Isocrates: (1) his recognition of the dependence between articulation and thought, and (2) his emphasis on aptitude, or native ability—a stance that cannot be understood without the Sophistic distinction between *nomos* and *physis*, a central issue for the older Sophists and subsequently for Western rhetorical history.

In *Antidosis* and elsewhere Isocrates offers us an alternative to the concept that language is a container that holds meaning. The positivistic attitude that language is a thing out there, retrievable, tangible, and determinant, plagues not only our own scholarly and instructional endeavors; it was an issue in ancient Greek discourse education, which relied frequently on rule-bound handbooks, rote learning, and the imposition of static models of discourse. Isocrates' pedagogical theory consistently works against this premise, despite the repetition of numerous commentators who interpret Isocrates in this way.

A related issue is Isocrates' emphasis on aptitude, or native ability. This issue recurs in Isocrates' writings and in the stock critical responses to him (the dismissive kind that appear in passing as well as in the more complicated and interesting responses). This premise of his pedagogical theory needs to be interrogated and taken apart, because it is based on class issues that make for serious limitations in language education in our own time of educational reform. Isocrates' repeatedly written accounts of the importance of aptitude fit into education as a transmitter of the status quo, of the perpetuation of power as it already exists, of a *physis* that

43. See Arthur Applebee's *Tradition and Reform in the Teaching of English: A History*, pp. 158, 169–170.

actually is a *nomos*. "Aptitude," or native ability, frequently disguises a power structure that allows the dominant culture to reproduce itself and then to regard itself as natural (as part of *physis*). This aspect of Isocrates' agenda requires more scrutiny. Interestingly, and maybe even ironically, Isocrates' pedagogy enables people to subvert this system. His promotion of what some now call "critical thinking" could contribute compellingly to the dismantling of the class-bound issue that some people have more native ability than other people. Although Isocrates appears in places to designate aptitude as part of *physis*, he nonetheless at other, more dominant, places regards it as a human-made construct, as part of *nomos*. By converting standard interpretation from a *physis*-driven aptitude to a *nomos*-driven aptitude, we can analogize Isocrates' fluid ideas about the relationship between class systems and aptitude to current educational reforms. In other words, aptitude for Isocrates and for us is a social construction.[44]

Traditional Appropriators of Isocrates and Their Problems

Of the many persistent problems that confront a repositioning of Isocrates, one of the most perplexing is dealing with the continuation of an Aristotelian reception/agenda based on privileging a version of logic that is linear, precise, and dependent on syllogistic reasoning, and exclusive of other entechnic *pisteis*, *ethos*, and *pathos*. This tradition grows out of and contributes to the formation of a classical rhetoric canon that continues to minimize or erase the Sophists (particularly a nonplatonized Protagoras and Gorgias) and women rhetoricians such as Sappho, Diotima, and Aspasia. Recognition that all canons are human constructs that reflect ideology, including ideology toward such issues as gender politics and Cartesian dualism, has been slow, even though a rich group of books has excavated the constructions of canons of Literary writing with a

---

44. See Peter Smagorinsky's explication of kinds of intelligence in *Expressions: Multiple Intelligences in the English Class*, based on Howard Gardner's understanding of multiple intelligences. The key issue is that verbal and quantitative ability are not the only kinds of intelligence but are the ones privileged in many cultures, so that students with other kinds of dominant intelligences are marginalized early.

capital "L."[45] The inclusion of Isocrates and other Sophists as a central force of classical rhetoric, and not merely as a sideshow to the center ring of Aristotle, constitutes a radical act necessary for promoting literacy in our own time. Isocrates is explicit in claiming he is a Sophist, both in *Antidosis* and in *Against the Sophists*, even as he opposed some branches of Sophism: in at least two places in *Antidosis*, he refers to Solon as the first important Sophist, thereby placing himself in outstanding company and rehabilitating "Sophism," a term that even in the fourth century B.C.E. caused difficulty, much as it does now.

The Next Rhetoric

"New rhetorics" have proliferated at various moments in the 2,400 year construction of traditional Western rhetorical history. We appear to be at another crucial historical moment for a "revival" of rhetoric, so I have chosen the phrase "Next Rhetoric" to indicate that the current wave is the latest; it doesn't necessarily supplant the old ones or suggest that it is the one and only rhetoric.[46] Rather, it indicates that there will be other revivals of rhetoric. This designation does not diminish the importance of the current explosion of rhetorical inquiry across many disciplines.

Next classical rhetoric (that is, classical rhetoric reconstructed by recent theory) and literacy (as consciousness interacting with materiality, both of which are conditioned partly by communication technology) function together in ways the world has not seen before. Unelectrified traditional historians of rhetoric such as Douglas Ehninger, while providing important resources for current historicizing, have not acknowledged this change; in this way, the status quo of Ramist rhetoric remains entrenched, even though such historians are, of course, opposed to that view of rhetoric. The problem is that rhetoric without conscious theory is destined to remain in the world of Ramism. This destiny is not a quaint academic issue for a few professors to be exercised about. Rather, it is the intellectual underpinning of current upheavals in the academy and a source of productive response (as opposed to reaction). In addition,

45. See note 22, chapter 3.

46. Consider Richard McKeon's point in "Rhetoric in the Middle Ages" that reactions to rhetoric incorporate much of the rhetoric supposedly rejected.

unelectrified Ramist rhetoric remains at the very core of a large number of freshman writing programs and the language-killing current-traditional textbooks that drive them. A writing requirement remains in place at many colleges and universities because of an awareness of its importance. *Nonetheless, it remains in place in a theory-unconscious way* in many places. One consequence of this unconsciousness is that many writing teachers cannot articulate why teaching writing is important. They cannot articulate this to themselves, to their students, to academic administrators, or to the general public. While bromides flourish ("Good writing is necessary for good citizenship," "Writing empowers a student to discover who she is," "Writing helps the student to understand his thoughts and feelings," "It is self-evident that taking writing courses is good for you"), grounded reasoning does not flourish. It does not take an advanced degree to realize that each of the four bromidic assertions offered above relies on theories and ideologies that drive the writing courses and so condition public perceptions of what English teachers do in college. Bromide 1 is grounded on the ancient connection that an educated citizenry provides the basis for representative democracy. Bromides 2 and 3 are pseudo-Romantic modernist ideas that an individual is self-evident, locked up within himself (a herself is an afterthought in this construction), and needs to explore these rather definite boundaries; expression of spontaneous emotion is held to be a good, as is the teacher as untrained psychotherapist.[47] Bromide 4 is based on the idea that college students do not know what is good for them, that they are empty vessels who await filling with Knowledge by the teacher who pours it in. These four representative bromides currently drive much writing instruction and, in fact, other areas of the humanities as well.[48] Next Rhetoric offers the basis for a reform of these courses and a repositioning of the humanities and the techno-liberal-arts. This new agenda must be based

47. The last phenomenon proliferates, and endangers our students with, a pedagogy of disclosure, in which teachers become untrained, unrestrained psychotherapists, sometimes exploiting the transference relationship that is inevitable in much effective teaching. See *Fragments of Rationality*, by Lester Faigley, who criticizes this pedagogy.

48. These and other intellectually suspect bases have led many scholars to call for doing away with the required freshman writing course, a well-intended but dangerous recommendation.

on a literacy that centers on the performance of writing and speaking, including inner voice and its inevitably multiple constructions.

Literacy and Oralism/Auralism

To understand Ong's position, which has stirred extensive and emotional controversy, I believe it is necessary to return to the issues that he engaged in *Orality and Literacy*, a 1982 synthesis of earlier work. This move necessarily includes an analysis of much of Ong's earlier work. The book grows out of Ong's entire research effort, beginning with *Ramus: Method and the Decay of Dialogue*.[49] The book also connects to a body of material that has influenced many fields: the oral-formulaic theory.

I present here an interpretation of Walter J. Ong's and Eric A. Havelock's orality and literacy and secondary orality stances. After splitting Havelock's work from that of Ong, I move to an interpretation of the critical reception of Ong's thesis of movement from primary orality to literacy to secondary orality by examining two schools of reception of Ong's theories. I privilege the reception of Ong's work because it is more complicated and addresses gender issues; he has also been more heavily appropriated in rhetoric/composition studies. Havelock's hierarchies make women and other marginalized groups disappear with his version of universalizing. My third move in this section shows that a reconstruction of Ong's theory of movement from orality to literacy to secondary orality offers us possibilities for understanding and performing electric rhetoric. I then apply a theory of oralism/auralism/literacy/electric consciousness to the late text *Antidosis* in a redeployment of Isocrates. I suggest a repositioning of Isocrates' so-called apology that is frequently given short treatment even in standard works.[50] I do this by interpreting *Antidosis* through two schools of response to Ong, schools that have been forming most noticeably since 1982, when Ong published *Orality and Literacy: The Technologizing of the Word*, and that continue to form with increasing frequency and that are in themselves fascinating in

49. For an overview of the themes of Ong's work, see Gronbeck et al., *Media, Consciousness, and Culture*.

50. See, for example, Edward P. J. Corbett's *Classical Rhetoric for the Modern Student*.

how they reveal the complexities of the reception of oralism/auralism and literacy and the new electric rhetoric. My aim is to suggest how to integrate current theoretical material (in this case Ong's work) into what we have received as classical rhetoric, so that we can reconstruct Isocrates' late text with different values in mind, a reconstruction that would include a new *paideia*.

The genre of ancient apology, which includes *Antidosis*, reveals little to many modern educated readers trained in formalist reading in the United States and Great Britain.[51] Those readers, relying (consciously or unconsciously) on standards of judgment such as unity of thought, carefully constructed "textures" (to use a metaphor deployed so well by New Critics such as John Crowe Ransom in "Criticism as Pure Speculation"), the linearity of a logical argument, and other formalist features, will be disappointed by *Antidosis* and may be led to conclude (legitimately, according to this way of reading) that Isocrates' writing is characterized primarily by tedium, numbing repetition, and semi-embarrassing self-indulgence. Isocrates as windbag is in fact a recurrent idea in many strands of reception. It has, in fact, become a leitmotif in many lines of rhetorical research. Even those scholars who recognize importance in Isocrates' writings and explicate the intelligence operating in Isocratic texts (for example, George Kennedy and Werner Jaeger) sooner or later tend to assume that Isocrates never belongs in a higher category with Plato and Aristotle, both of whom, of course, denounced the Sophists, which Isocrates claimed at times to be. The anti-Sophistic agenda set by Plato and Aristotle for understandable local, theoretical, and competitive reasons continued until the nineteenth century, following a by now well-known story.[52]

51. The English-language formalisms that have so dominated twentieth-century U.S. and British reading habits are, of course, very different as well as very similar. For a cogent explanation of the British variety, see especially Terry Eagleton, "The Rise of English," in his *Literary Theory: An Introduction*, pp. 17–53, and his analysis of the Scrutineers.

52. See, for example, Jarratt, *Rereading the Sophists*; R. Enos, "The Epistemology of Gorgias's Rhetoric" and *Greek Rhetoric before Aristotle*, pp. 91–131; J. Poulakos, *Sophistical Rhetoric in Classical Greece*; T. Poulakos, "Towards a Cultural Understanding of Classical Epideictic Oratory"; Swearingen, *Rhetoric and Irony*, pp. 22–94; Jasper Neel, *Plato, Derrida, and Writing*, pp. 1–29.

Two kinds of dominant orality make up Ong's thesis, not one, as is so frequently thought. Primary orality existed in cultures where writing was unknown, where cultural values were transmitted orally, and where consciousness was formed by reliance on oral discourse and the necessary use of discursive features such as formulas, repetition, the addition of phrases rather than their subordination, the aggregation of ideas rather than their analysis, concreteness rather than abstraction, agonistic verbal behavior, and audience participation.[53] Primary orality is a dominant kind of consciousness and is characterized by an emphasis on speaking not only for instrumentalist communication but for the transmission of cultural values, norms, and behaviors through shared consciousness. Primary orality indicates a kind of consciousness in which the dynamism of the spoken word is powerful but evanescent; its very burst of energy plays it out. It ends. Only spoken repetition keeps it going, but at the price of loss of the exactness that we print-based interpreters take for granted. The Homeric epics are standard examples of this kind of oral consciousness. Repetition of the poems leads to changes in various details. Native North American written-down stories provide other powerful examples. However, it must be remembered that our access to primary orality is profoundly limited, influenced as we are by the structures of literacy consciousness and secondary-orality as consciousness.

Literacy, the second of the three stages of consciousness, began in about 720–700 B.C.E. (according to Rhys Carpenter's widely accepted formulation)[54] as the gradual result of the invention of the phonetic alphabet in the eighth century B.C.E. provided new ways of thinking as the written word became gradually interiorized (as it had been by the time Plato was writing). Writing led to the development of abstraction,[55] according to Ong (and Havelock), and therefore to the burst of abstract writing that characterized fourth-century-B.C.E. Greece. Literacy accel-

---

53. Ong, *Orality and Literacy*, pp. 27–60 and passim.

54. See "The Antiquity of the Greek Alphabet" and "The Greek Alphabet Again." See also Denise Schmandt-Besserat, "The Envelopes That Bear the First Writing," and Martin Bernal, *Black Athena*, vol. 1. Schmandt-Besserat places Carpenter's dating in a much wider context, with examples of literacy in the Middle East, China, and Egypt at about 3000 B.C.E.

55. See note 15, chapter 3, for problems with this concept.

erated in the fifteenth century with the establishment of print discourse. Secondary orality, Ong's third stage, began in the nineteenth century, when various electronic devices revolutionized communication, beginning with telegraphy in 1844 in the United States. Our position now is in secondary orality, in which there is a new emphasis on the ear and a change in the emphasis on the eye. The spoken word is now electrified, instantaneous, repetitive, and so familiar that we have normalized it. Many group consciousnesses depend now to a great extent on secondary orality. Like the air, it exists and sustains us and is us. Secondary orality is "present-day high-technology culture, in which a new orality is sustained by telephone, radio, television, and other electronic devices that depend for their existence and functioning on writing and print."[56] This concept of secondary orality, which, as with primary orality and literacy, depicts a stage of consciousness, rather than the individual acts of, say, working on a computer or speaking on the telephone. Secondary orality, for Ong and Havelock, finds its existence as a stage of consciousness that depends on the previous stage of primary orality and the still strong stage of literacy.

This rehearsal of Ong and Havelock remains important because the appropriation of their work has frequently been characterized by factual errors, as well as by legitimate and important interpretive disagreements.[57] Partly as a response to theorists who reject Ong's three-part theory, I turn to the precursors of his theory.

The approach used by Ong and Havelock needs to be seen in the context of the oral-formulaic theory, which has generated so much theoretical response in so many fields since the early 1980s.

The Oral-Formulaic Theory and Oral Structures of Articulation

Ong's theory is a dynamic synthesis of enormous previous research in oral-formulaic theory across many fields. Many respondents of Ong's theory, perhaps unaware of this voluminous earlier research, have

56. Ong, *Orality and Literacy*, p. 11.

57. For the latter, see Mary Carruthers, *The Book of Memory*, pp. 30–32, in which a significant disagreement with Ong is based on a complex interpretation and not the more familiar bifurcated, reductive interpretation.

claimed that he makes a binary opposition of vaguely imagined versions of orality and literacy and that he favors one over the other. I will quickly sketch Ong's system of consciousness in primary orality, literacy, and secondary orality as he analyzes it particularly in *Orality and Literacy* and to a certain extent in the 1967 *Presence of the Word* (in many ways a precursor of *Orality and Literacy*), *Rhetoric, Romance, and Technology,* and other places.[58] Ong transforms the oral-formulaic theory of Milman Parry and Albert Lord to identify two kinds of orality, primary and secondary, discussed above. Many versions of some Native North American orally transmitted cultural communications (e.g., the Acoma Pueblo *Origin Myth of Acoma*, a spoken text that existed in primary-oral form until the encroachment of White people in what is now the U.S. plains) have to be understood according to oralist theory. Their suppression in White U.S. schools and canons has been partly a product of racist attitudes toward orally dominant writing.

Residue of discursive features from primary orality can be found in the primary texts of classical Greek rhetoric as well. Ong's construction of literacy, a kind of consciousness that is the gradual result of the Greek adaptation/invention of the phonetic alphabet in the eighth century B.C.E., provided new ways of thinking as the written word became gradually interiorized (as it had been for part of the population by the time Plato was writing). Ong clearly claims and demonstrates that there is not a loss with the movement from one kind of consciousness to another. He analyzes the changes and the residue of, say, primary orality within various post-primarily-oral cultures. Significantly, Ong in his book does not construct a binary opposition between orality and literacy, making them mutually exclusive, competitive, and reductive; rather, he emphasizes their mingling and the tenacity of established forms as new ones occur. Ong's contribution to the great-divide theory resides in his bifurcated title *Orality and Literacy* and in various references.[59] While he has not yet elaborately explored the situation of secondary orality, he has nevertheless set forth some of the theoretical bases for further theorizing. His

58. See, for example, *The Barbarian Within* and *Interfaces of the Word.*

59. See, for example, his foreword to Paul Zumthor's *Oral Poetry:* "Paul Zumthor's work here belongs in the new tradition studying orality-literacy contrasts" (p. ix).

work could strengthen the postmodernized rhetoric of television, or electric rhetoric.

Tripping over the Great-Divide Theorists of Orality/Literacy

The great-divide theorists tend to see two mutually exclusive categories in Ong's three stages. For example, Patricia Bizzell, in "Arguing about Literacy," an article that has many important things to say about the hegemony of academic dialect at the expense of other dialects, contends, "Humanists tend to dichotomize non-literate and literate states of being, and to reify the two states into all-embracing conceptual universes of orality and literacy (see Ong)."[60] Bizzell finds a conflict between what she posits as a humanist position and a social-scientific position assumed by people such as the ethnographer Shirley Brice Heath. Bizzell's essay reveals no awareness of the merger of literacy and secondary orality or, in fact, of the construction by Ong (along with Havelock, Parry, Lord, and many others). She charges Ong with privileging the written word (in the form of academic literacy) over the oral word. The interpretation that Ong privileges the written word over the spoken word recurs in the reception of *Orality and Literacy*.

Brandt, in *Literacy as Social Involvement*, also characterizes Ong's theories of consciousness as a great divide in which Ong privileges writing. As with Bizzell, she establishes mutually exclusive categories and contends that Ong—along with Jack Goody and David R. Olson—promotes what she names a "strong-text view of literacy." The strong-text view is a variation on the Bizzell stance: Brandt writes, "Strong-text accounts of literacy are product-centered, defining literacy by working backward from the nature of finished texts" (p. 8).

Both Bizzell and Brandt, following what has become virtually a tradition in anthropological literacy studies and in some areas of rhetoric/composition studies, locate a binary opposition and find the privileging of one of the terms. Bizzell and Brandt conduct a kind of tacit and partial deconstructive reading in which they identify the dominant term in the

60. P. 142. The influence of this essay is indicated by its reprinting in *Professing the New Rhetorics*, ed. Theresa Enos and Stuart Brown, pp. 446–460.

orality-literacy binary and then expose the power of the dominant term. But they stop there. This binary thinking, however, does not account for the merger of and mutual dependence of, for example, literacy and secondary orality, or primary orality and manuscript literacy. The great-divide theorists have also tended not to historicize adequately. They universalize literacy, a charge made by some of them against Ong. Fortunately, Brandt moves her case forward into a compelling case for literacy and social interaction. This interaction has important implications for literacy and its historicizing.

The Consciousness Theorists

A second school of response to Ong is exemplified by Henry Sussman and Michael Heim and may be called the consciousness theorists. This reception of Ong avoids the familiar dualism of orality and literacy and the consequent privileging of one mode over the other; as such, it is more complex than the work of the great-dividists.

Heim, a philosopher who investigates the changes in mind brought about by word processing, names Ong's orality, literacy, secondary-orality construction a transformation and places it within familiar western philosophical traditions. Before he absorbs Ong in that line, he presents a complex reading of Ong on psychic changes brought about by communication technologies.[61]

Sussman, a literary theorist, deploys Ong in the following way: "The constellation of oral behaviors, skills, and attributes that he assembles throughout the main part of his book constitutes a major contribution of the theory of linguistic behavior. Within Ong's scenario, orality and literacy do not so much threaten as condition, extend, and in some cases stimulate each other" (*High Resolution*, p. 216). Sussman avoids the binary interpretation of the great-dividists and can see the interactive capacities of literacy and secondary orality, in much the same way that

61. Heim, *Electric Language*. The concept "transformational" does not ultimately work, because it suggests rapidity or conversion experience, and not the imperceptible slowness of change that Ong works through for the three stages he examines, two of which are utterly intermingled. See also Heim's *Metaphysics of Virtual Reality*.

Tony Lentz, in *Orality and Literacy in Hellenic Greece*, sees the interaction of primary orality and literacy.[62] Sussman's case falters, however, when he relegates work of low-art texts, particularly television texts, to the land of kitsch. This dismissal is as unselfconscious as it is classbound. Sussman privileges a familiar version of the canon of "American" literature, providing separate readings of Nathaniel Hawthorne, Herman Melville, Wallace Stevens, Ezra Pound, and William Carlos Williams. In other words, Sussman understands Ong's position and avoids the familiar binarizing of orality and literacy, but he cannot apply it to television because he lives, in this book, in an unexamined high-art/low-art world. The all-white, all-male canon of nineteenth-century American great writers juxtaposed with some of the high priests of modernism—in this case, also all-white, all-male, and all-dead—reveals a sensibility that relegates the texts of a symbol system such as television to the realm of kitsch, where ever after they must languish, unexplored and so not understood or synthesized into larger cultural agendas. Sussman offers helpful exegesis of Ong, particularly in his understanding of orality, literacy, and secondary orality as kinds of consciousness. However, the formalist, or Brandt's strong-text, readings in the middle of his book appear to have little to do with the beginning and the end.

The book is a sandwich in which the meat is a well-done formalism applied to Male Master texts and the bread is some orality, literacy, secondary-orality theory. We need the bread. If the middle chapters had been informed by the beginning and ending literacy chapters, they might have been less formalistic. Given the elitism, the exclusivity inherent in the Male Masters approach, however, television as an oral/aural form cannot be adequately analyzed. Had Sussman persevered with Ong's theories, he could have made a difference in the teaching of literary texts. Ong's merged triad of orality, literacy, and secondary orality, when addressed with complex sophistication, can be used to demarginalize U.S. groups that have oralisms different from those of White U.S. citizens. Sussman sees the power and possibility of Ong's construction, but his ideological commitment to Whiteness and Maleness as the identifying

62. See, for example, pp. 11–45, 71–89, and 100–102 of *Orality and Literacy in Hellenic Greece*.

attributes of Important Culture and his traditional canonicity prevent him from making the substantial analysis that he could have made.

He remains firmly behind the invisible but powerful boundaries of one version of the academic/museum world. A more complicated analysis of orality, literacy, and secondary orality would require a radical reconstruction of "American Literature," an elaborate restructuring of U.S. writing. Part of this reorganization would have to include women writers and readers and the particular discourse communities they inhabited.[63] Sussman cannot break away from the text-bound, race-bound, class-bound books that he and others valorize and maintain in our schools and universities and on the margins of general culture.

Sussman, who explicates Ong's stages of consciousness with complexity, nevertheless resembles the great-dividists in that he privileges literate consciousness over oral consciousness. His high-art, traditionalist stance, revealed by his strong-text accounts (his close textual analyses) of U.S. canonical authors (excellent analyses that are not taken anywhere and so stand alone), along with his felt abhorrence of what he characterizes as television kitsch, prevent him from applying his considerable insight to the oral features of the discourse he has chosen to analyze in detail. In spite of his insight into Ong's construction and its implications, he is pulled back into what for so many remains the comfort of traditional American Literature, redolent now with its Arnoldian underpinnings, which cannot question the ideology and its adherents that made this group of strong-text books. Had Sussman persevered with Ong's theories, he could have made a difference in the teaching of literary texts and so in the construction of the national identity that has preoccupied so many White intellectuals and that has been thoroughly challenged by various schools of feminist theorists and African-American theorists.[64] Part of this difference is capsulized by Toni Morrison, who unveils the public secret of "American literature":

63. See Hobbs, ed., *Nineteenth-Century American Women Learn to Write.*

64. Residing in a White culture and a tribal (or national) culture, native American writers tend to be more bicultural, for example, the Quapaw Tribe now centered in Arkansas and Oklahoma. The tendency toward invisibility of these groups by Whites is far different in kind and degree from the invisibility conferred on many African-American communities.

Deep within the word "American" is its association with race. To identify someone as a South African is to say very little; we need the adjective "white" or "black" or "colored" to make our meaning clear. In this country it is quite the reverse. "American" means white, and Africanist people struggle to make the term applicable to themselves with ethnicity and hyphen after hyphen after hyphen.[65]

The ideology of the word "American" remains entrenched in U.S. discourse communities of every kind, and it is a danger because it strives to make invisible many communities of people.[66]

Interpreting *Antidosis* with a Great-Dividist Interpretation and with a Consciousness Interpretation

So we can see two kinds of resistance to the intermingling of orality, literacy, and secondary orality, the first a rather simple move, the second a complex move that does not go far enough but does offer possibilities. Historical rhetoric necessarily includes oral texts and oral consciousness and offers a great deal in understanding the forces of literacy now. Classical rhetoric in particular offers us the opportunity to reconstruct literacy now; the case of Isocrates is compelling for literacy studies in general and for classical rhetoric in particular.

The binary opposition at the center of great-dividist interpretation erases the distinction between primary orality as it might have affected Isocrates (although he would not have experienced it directly, since versions of Greek writing had been in use for at least three hundred years) and the still-burgeoning literacy of Isocrates' rapidly changing fourth-century-B.C.E. context. A strong-text interpretation of the kind characterized by Brandt leads to an exclusion of the occasion for writing (the context or ideology) in which Isocrates worked. It fits in with familiar stylistic analyses of Isocrates' way with a periodic sentence. It erases Isocrates' central connection to a highly oral culture that valorized repetition, aggregation, copiousness, redundance, conceptualization close to the human lifeworld, situationalism, group participation (notice Iso-

---

65. *Playing in the Dark: Whiteness and the Literary Imagination*, p. 47.

66. For this reason and others, I refer to U.S. writing and citizens, foregoing the coded word "American."

crates' repeated use of the second person), agonism, homeostasis, the establishment of traditionalism, and the other discursive features discussed above that Ong establishes as central features of writing that contains a substantial residue from primary orality. These features recur, as Ong points out, in secondary orality.

A great-dividist interpretation—with its rigid bifurcation of orality and literacy and its frequent blurring of spoken and written texts with forms of consciousness—leads to closure in the reading of *Antidosis*. The oral features are erased, and therefore the situation is obliterated. The force of the binary and its inevitable lunge toward privileging one term over the other makes Ong's thesis of primary orality, literacy, and secondary orality simplistic for this group. This stance effectively terminates the inquiry in a way that is strategically similar to terminating inquiry through deconstructive reading by claiming that it kills meaning and removes the reason for interpretation. Each reading is too simple and does not accord with the texts/contexts/ideologies that operate. These literacy theorists need to reconsider Ong's writings, particularly the books before *Orality and Literacy*.

Ong explicitly and repeatedly writes that orality exists in all the states he sets up, that secondary orality does not cancel out literacy but in fact utterly depends on it epistemologically. Ong writes,

The interaction between the orality that all human beings are born into and the technology of writing, which no one is born into, touches the depths of the psyche. Ontogenetically and phylogenetically, it is the oral word that first illuminates consciousness with articulate language, that first divides subject and predicate and then relates them to one another, and that ties human beings to one another in society. Writing introduces division and alienation, but a higher unity as well. It intensifies the sense of self and fosters more conscious interaction between persons. Writing is consciousness-raising. (*Orality and Literacy*, pp. 178–179)

Here and elsewhere Ong claims repeatedly that orality as consciousness lives on, and in fact has to. He argues that literacy does not cancel out orality. The question that remains in this section is, Why are the great-dividists such as Patricia Bizzell, David Bleich, and Beth Daniell so vehement in their opposition to Ong? On another side, why does Sussman respond so energetically against the artifacts of secondary orality, even as he understands the power of Ong's stance?

Joyce I. Middleton, in discussing these phenomena, has worked "to expand upon Ong's examples and details to illustrate the historical integrity of his concept of 'residual orality,' an implicit value for speech in a culture that writes.... I argue that writing teachers and scholars must explore the significance of oral-literate relationships to our current theories about writing and pedagogy."[67] By using Ong's list of oral features, Middleton deploys a vocabulary with which to write about and discuss what I refer to as oralism.[68]

One key to the problem of understanding orality versus literacy and new ways of interpreting orally infused texts such as *Antidosis* is to concentrate on the consciousness issue explored by Ong. David Heckel, in "Ong and Derrida," has written, "It should be carefully noted that the terms speaking/writing and orality/literacy are not interchangeable; one describes two means of communication and the other two mentalities or sets of intellectual habits and predispositions inferable from relationships between cultural phenomena and [dominant] communication technologies" (p. 2). This crucial distinction is understood by Sussman and dropped because of his resistance to his uncritiqued conception of low art; the distinction appears to be merged in Bizzell's argument; and Brandt, who understands the distinction, erases context in communication acts and so herself becomes in some sections a strong-text theorist of the kind she challenges.

Sussman's high-art orientation, his deeply felt aesthetic formalism, will act as a synecdoche in chapter 3, where I will analyze Fredric Jameson's "windless closure of the formalisms" from the critical stance of rhetoric and composition.[69]

Isocrates' written performances offer us a way to apply the oral-formulaic theory and to reposition Isocrates in the various constructions we have available of fourth-century-B.C.E. rhetoric. His repositioning using various twentieth-century theories, including Ong's, is an impor-

67. "The Psychodynamics of Orality in Written Texts," p. 1.

68. Her work of applying Ong's theories to the fiction of Toni Morrison and other African-American writers has provided trenchant new interpretations for U.S. writing.

69. *The Political Unconscious: Narrative as a Socially Symbolic Act*, p. 42.

tant scholarly task and part of a continuing reconstruction of classical rhetoric according to new theories. But it is not just that. In his differently oral state (different from previous Greek rhetoric and different from our own rhetoric now), Isocrates' "mentality" as revealed in his writing can provide strategies for partially analogizing twenty-first century "mentality," or consciousness.[70]

By "literacy" I mean, as I elaborated on in chapter 1, not only the ability to read and write but an activity of minds (the plural is required) capable of recognizing and engaging substantive issues along with the ways that minds, sensibilities, and emotions are constructed by and within communities whose members communicate through specific technologies. In other words, literacy has to do with consciousness: how we know what we know and a recognition of the historical, ideological, and technological forces that inevitably operate in all human beings.

"Consciousness," of course, is a problematic term. I deploy it here partly because other keywords for the phenomenon do not work. "Cognition," for example, resonates in a way that is important in the social sciences; its limitation resides in its usual avoidance of the unconscious, a move I cannot make. "Mentality" similarly resonates in directions that are not the ones I pursue, and I wish to avoid a mentality/materiality binary, which would not be helpful here. The word "consciousness," as I use it, works to include language/thought/subvocalization and signifies an awareness and activity that depends on language. It rejects firmly the commonplace that thought is speech that is not uttered and instead adheres to the Vygotskyan idea that language and thought have different roots and that they interact at about the age of two along with social behavior, which of course includes speaking and other bodily movements. I further contend that a recognition of this issue (whether one agrees with my version or not) is central to any teaching of writing, speaking, or other verbal performance at the college level and to other fields of study as well. The tacit stance that one assumes on this issue

70. See chapter 1. I deploy "consciousness" as a synonym of Roger Chartier's "mentalité," a keyword that does not translate adequately as "mentality." Chartier, in *Forms and Meanings: Texts, Performances, and Audiences from Codex to Computer*, p. 13, aligns his work with that of Ong.

drives pedagogical theory to a substantial degree and so cannot be ignored.[71]

Standard treatments of Isocrates (for example, by Norlin, Jebb, Jaeger, and Ijsseling) continue the logic-dominant traditions of one Platonic and Aristotelian agenda (there are others) that privileges one version of logic over other forms of human communication and that divides the public from the private and then privileges the public, as we see in Aristotle's *Rhetoric*.[72] This stance does not acknowledge the possible and inevitable merger of the two, particularly in the minds of individual encoders. Moreover, it promotes a relentless logic that denies what we have learned about interior discourse in the twentieth century from such theorists as Walter Ong, Lev Vygotsky, Susanne Langer, and many others. The hegemony of Aristotle in the Western tradition and the attendant devaluation of Sophists such as Isocrates until the nineteenth and twentieth centuries contributes to the current problems in cultural literacy, a phrase I appropriate elsewhere as diametrically opposed to the ideas of E. D. Hirsch and similar thinkers, whom C. Jan Swearingen has characterized as "bully boys in their bully pulpits."[73] Genuine cultural literacy resists the bully consumption of high art as commodified in Hirsch's dictionary of cultural literacy, in Sussman's strong-text reading of submerged whiteness, and by proponents of canons that are presumed to be self-evident.[74] The artifacts proposed by Hirsch and his collaborators promote one of the most intellectually and politically dangerous issues of our time: the idea that knowledge is a retrievable reality out there in the world (for example, on a list devised by Hirsch or anybody else), an idea appropriated in ways that suggest the workings of machines rather than the interactions of human beings with various constructions of the world. The idea that knowledge and one's own encoding (in speaking, writing,

---

71. One's stance is, of course, easy to ignore when institutions of higher learning hire writing teachers who are not trained in any of these issues. These teachers tend to replicate the freshman writing courses they had in college and so usually reproduce the modernist ideology of a split between thought and language with its Ramist tradition of rhetoric as decoration.

72. See book 1, chapter 2, for example.

73. "Bloomsday: Doomsday for Literacy?"

74. See Lunsford, Moglen, and Slevin, eds., *The Right to Literacy*.

or any symbol system) are separate entities disconnected from the decoder remains a general received opinion even among thinking people and is reflected in many school and university curricula. Perhaps one of the most debilitating sites of this tacitly accepted stance toward the nature of one's own discourse lies in general perceptions toward writing: that it is a tool (a skill in the sense that the ability to work with a machine is a skill), and that it is outside the self. Pseudoromantic perceptions reject the tool-machine model for an organic one but make an equally false move when they view writing as a completely interior activity. The denial by both groups of the inevitability of a discourse community or communities remains strong.

The current reception of Isocrates' writing—how his writings are read in particular scholarly-discourse communities (for example, Takis Poulakos and Susan Jarratt)—offer powerful ways out of the Cartesian ideology that knowledge and writing are things out there in the world and that reality is a self-evident and self-explained issue. Isocrates' development of general education depends on the continual interaction of the student (who inevitably interacts within discourse communities and within particular scenes) and on challenges to mind and sensibility through the study of philosophia (not philosophy in the Platonic sense). His agenda provides one powerful alternative to the dangerous current public view—reinforced tacitly in schools and universities—that knowledge is merely a retrievable reality out there in the world and available for consumption by discrete individuals who operate as self-enclosed units not susceptible to forces unless they choose to be. Isocrates' general education (tainted though it is by misogyny and imperialism) also offers an alternative to the pseudoromantic writer who believes (or teaches) that an organic meaning is locked within a discrete individual and can be unlocked, discovered or even released through artistic endeavor.

These stances are the ones most of our students walk into our classrooms with and the ones we struggle with as they not infrequently claim that all points of view are equal and valid, that language is a neutral tool (or organic matter), and that differences among people arise from taste. These students, most frequently coming from dominant middle class U.S. culture, harbor an intellectual stance toward the world based on a largely unacknowledged belief that language is a neutral tool used by human beings when they need it or is a powerful interior organic essence. As a corollary to these ideas, these students (and others) believe that mind and thought are prior to and superior to articulation of any kind. These students need to study Isocrates and to do so in a new way. They need to become aware of the histories in their heads and of how they relate to their articulations as intersubjective performances within discourse communities.

A genuine revivifying of the liberal arts tradition, of which Isocrates is routinely and rather boringly designated as the progenitor ("father"), requires that we recognize how the mind interacts with discourse communities—one's own and others—and that we dispense with the consuming of artifacts. Over and over Isocrates offers us a way of treating this issue.

A retheorized Isocrates offers us an agenda for critical performance, or the ability to develop and apply sound judgment to issues that cannot be predicted with certainty. Isocrates' critical thinking is usually mistranslated as "philosophy," because of the Platonic construction of the Attic Greek word that had no such sense in Isocrates' work. Rather, Isocrates' sense of "philosophia" is what Jebb translates as a "theory of culture," what Norlin translates as "judgment," and what Isocrates himself refers to as "power." The ability to meet and negotiate issues that confront individuals who operate intersubjectively in discourse communities is one of the most compelling needs of human beings after the basic necessities of shelter, food, clothing, and so on, are met. Like Isocrates' students, our students need careful, intense instruction in the production of discourse as a way of negotiating unpredictable issues—issues such as judgment, passion, and sensibility—that confront human beings throughout life. In our time the rigorous study of writing, the development of a writing repertoire, and the intensive and extensive study of how to articulate in oral discourse are essential for critical thinking and literacy of the kind advocated here. The two forms of articulation—the written and the spoken—can most profitably be studied together and, as Isocrates recommends in *Antidosis*, with a teacher proficient at producing the kinds of discourse the students will need to produce.[75]

75. I address the limitations of video teaching in chapter 6.

With his work on *logos* in *Antidosis* and other places, Isocrates shows how *logos* can be developed now within individuals through practice and production in what can be called a dialectic (a Platonic dialectic with unequal discourse partners). In other words, his work on interiorized *logos* enables us to understand that knowledge is not a retrievable reality out there in the world somewhere, not a mere skill or tool (the former based on rote memory, the latter based on an exterior applied object). Nor is it a locked-up force residing in a discrete individual who awaits romantic unlocking. The activity of Isocrates' *logos* and *paideia* is appealing because it disintegrates the current-traditional paradigm and the literary formalism that goes with it. A current conceptualization of literacy must be based on activity, not passivity; that is, it must be based on informed intersubjective performance.

The construction of language in the mind and the obliteration of the public and the private are treated by Isocrates in *Antidosis* and else-where. One could add here that Plato is far ahead of Aristotle in understanding the merger of the public and the private. In *Phaedrus*, for example, Plato's Socrates carefully explains the idea that rhetoric is for the household and the personal, not just for public venues,[76] an idea I elaborate on in chapter 3 when I examine more closely the competition between the Isocratic and Platonic schools (which in turn competed with other new schools of the time).

Isocrates' work needs to flow into a canon of classical rhetoric and techno-liberal-arts study in a way that supplants the Platonic-Aristotelian hegemony, particularly the logic so dominant in one version of Aristotle. This proposed canon must be interrogated relentlessly and viewed as in flux. Because Isocrates promotes (partly through example) elaborate training in critical language performances and shows its necessity, his work—along with that of Plato, Aspasia, Aristotle, Protagoras, Gorgias, and Diotima—should be studied in schools and in universities in a way that challenges the usually assumed dominance of Plato and Aristotle.

What, specifically, are the obstacles? A large problem here lies, of course, in the fact that many young students do not study even old-fashioned Isocrates, Plato, and Aristotle, much less such re-uncovered

76. See *Phaedrus*, 261.

rhetoricians as Aspasia and Diotima and the new interpretations of all of these thinkers and their receptions/constructions from such scholars as Cheryl Glenn, Susan C. Jarratt, C. Jan Swearingen, Richard Leo Enos, James L. Kinneavy, and others. In other words, school students in most settings are not even trained in the ways I am arguing against. The training of students in a newly historicized rhetoric, with an emphasis on the production of discourse, on activity more than on passivity, can become the center of a new, rigorous liberal-arts education. The study of the Sophists, including Isocrates, would be one addition to a rigorous curriculum made available to all students, not just the privileged ones. With this new curriculum, students could examine how the Aristotelian agenda has dominated so-called Western thought for over 2,000 years, how it operates in their own lives, whether they are aware of it or not, and how other possibilities await them. In other words, students can learn the construction of the modern and how they too have been constructed and replicate the modern without knowing it. With this *paideia*, they can situate themselves and learn to what extent they are situated in ideology.

This agenda will not work unless a concerted effort is made to coordinate a deconstructed/reconstructed liberal-arts curriculum in which the trivium (rhetoric, grammar [language structure], and dialectic [philosophy]) and the quadrivium (geometry, astronomy, music, and arithmetic) are retheorized and redeployed. The trivialization of the trivium must, of course, be addressed.

Such a new path of study would enable students and scholars to recognize the false binary opposition of the public and the private. With the advent of electronic forms of discourse, the public and the private have been reconstructed yet again, much as they were in the fourth century B.C.E. with the advent of a widely used kind of writing and as they were again with the invention of the printing press in the fifteenth century and the subsequent rise of print literacy in the western European Renaissance. Working at home with computer, modem, facsimile machine, electronic mail, and the Internet, writers now conduct work in a new public. Another electronic machine, the television monitor, has been with us in the United States for nearly a half century. Humanists need to be part of the critical conversation and the legislating of media issues. We are not now in this conversation and legislation. Historicized (which is to say theorized) rhetoric offers some powerful theories for dealing with these issues. But they are not sufficient without new (including postmodern and after-postmodern) theory.

A new agenda lies before us. Isocrates needs to be rescued from his placement as an educationist, a designation that allows him to be dismissed by those who, for whatever reasons, dismiss the field of education. Marjorie Curry Woods has made the point that the histories of universities have been ignored at times because of the tendency to cordon off this important history in an area for education specialists only. Isocrates also needs to be reinterpreted through the new intellectual sensibility brought about by the last twenty years of language theory. Isocratic classical rhetoric offers us one powerful means of reconstructing a techno-liberal-arts curriculum that goes beyond the merely genteel and tolerant ideas that a construct of a liberal-arts education is a retrievable thing out in the world that one stores up and goes to as needed and that the liberal arts provide wholesome pastimes that are somehow vaguely good for everyone. Instead, we can construct a techno-liberal-arts education based partly on Isocratic ideas about how producing discourse in writing, speaking, and other ways is central to developing considered action in the newly emerging constructions of private and public worlds and about how intelligence, sensitivity, and emotional well being are cultivated by advancing our awareness of them.

An aim of this book is to help language students, including scholars, understand rhetorical/compositional principles as they produce them, including interior discourse and its multiple constructions. The study of rhetoric is to a large extent the study of ways of presenting oneself in a variety of subjectivities to the world, of recognizing and deflecting the barbs of hostile rhetoric, and of coming together with other people in a variety of contexts. The agenda has been and is being set forth in scholarship in English, communication studies, and other disciplines in the humanities and social sciences. It has not been worked out elaborately enough in the classroom, with the prominent exception of rhetoric and composition studies, a field where pedagogy has always enjoyed the prestige, power, and commitment that scholarly activity has long enjoyed.

One of the most effective ways to put aside the binarism (rather than to reject it outright, something that may be impossible anyway, as numerous writers have pointed out) is to move beyond dominant receptions of Aristotle and his desires for logic or even his less rigid desire for order in the enthymemes that characterize so much of his writing. The Sophists stand ready again to show us alternate ways of becoming *logos* users. The work of such thinkers as Aspasia and Diotima await the rigorous critical scrutiny that has been accorded Plato and Aristotle and, one must add, the equally textless Socrates. This strategy enables interpreters to avoid binarism (even if only for the rhetorical moment) and to think about performance, activity, and intersubjectivity as the bases of cultural literacy and writing practices.

Isocrates' work and an analysis of the traditions, or narratives, that grew up in response to that work, can show us some alternatives. In chapter 3, I analyze the dominant, received historicizing of Isocrates and discuss how his work has been interpreted and fits particular agendas. As I do so, the gendered and raced nature of classical rhetoric in the post-modern and after-postmodern era emerges. Diotima, perhaps another competitor of Isocrates, can rescue him as well.

3

Disciplining Isocrates

To deploy Isocratic rhetoric and its pre-Aristotelian power for current literacy activities (electric rhetoric), Isocrates needs a home, a disciplinary home. His work has been studied in the twentieth century in classics, in communication studies (where Isocrates is studied in traditional and revisionary rhetorics), in English (where rhetoric and composition studies have appropriated him), and in philosophy (where Isocrates is studied as a canonical orator). These locations of the study of Isocrates have driven his reception.[1] While these fields, of course, overlap, each one nevertheless possesses its own agendas and institutional practices that condition responses to Isocrates and perpetuate his marginality. In this chapter I present representative twentieth-century receptions of Isocratic rhetoric and then retell his story with theories of oralism that I developed in the previous two chapters. I then move to the issue of a gendered Isocratic-rhetorical theory that can be put to use for electric rhetoric. I emphasize that Isocratic rhetoric and electric rhetoric are performative. They are not merely important ideas. In other words, I seek to historicize part of literacy studies so that we can move away from the whatness of the modern period and get on to postmodern performance. I do not deploy Isocrates to "correct" current literacy studies, a move that would reinforce a philological-Golden-Age idea of classical rhetoric and culture (and thus be unproblematic for the general public). Rather, I seek to locate rhetoric and writing issues in Isocratic oralism and writing practices in a way that will empower current literacy studies, not merely refute any part of it. Historicized correspondences will emerge. My particular focus will be

---

1. Martin Bernal makes this point in volume 1 of *Black Athena*, where he writes from the rhetorical stance of a disciplinary outsider.

Antidosis, since it incorporates so much of Isocrates' theorizing on rhetoric and *paideia* and since it reveals so well Isocrates' cultural/ideological positioning.

Making Bears Dance

In section 210 of *Antidosis*, Isocrates teaches us an important lesson about pedagogy and its cultural implications:

But there remain still other reasons why everyone may well be astonished at the ignorance in men who venture so blindly to condemn *philosophia*. For, in the first place, they know that pains and industry give proficiency in all other activities and arts, yet deny that they have any such power in the training of the intellect; second, they admit that no physical weakness is so hopeless that it cannot be improved by exercise and effort, but they do not believe that our minds, which are naturally superior to our bodies, can be made more serviceable through education and suitable training; again, they observe that some people possess the art of training horses and dogs and most other animals by which they make them more spirited, gentle, or intelligent, as the case may be, yet they do not think that any education has been discovered for training human nature, such as can improve men in any of those respects in which we improve the beasts.... But most absurd of all, they behold in the shows held year after year lions that are more gentle toward their trainers than some people are toward their benefactors and bears that dance about and wrestle and imitate our skill, and yet they are not able to judge even from these instances the power that education and training have, nor can they see that human nature will respond more promptly than the animals to the benefits of education. In truth, I cannot make up my mind which should astonish us more: the gentleness that is implanted in the fiercest of wild beasts or the brutishness that resides in the souls of such men.

Isocrates' pedagogy and world view are revealed partly by his reliance on binary oppositions such as physical/mental, animal/human, and knowledge/ignorance, binaries that defined Greek thought for Derrida and others but that have received different treatments in recent rehistoricizing of classical rhetoric. Pedagogy as "aptitude" versus no aptitude acquires new meaning when dancing bears are considered, as Isocrates asks us to do in this passage from what is arguably his most important work. Throughout *Antidosis*, and indeed throughout all of his writing, from about 404–403 B.C.E. (*Against Lochites*) to 342 B.C.E. (*Panathenaicus*), Isocrates displays "aptitude" in revealing ways.[2] Like most

2. See, for example, *Antidosis*, passim.

objectivist stances, traditional twentieth-century receptions of Isocrates tend to universalize this strange trait, as they have tended to universalize many traits. Through recourse to the trope of aptitude, people such as women were not and frequently are not included in the categories of philology, and people such as Blacks were and frequently are automatically assumed to be Others, whose very contrast enabled the universal, property-owning, white, male subject to be constructed and reconstructed.[3] The same universalizing move enables objectivist historians to regard Isocrates' virulent imperialism as a quaint and secondary trait.[4] These moves converge, as only some things get to be universal, while others get to be unique. So in standard Western receptions of Isocrates, the terms "philosophy," "education," "man," "Greek," and other categories are assumed to be static and knowable. However, more fluid meanings of keywords (concepts such as *logos, physis, dike, ethos*) lead to more complex interpretations. Traditionalist constructors drive the meaning of Isocrates. In particular, George Norlin in his hegemonic English translation and editing of Isocrates and Werner Jaeger in his devotion to the goldenness of ancient Greece have constructed the "reality" of Isocrates for four generations of English readers in the first case and for about three generations of German, English, and other readers in the second case. Their particular philological constructions—regarded as truth more than as interpretation embedded in ideology—partly construct the discourse communities that receive the knowledge. The receptions of Isocrates are determined by these philology-driven communities as much as they are by anything inscribed by Isocrates (or his scribe). Much is left out, or as Foucault puts it, only some material is let into the discourse.[5]

3. See Paul Gilroy, *The Black Atlantic: Modernity and Double Consciousness* for an analysis of modernity and race and the limitations of writing about a white, male subject, especially pp. 68–71.

4. The universalizing and deuniversalizing of particular traits by traditional constructors accounts, of course, for the ideological veiling that characterized these accounts. See Foucault, "The Discourse on Language," in *The Archaeology of Knowledge*, pp. 215–237.

5. See "The Discourse on Language," *The Archaeology of Knowledge*, p. 216, for example.

Let us look for a moment at some passages. First look at one from Norlin:

Thus Isocrates took from Gorgias a style which was extremely artificial and made it artistic. In so doing, he fixed the form of rhetorical prose for the Greek world, and, through the influence of Cicero, for modern times as well. And if the style of Gorgias lost something of its brilliance and its fire in being subdued by Isocrates to the restraints of art, perhaps the loss is compensated by the serenity and dignity of that eloquence which Dionysius urged all young orators to study who are ambitious to serve the state in a large way. (*Isocrates*, Norlin's Introduction, vol. 1, p. xvi)

Norlin thus delineates the seamless history from Gorgias (who is bad) to Isocrates (who is good) to Cicero (also good) to modern times (really good as well, following the construction of progress). Its teleology is assumed in the philological assumptions Norlin believes are true, as was the fashion of his time and as has been the fashion of our time as well.

Jaeger too reinscribes this definite historical line:

Greek literature of the fourth century reflects a widespread struggle to determine the character of true paideia; and within it Isocrates, the chief representative of rhetoric, personifies the classical opposition to Plato and his school. From this point on, the rivalry of philosophy and rhetoric, each claiming to be the better form of culture, runs like a leitmotiv throughout the history of ancient civilization. It is impossible to describe every phase of that rivalry: for one thing, it is rather repetitious, and the leaders of its opposing sides are not always very interesting personalities. All the more important, therefore, is the conflict between Plato and Isocrates—the first battle in the centuries of war between philosophy and rhetoric. Later, that war was sometimes to degenerate into a mere academic squabble, in which neither side possessed any genuine vital force; but at its beginning the combatant parties represented the truly moving forces and needs of the Greek people. The field on which it was waged lay in the very centre of the political scene. . . . In retrospect, we realize that in this conflict are symbolized the essential problems of that whole period of Greek history. (Jaeger, *Paideia*, vol. 3, p. 46)

Jaeger's binaries, his originary war between rhetoric and philosophy (a binary in which "rhetoric" is inevitably the oppressed term), and his narrative of the vanquished similarly follow the teleological imperative that Norlin believes in as well, although Jaeger, in this passage, is less explicit about the march of progress to the modern period.

These representative and powerful classicists who have contributed so much have also to a large extent constructed who Isocrates is for us in Next Rhetoric at the rhetorically exuberant closing of the current millennium. I suggest alternative deployments based on the elaborate historicizing of rhetoric and composition studies of the last thirty years and on recent feminist interventions into narratives of the West.

In the *Antidosis* passage above, Isocrates seems to be saying (with his stylus or to his scribe) to take a look around; figure out which way the wind is blowing. *Paideia* enables human beings to train bears to dance for the entertainment of other humans (not, presumably, for the bears, but who knows), so education can train virtually anybody to do anything—a lesson that has to be relearned over and over in various cultures. The dancing-bear episode of *Antidosis* needs to be kept in mind as we consider Isocrates' five-part system of *paideia* discussed in chapter 2 and our redeployment of it: aptitude, knowledge of different kinds of discourse, practice, a teacher who provides instruction in the principles of discourse, and last, a teacher who models a mastery of discourse (*Antidosis*, sec. 187–188).[6] This system is consistently truncated by later commentators, such as Jebb, who delete the last item, the teacher as rhetor—surely an erasure very telling about the construction of knowledge, the nature of teaching, and life in the contact zone.

Like most writers, Isocrates instructs his readers in how to read his text:

I beg you now to listen to my defense, which purports to have been written for a trial, but whose real purpose is to show the truth about myself, to make those who are ignorant about me know the sort of man I am and those who are afflicted with envy suffer a still more painful attack of this malady; for a greater revenge upon them than this I could not hope to obtain.[7]

An occasional piece of the then déclassé genre, prose,[8] *Antidosis* assumes the fiction that the historical Isocrates is challenging another rich person

---

6. The system is more explicitly listed in *Against the Sophists*, sections 17 and 18.

7. *Antidosis*, sec. 13.

8. See chapter 1, n. 10, on the hegemony of poetry and how that difference causes many current discourse communities to view classical Greek rhetoric in odd ways.

to fund a warship or to exchange property after he has been assigned to fund one because he is perceived to be rich.[9]

Today's readers frequently find texts such as this long-winded, repetitious, digressive, and, finally, annoying. *Antidosis* may be in the common genre of an apology, but its conventions depart from that type in many ways.[10] Isocrates, in the conventional guise of a legal fiction and an autobiography, expounds particularly on the following seven themes: *philosophia*; hegemonic *paideia* and what is wrong with it; his own *paideia* and what is right with it; the negative aspects of the eristic (wrangling) Sophists; the importance of *logos* study; brief biographies of some of his successful students, deployed to display Isocrates' success as a teacher; and imperialistic exhortations to hate Persians and love Greeks, real Greeks.

Inquiry in *Antidosis*

In *Antidosis* as well as other places, including the letters, Isocrates writes in clusters as well as in careful lines, an oral feature. So, for example, he tends to present an issue, say what is wrong with hegemonic *paideia*, segue into his (good) *paideia*, and move to an example of one of his successful students. Thus the prose is associative, as of course so much important prose has been, so for him the kind of logic invited by linearity is not privileged.[11] Isocrates introduces issues, leaves them, returns to

9. Norlin explains: "The wealthier citizens of Athens were required by law to bear the expense of public services known as 'liturgies.' One of these was the 'trierarchy'—that of fitting out a ship of war. Anyone allotted to such a duty might challenge another to accept the alternative of either undertaking this burden in his stead or of exchanging property with him. Such a challenge was called an 'antidosis.' If the challenged party objected, the issue was adjudicated by a court" (*Isocrates*, vol. 2, p. 181).

10. For more on the genre of the apology in classical Greek, see Plato's *Apology*. For its relationship to modern autobiography, see Welch, "The *Pisteis* and Composition Theory."

11. The associativeness of Isocrates' prose resembles that of the U.S. Romantic rhetorician Ralph Waldo Emerson, whose work James A. Berlin explicated in *Writing Instruction in Nineteenth-Century American Colleges*. Although Berlin errs in dichotomizing Emerson and his transcendental mentor Plato, he nevertheless makes an important case for the inclusion of Emerson in U.S. rhetorics

them, leaves them again, and cumulatively builds on them, in a manner not unlike the speech genres of a lecture or a sermon. The reader will be disappointed if she expects a discernible progression (as we can see in, for example, *Phaedrus*, even when Plato waxes eloquent about aching, sprouting wings poking out of the backs of quite unusual horses[12]). She will find instead these clustered issues, all of which are tied together by the tonal strength of Isocrates' commitment to *logos* and its development, a commitment that we can see and feel subtextually. The reader both ancient and nonancient will find as well an absorption with the lines that Isocrates writes, lines that are worked over, woven, in ways that are beautiful to decode when one stands away from print-dominant formalism that necessarily mocks this writing.

The rhetorical importance of the beauty of Isocrates' periods is frequently overlooked in Isocratic studies as they occur in rhetoric/composition studies in English, communication studies, and classics, all of which bring great modernist burdens to Isocratic rhetoric. In the first two areas, Isocrates' periods are dismissed because Attic Greek is taken for granted, which thus reinforces the familiar idea that language is a container that holds meaning and that one container is virtually the same as any other container and so, that the language is of no consequence.[13] In all three fields, his periods are viewed as "style," that formalist commodity that exists to be cordoned off into the Ramist split of rhetoric, where the canons of style and delivery substitute for the meat of the full five canons—functions that give rhetoric its great strength and whose diminution can be seen to be a lingering problem for the study of language in all its manifestations.[14] The divorce of "style" from ideology

---

and histories of writing. See "Emerson and Romantic Rhetoric," pp. 42–57. Emerson's Scottish counterpart and friend Thomas Carlyle also writes associatively and with much of the bombast that typifies Isocrates' prose. These writers have yet to be rhetorically historicized, but see Jacqueline Jones Royster, "Perspectives on the Intellectual Tradition of Black Women Writers."

12. See 251–255.

13. A similar stance holds that devising an efficient alphabet or the burgeoning communicative power of electronic mail and Internet dialectic make no difference.

14. For an important exegesis of the five canons and medieval drama and rhetoric, part of the long and twisting history of the canons, see Jody Enders, *Rhetoric and the Origins of Medieval Drama*.

and culture continues to be one of the biggest problems in all current *logos* studies. The desiccation of style makes it a feeble and unimportant part of culture and education. To cordon off style is to promote the content/form binary that disempowers *logos*. This pervasive binary reempowers the hegemony of whatness and makes rhetoric a mere decoration.

An exception to this reception is George A. Kennedy's analysis of an Isocratic period in *Classical Rhetoric and Its Christian and Secular Tradition from Ancient to Modern Times*, deployed partly to demonstrate the Gorgianic figures that Isocrates also wrote.[15] In presenting the English version, Kennedy explains the operation of the Greek text and the limitations of translation into English. Nevertheless, Kennedy tends elsewhere to treat style more as part of a form/content binary than as a central issue for decoding Isocrates.[16]

The first four themes—*philosophia*, negative *paideia*, good *paideia* (that is, Isocrates'), and the attack on the eristic (wrangling) Sophists— intertwine around the spiraling sense of Isocratic *logos*. The other two dominant themes of *Antidosis*—raw imperialism and biographies of successful students (rhetoric as self-advertisement)—are less directly related to *logos*. Jaeger's philological analysis remains powerful and helpful in this respect, and Norlin's analysis offers some aid in decoding Isocratic rhetoric. Traditional, philological readings of Isocrates and other writers and texts offer us powerful interpretations and represent centuries of inquiry, of careful work conducted by serious scholars across disciplines and across centuries. This work is important and should be continued to be studied and deployed. Nevertheless, the work has obliterated gender and race in similar and in different ways. The Great Man theory of history writing, with some token women thrown into the same underlying theoretical structure, dominates not only much of our scholarly lives but also the daily lives of regular people. The little histories we walk around with in our heads continue to be constructed according to the nineteenth-century fount metaphor of Western Civilization (all male, all white, and all socially privileged) and unacknowledged constructions

15. See chapter 2.

16. The form/content binary and its continuing stranglehold over English studies, as well as other areas of the trivium, are discussed more thoroughly in chapter 6.

of gender and racial difference. The familiar philological readings that assume that woman is merged with man (so that, for example, the word "man" signifies "man and woman") and that racial construction is a part of *physis* and not *nomos* reinforce this cultural illness.

When we examine Isocrates' *paidea* and his contra-Platonic *philoso-phia*, we see important material that has come to us from such philological approaches as those of Norlin, Jaeger, and Benoit. The formalism of these approaches and its underlying erasures of gender and race must, however, be addressed and refuted. In classical Greek rhetoric, simultaneous moves must be made to regender rhetoric. These include the addition of silenced rhetors such as Sappho, Aspasia, and Diotima and a retheorizing of classical Greek rhetoric based on its regendering and recoloring.

Traditional analyses of classical Greek rhetoric reproduce the ideology of gender construction that the modern has reinforced for us but that existed powerfully in classical Greece despite its alleged progress. The condition of women in all social classes deteriorated markedly as the condition of selected groups of males improved substantially. This previously buried fact, excavated by feminist theorists in cultural studies, rhetoric, classics, and other areas, remains central to the historicizing of the West, of which classical rhetoric is, of course, a dominant part.[17]

Jaeger, Norlin, and many of their contemporary philologists reproduce this womanless, white-male-assumed ideology. One of the reasons for the erasure of woman is, of course, the belief that "man" allegedly signifies "man and woman." The last twenty-five years of Anglo-North-American and French feminisms has dispelled that lie for many, even though it continues as a dominant ideology in daily life, much of the academy, and elsewhere.

One of the reasons woman has been erased is that women for the most part did not get to learn to write, and when they did, their writings were not regarded as important enough to preserve and transmit. While many of the texts of the great writers of the classical West were reproduced and transmitted, the texts of great and nongreat women speakers and non-

17. For two important treatments of the regendering of classical rhetoric, see C. Jan Swearingen, "A Lover's Discourse: Diotima, Logos, and Desire," and Susan Jarratt and Rory Ong, "Aspasia: Rhetoric, Gender, and Colonial Ideology."

great men speakers were not preserved. And, of course, many of the "great" works were lost as well (for example, much of the work of Aeschylus). In addition, oralism plays a significant role as well. The burgeoning hegemony of the written word had the strong effect of silencing women even more than they had been.[18] Depriving women of access to writing deprived them in yet another way: it allowed selected categories of males to progress through the growing power of literacy as consciousness to develop different ways of thinking.[19] Women lost much in the changes brought about in the movement from oral dominance to literacy.

The Limitations of a Close Textual Analysis of Isocrates' Writing

Since Isocrates wrote his texts or had them written down, in contrast to his elder teacher Socrates,[20] and in contrast to many of his peers who appear not to have grasped the power of the technology of writing, we can conduct a close textual analysis of his writings. Such analysis, however, does not necessarily work on long pieces of writing. As the hegemony of New Criticism has displayed and does display, close textual analysis works best with short poetry, drama, and the novel—the trium-

18. See Susan Jarratt and Rory Ong, "Aspasia: Rhetoric, Gender, and Colonial Ideology."

19. I reiterate that not all males benefited from this situation. See chapter 1, n. 30.

20. Socrates supposedly would not engage the technology of writing, and so his protégés, such as Plato and Xenophon, wrote in his name by using the figure of prosopopoeia, or ventriloquism (putting words into someone else's mouth). We have no writing by Socrates. Nevertheless, many scholars—from English, classics, communication, and philosophy, for example—continue to refer to Socrates as if he had written the material in Plato's dialogues. When challenged on this attribution of authorship, the response invariably is that Plato is the author and that fact is so obvious that it need not be stated. The construction that underlies this view reinforces objectivist stances toward knowledge: the texts of Plato that invoke Socrates—that ventriloquize Socrates—are regarded as objects that can be consumed. Given the thingness of these objects, it does not matter in this deployment who the writer is. It is difficult to argue against the contention that something does not matter or that something is so obvious that it need not be stated. See Dominick LaCapra, "Introduction," in *Soundings in Critical Theory*, p. 4, who writes on the obviousness argument among historians.

virate of genres that has reigned in the United States.[21] The problems of formalism and close readings have been investigated by literary theorists with great persuasiveness. Nevertheless, close reading and its writing-pedagogy twin, the current-traditional paradigm, remain entrenched in our schools and many universities, as I discussed in chapter 2. Both institutions act to dehistoricize, deideologize, and replicate an assumed modern male subject into which marginalized Others will inevitably not fit.[22] At the same time, textuality as situated and historicized and explicitly theorized remains a powerful force that we need. Formalist analysis can, in fact, be conducted on anything that is textualized, as we can see from, for example, studies in semiotics.[23]

Isocrates' work has, of course, been textualized by being preserved, transmitted, and studied according to various rhetorical and other stances. In the last one hundred years in particular, the writing of Isocrates has been studied according to the reigning formalisms, all print-based and all print-biased. However, the oralism of his prose is so strong that it does not conform to readerly expectations as they have been trained to respond in our era. One way to approach this oralism is to recognize it, acknowledge it, and then analyze it, as I do in the following pages.

It is important to realize that a close textual analysis cannot be performed on a spoken text unless that text is preserved for repeated scru-

21. While virtually every English department has expanded the privileged genres included in the curriculum, a branch of English studies continues to be partly dominated by the New Critical/Modernism triumvirate: creative writing tends to maintain the three-part hegemony by focusing on these genres, especially poetry and fiction, often to the exclusion of other genres. Teaching the writing of drama usually resides not only in departments other than English but in different colleges as well, since playwriting is located within colleges of fine arts. This anomaly has received inadequate critical attention. However, since this important field teaches so many important issues, it naturally remains very important.

22. John Guillory has written, "The problem of the canon is a problem of syllabus and curriculum, the institutional forms by which works are preserved as *great works*" ("Canon," p. 240).

23. See, for example, Julia Kristeva, "The System and the Speaking Subject"; Umberto Eco, *Travels in Hyperreality*; and Thomas S. Sebeok, *The Tell-Tale Sign*. See also Aristotle on *semiosis*. The relationship of rhetoric and composition studies to semiotics has not been worked through yet, and needs to be made. Berlin claimed that they are nearly the same. In this book I assume that pantextualism exists, is important, and should not be hidden from our students.

tiny. Analysis proceeds from some kind of preservation, an act that brings with it repeatability. This preservation derives from the apparent permanence offered by the handwriting Isocrates and his peers practiced. Papyrus and stylus can be used to record something spoken. However, as "transcriptions" of Aristotle by his students and many other examples indicate, these records frequently are inaccurate.[24] Repeatability in reading is the key to constructing a situation in which a close textual analysis can occur. The repeating of the *Origin Myth of Acoma* by Acoma Pueblo people and of the prerecorded *Odyssey* enabled those spoken performances to be preserved and transmitted, as I discussed in chapter 2. This obvious connection seems not to have taken hold in the academy or general culture, as Henry Sussman's *High Resolution* served to demonstrate in the previous chapter. Only after they are recorded can spoken texts be scrutinized formalistically. With scrolls at hand, a writer can mull over his or her writing, revise it, and hold sections in abeyance as she or he intensively works over a particular area.[25] Memory, and thus psychology, changes, as Plato correctly predicted.

In the fourth century B.C.E., Isocrates and Plato recognized the repeatability and permanence offered by the far-from-new technology of writing. The story of Plato's paradoxical relationship to the technology of writing has been told in rhetoric and composition studies, and it has been told in poststructuralist literary and philosophical studies.[26] The story of

24. For different historical transcriptions in rhetoric and composition studies, see Winifred Bryan Horner, *Nineteenth-Century Scottish Rhetoric*, and Thomas P. Miller, "Teaching the Histories of Rhetoric as a Social Praxis." Obviously, the paleographic traditions in classics, medieval studies, history writing, anthropology, and other fields are of central interest here and need to be more fully incorporated into rhetoric and composition studies. See also Armando Petrucci, *Writers and Readers in Medieval Italy: Studies in the History of Written Culture.*

25. Revising strategies in historicized periods other than the present have recently received helpful critical analysis. See, for example, Lucille Schultz, "Elaborating Our History: A Look at Mid-Nineteenth-Century First Books of Composition." Revising strategies for other historical periods, including the classical Greek period, need to be addressed by rhetoric and composition studies. The extensive research conducted on writing since 1963 could operate as a model for earlier periods as well.

26. See, for example, Jasper Neel, *Plato, Derrida, and Writing*, and Welch, "Appropriating Plato's Rhetoric and Writing into Contemporary Rhetoric and

Isocrates' nonparadoxical (to most current discourse communities) relationship to the technology of writing has not been told. Instead, his story has been rewritten in standard, philological ways, ways that help us understand a number of issues and are valuable but that at the same time repeat the silences that speak so loudly.[27]

Isocrates and Audience Analysis

In addition to repeatability (preservation) of text, oralism in prose requires a particular construction of audience. Who is Isocrates addressing in *Antidosis*? Beyond the antidosial construction of the immediate legal and fictional audience, Isocrates addresses an audience of readers (already an exclusive group[28]) who could be influenced to join him in his new *paideia*, his *philosophia* of wisdom developed through education. Surely some of these readers were Plato and his circle; surely another group were the eristic (wrangling) Sophists, those who, according to Isocrates,[29] gave Sophism such a bad name and whom he reprimands, at least in writing. The cognoscenti were reading (or being read to), and the reading was done aloud; in other words, reading was more self-evidently performed.

Composition Studies," in *The Contemporary Reception of Classical Rhetoric*. In philosophy, see Catherine H. Zuckert, *Postmodern Platos: Nietzsche, Heidegger, Gadamer, Strauss, Derrida*.

27. See, for example, Edward Schiappa, "Isocrates' *Philosophia* and Contemporary Pragmatism"; Tony Lentz, *Orality and Literacy in Hellenic Greece*; and William L. Benoit, "Isocrates on Rhetorical Education." These scholars, all located within communication studies in the United States, are trained in a powerful version of rhetorical studies that tends to discount writing practices as mere skills, in much the way that traditional western European receptions of Isocrates have done. See, for example, Ijsseling, *Rhetoric and Philosophy in Conflict*, and Chaim Perelman and Lucie Olbrechts-Tyteca, *The New Rhetoric*, and many other texts. By making this move, these scholars have effectively aligned themselves with scholars in U.S. literary studies who similarly discount writing pedagogy and the study of writing practices as mere skills or instrumentalist activities.

28. See William V. Harris, *Ancient Literacy*, pp. 3–24.

29. See, for example, *Antidosis*, sec. 148.

The wider audience, including us, is much more difficult to assess, and that is always the case with writing. The disembodiedness of a text allows it to go off by itself to be decoded by various ideological positionings.

Tellingly, two very different current reader groups[30] tend to find the text annoying: hyperliterate readers and underprepared readers.[31] Both groups have been trained (for at least three generations in the United States, say, under the hegemony of such New Critical textbooks as *Understanding Poetry*, *Understanding Drama*, and so on[32]) to be formalist readers who ipso facto desituate, depoliticize, and generally wring out many (but not all) the juices that make any reading fascinating. In a similar move, hyperliterate formalist readers—professors, for example—were trained to be careful formalist readers and frequently still are. One difference, of course, is that the latter group is trained intensively and extensively, so that historical, ideological, and cultural questions are woven into the study of language and literary studies.[33] Even when formalism officially reigned, graduate students received extensive and expansive nonformalistic training in the histories of ideas and so on. So when we have formalist underprepared readers and hyperliterate formalist readers, we get a similar reader response: these two very different current groups are strongly put off by Isocrates' orally influenced prose. Formalists resist the oral features that Isocrates displays even as he advanced prose composition.

It is not difficult to see why formalist, underprepared readers and formalist hyperliterate readers would tire of Isocratic prose, particularly in the more-than-sixty-year-old English translations on which so much Isocratic scholarship is based. Instead of getting on with his exposition,

30. While I would like to use "discourse communities" here, I cannot, because the groups are too large and do not cohere in ways that would identify them as discourse groups. See Porter, *Audience and Rhetoric*.

31. For the term "hyperliteracy," see C. A. Perfetti, "Language, Speech, and Print: Some Asymmetries in the Acquisition of Literacy." The term applies to most academics. For further similarities between hyperliterate and underprepared readers, see chapter 6.

32. See Arthur Applebee, *Tradition and Reform in the Teaching of English*, pp. 158–166.

33. Of course, this issue could be addressed at length.

Isocrates writes and writes. While his cuing is helpful in some cases, he seems never to stop.[34] Unlike what we now call the tight, patterned, controlled prose of Isocrates' rival Plato, the strung-out prose of Isocrates appears to be a blob, oozing out into corners and never coming back.

In fact, these features constitute Isocrates' homage to and dependence on oralism, a performance that derives from his placement in the history of manuscript literacy (the historicizing of writing) and his placement in the history of consciousness (literacy as a language-embedded activity of consciousness). In this placement, Isocrates is, at the age of 82 in 354–353 B.C.E., when most of *Antidosis* was composed, only three and one half centuries away from the devising of the Greek alphabet, which occurred between 720 and 700 B.C.E.[35] This great change may or may not be regarded as revolutionary, but the transition of cultural memory from repeated speaking and hearing, as in assumed performances of the Homeric poems, to a combination of performance speaking, ordinary speaking, and craft literacy (that is, writing used for ordinary record keeping) contributed to considerable changes in structures of articulation.[36]

Symptoms of some of these changes can be detected in Isocrates' apparently windy prose. Isocrates' particular cultural moment—he had recovered financially from the Peloponnesian War, acquired and

34. See, for example, *Antidosis*, section 9.

35. Isocrates' writing process included a form of what we would now call sampling: he not only quotes his previous writing extensively; he places long sections in word for word. These segments are exact repetitions of earlier writing. They differ radically from the spoken repetitions detected by Albert B. Lord, Milman Parry, et al.; those repetitions were far from exact repetitions. Norlin (and probably his editors) chose to excise Isocrates' quoted sections from *Antidosis*, referring the reader to another text and frequently another volume of the Loeb three-volume Isocrates. This decision, made perhaps for reasons of economy, constitutes a large error because readers tend not to refer to the other (quoted) text if it is in fact published in a different volume. Even when a reader does turn to the cited passage, the flow of reading is interrupted in a negative way. On the other hand, this publication move reflects print dominance. So the dominant English-language presentation of Isocrates' writing (in print since 1928, 1929, and 1945) contains hidden histories of writing and distribution practices.

36. See, for example, Eric A. Havelock's titles, such as *The Literate Revolution in Greece and Its Cultural Consequences*. It is obviously difficult to determine what constituted ordinary speaking.

developed a vision of rampant Greek imperialism, and realized the power available to him in writing—enabled him to seize a new communication technology and to use its power in a number of ways, including establishing it in his school.[37] Inscribing a papyrus or an ostracon with a stylus, or speaking to a scribe who handled those technologies, Isocrates encoded prose that took advantage of the inherent disembodied communication that writing offered him and at the same time maintained and changed the patterns of writing that tapped into the ears of his immediate Greek audience.

So did Plato. However, they performed writing in entirely different ways. Their writing and rhetorical strategies/performances worked toward very different agendas. In addition, the receptions of each writer led this work in very different directions.[38] As I discussed in chapter 2, Plato's version of philosophy became our own in the West, making translations and therefore receptions of Isocrates' deployment of *philosophia* quite inaccurate. Isocrates' *philosophia* signifies a lettered wisdom, the making of a better person who can conduct self-deliberation about difficult issues. From these qualities it is possible to see how lines of reception constructed Isocrates as the "father" of the liberal arts. In addition, one can see how Isocrates became an early romantic in the romantic composition movement that continues to hold so much power in U.S. writing theory.[39] Less easy to detect have been Isocrates' innovative

37. Isocrates' father, a flutemaker (an important communication technology of the time), lost his fortune in the war, and so Isocrates had to go to work as a logographer (a speechwriter for people who took claims to court—an activity that, of course, had become more and more popular).

38. It is important to use the word "writer" here because standard terms such as "thinker" (the obvious, discrete individual) or "mind" (as in the Western mind) lead us back to the nonperformative, this-is-good-for-you construction of the Western Tradition, which is, of course, written nonconsciously as a mass of material that excludes those who are not property-owning, white, and male and that is to be consumed by students in training for entry into this particular social class and gender role.

39. The term "romantic writing" for rhetoric and composition studies was devised by Frank D'Angelo and has become a standard issue in rhetoric and composition studies, more commonly described as "expressivism." See Berlin, *Rhetoric and Reality*, and Faigley, "Process Composition: Three Views." See also chapter 6.

prose moves and educational strategies, both of which he mastered and combined in a way that offers us possibilities in our postmodern cultural moment, or in Next Rhetoric. Isocrates, like his later Roman follower Quintilian, knew that if you can teach bears to dance, you can teach humans virtually anything. At the center of his *paideia/philosophia*, including the sense of a healthy culture, resided an interlocking educational system that covers many aspects and crosses the stages of development of the person being educated.

The Regendering of Rhetoric[40]

In most locations rhetorical study remains loudly silent on the tacit masculinizing of traditions of rhetoric and writing practices. The silence is loud because it is so forcefully not spoken. The denial of its existence shouts to many of its readers, females and males, who have chosen to listen to the silence. Nevertheless, most historians of rhetoric (across the disciplines that study it) believe in the modern idea of disinterested, neutral language in which "man" signifies woman too and in which the claims of marginalized Others are said to be already, always there. This issue is regarded as the natural, normal state of affairs. There is no problem for these appropriators, aside from uncovering the origins of meanings, so there is nothing to be changed. Philology in particular continues to suffer from this wizened principle of origins.

Isocrates' biggest problem lies in his and his culture's erasure of women, a form of colonization that fits in well with his imperialistic agenda. Historical receptions have, in one way or another, replicated and reinforced these two large problems. In addition, nineteenth-century German and English philological scientism constructed Isocrates and other ancient Greeks as Aryan. All three interpretations continue to damage our students, ourselves, and so the culture. While Isocrates' performances in writing, still tied to the mentalité of oralism, offer us useful theory for current literacy studies, at the same time it is necessary to unveil his misogyny, colonialism, and philologically constructed racism. To make this move, let us turn to Socrates' teacher, a figure so important

40. The phrase is Cheryl Glenn's in *Rhetoric Retold*, where historicized Western rhetoric from Sappho to the early modern era is retheorized according to gender.

that she was deployed in Plato's *Symposium* as the teacher of one of the most important intellectuals. Let us turn to Diotima, whose textual existence enabled her to persist, lodged in the Attic Greek letters, inscribed in manuscript writing, and then in the printed writing of Plato, who deployed her to instruct the Socrates that Plato inscribes in the *Symposium*. Through the power of the written word and, just as important, through the power of the preservers, transmitters, and translators of Plato's manuscripts, Diotima has continued to live, even as she was marginalized. Various historical epochs tried to erase her; her preservation in writing, however, kept her alive so that the current generation of historicists could find her, explicate her, and so rewrite one of the Masters—perhaps *the* Master—of the West. The Great Male Teacher, Socrates, is shown to have been instructed by a woman, Diotima, whose very name signifies godliness.

Rehistoricizing Isocrates' Oralism with Diotima

New constructions must be made self-consciously and must be accomplished by including representative accounts of previous relevant constructions.

In the same way that the Sophists are being incorporated into standard publications and seminars, the historicizing of classical-Greek rhetoric can take more elaborate account of how ordinary women operated and were operated on, including their ability or inability to write, to engage in that burgeoning power. In a second move, classical-Greek rhetorical studies must take more elaborate account of how representations of women have been presented as mythical and so as not important—an issue I will elaborate on below. In a third move, the structural oppression of women as a class and the institution of slavery need to become centerpieces of the study of classical Greek rhetoric and not merely remain as withered "additions." These additions too easily appear as afterthoughts.[41] Eva C. Keuls has substantially advanced this project with *The Reign of the Phallus: Sexual Politics in Ancient Athens*, as have other

41. Is is especially important in the United States to study the slavery systems of other cultures, since enslavement by racial construction continues to define what the United States is.

feminist scholars. We have a problem now with institutionalizing these issues, in other words, with working them into school curricula and syllabi as standard issues and, eventually, into general culture.

The Strange Case of Diotima

Diotima was a Sophist. But where is she now in the canon of classical rhetoric? She is almost not even marginalized. Following the negative pronouncements of the early modern rhetorician Ficino, she is frequently dismissed as a "legendary" person or perhaps a superhuman person (in other words, not like any ordinary women) and made to be a character devised by Plato, a writer who persistently constructed his characters from historical people. I want to suggest three ways to rethink Diotima as she is deployed in the disciplines of English, communication, and classics. (In each of these disciplines, she will be appropriated in different ways; however, there will be some effective interdisciplinary moves as well.)

• The basic scholarly apparatus on Diotima needs to continue to be rewritten. The *Oxford Classical Dictionary* provides a standard example of a dominant reference problem that is a symptom of general belief. In five lines on Diotima, an unsigned writer mentions in three lines and in four ways that she is not "real." This writer assumes a know-nothing stance encased in the appearance of objectivity. One of the best apparatuses is Mary Ellen Waithe's entry "Diotima of Mantinea" in *A History of Women Philosophers*, vol. 1, *Ancient Women Philosophers, 600 B.C.– 500 A.D.*, published in 1987. In this important essay, Waithe promotes the idea that Diotima is a historical person, partly because of Waithe's project to reinscribe the history of women in philosophy. In making her argument, Waithe supplies rhetorical studies with ample material, as C. Jan Swearingen has pointed out. Waithe shows us how to compensate for standard references such as the *OCD* that marginalize or erase women thinkers and do so as if it were normal, natural, and inevitable, or as a part of *physis* and not *nomos*. In the area of the available scholarly apparatus, then, some basic rewriting needs to be done.[42] In other

---

42. This project has begun. Theresa Enos, in *The Encyclopedia of Rhetoric and Composition*, confronts a number of these problems by recognizing the centrality of women and feminism in rhetorical studies. See also Covino and Jolliffe, *Rhetoric: Concepts, Definitions, Boundaries*, who construct Diotima and other women as central to rhetoric.

words, the *physis* of this situation has been restructured and requires much further effort.

• Another move that I suggest is the inclusion of the *Symposium* in classical rhetoric seminars and other pedagogical locations in a way that places Diotima on the same plane as Socrates. After all, we have nothing of Socrates from himself; we have Plato's version primarily (although not exclusively). We have, then, Plato's Diotima just as much as we have Plato's Socrates. We can position Diotima in a way that privileges her work. The issue of whether or not she is a historical person then becomes another issue for discussion. In other words, Diotima may be retextualized so as to be more central. Since the *Symposium* is partly a companion piece for the *Phaedrus*, it is not difficult to include.

• The third move that I suggest is that Waithe's article on Diotima in her *History of Women Philosophers*, Swearingen's "A Lover's Discourse: Diotima, Logos and Desire," Glenn's *Rhetoric Retold*, and Covino and Jolliffe's "What Is Rhetoric?" be included with the study of Diotima in the *Symposium*. This study would highlight the gender issues associated with studying her work along side of Plato's, and with how they have been appropriated. After this basic revision of the apparatus, new feminist readings of Diotima, particularly that of Luce Irigaray, can be included.[43]

Including the *Symposium* and Diotima (along with *Gorgias*, *Phaedrus*, and the Seventh Letter) in standard rhetorical studies works against the standard post-fifteenth-century reception that she is a fiction and does not have the pull of history that Plato's other characters possess. (For example, some early modern constructions regarded her as a mythologized character with no historical correspondence at all.)

The issues raised by Waithe that can be usefully appropriated by current receptors of classical rhetoric include the following two:

• Diotima's historicity. While, as I have mentioned, it is important to Waithe's argument that Diotima be regarded as a historical person, that importance does not hold for classical rhetorical studies. What does matter is that she be positioned as an important construction. In rhetoric we can bypass the issue of historicity, after acknowledging it, by saying that in this central dialogue of Plato there is a construction of not just a female teacher but a female teacher who resides on a pedagogical hierarchy higher than does the revered Socrates himself. This positioning is extraordinary and should be studied as a rhetorical issue. How does

43. See "Sorcerer Love: A Reading of Plato's *Symposium*, Diotima's Speech."

Plato construct her rhetorical strategies? How does she deploy language as an issue in power?

• False history. Waithe's examination of much of the reception of Diotima itself presents an important lesson on how reception in various historical eras creates "truths" that subsequently take on unexamined historical reality. One question that arises subtextually in Waithe's treatment is the question of dismissing Diotima because she is a woman but using the pretext that she is nonhistorical, fantastic, legendary, and so on, to do so. Waithe conducts a meta-analysis of standard appropriations of Diotima. Her way of conducting that analysis is a useful one for students to follow, whether or not her conclusions are accepted.

I want to redirect these issues of hierarchy, history, and gender to the daily issue of working with our students, all of whom live and study, as do we, in gendered worlds. One useful way of treating this problem is by appropriating some issues of audience-response theory from the discipline of English to take account of some frequently unseen problems in the study of classical rhetoric. While much of this theory is written for responses to literary texts in the standard sense—extraordinary written language (as opposed to ordinary written language), or written language that contains some hard-to-define aura of the special—some of the tenets worked out there can be applied to texts of classical rhetoric, including the *Symposium*. Nan Johnson describes it this way: a "basic assumption of reader-response criticism" is "the premise that the act of understanding of the meaning of textual features is affected by the predisposition of the reading mind" ("Reader-Response and the Pathos Principle, pp. 152–153). Johnson works as well on the theory of Louise Rosenblatt, one of the earliest reader-response theorists, who first published her work on this topic in 1939. (A particular irony resides in the fact that much reader-response theory erases Louise Rosenblatt's contribution to this material in favor of male critics.) We need to teach our students that all readers reside in discourse communities and that we must now include questions of gender and the erasure of women, whether they are historical, fantastic, or ordinary. In other words, the universalized reader—the white, male, propertied, philological, bookish decoder whose values, ideologies, and desires underlie many of the assumptions of standard readings—needs to be elaborated on. One elaboration is how various groups of late twentieth-century readers of texts such as the *Symposium* are treating exclusions of women. The recognition of the instability of texts should help to place women within the intersubjectivities of interpretation, rather than as marginalized bystanders.

If the text is not a monolithic object that contains transmissible knowledge but is part of what some audience-response theorists term transaction or transformation, and if women sometimes (but not all the time) make up particular discourse communities that differ from the discourse communities of men, then those communities need to be appropriated more fully in classes on historical rhetoric. In this way, the erasure or the marginalizing or even the ridiculing of a figure such as Diotima can come to be seen as a historical way of reading that worked to disempower women as readers, writers, and speakers. It is crucial that women readers see themselves in the texts they study, and it is crucial that they and male students be taught how to recognize and account for erasures. In other words, our male and female readers need Burkean identification, and they need it badly. However, these moves alone remain inadequate. The relationship of language and power that governed classical rhetoric needs to replace the model of study that privileges interpretation that leads nowhere. As Jane Tompkins points out in "The Reader in History," ancient language linked "language with power" (p. 203) and action; we link it in the twentieth century with interpretation, or a search for meaning. We privilege readings and rereadings. This stance is one of the things that is wrong with the discipline of English. It has privileged interpretation (in reader-response theory two of the favored words are "transaction" and "transformation"), and it stops there, as if interpretation will automatically lead to a different interaction with the world. This stance is one of the reasons that English studies so frequently consists of courses having transformations that do not affect material reality. As Tompkins puts it, the reader-response theorists' preoccupation with "meaning" makes these theorists as formalist as the critics they sought to depose, the New Critics who found "meaning" in texts and not in readers. She argues that reader-response theorists—including Norman Holland, David Bleich, Wolfgang Iser, and Stanley Fish—remain committed to "meaning" and so work from the same assumptions as the formalists.

Because her story is told in the technology of writing, Diotima endures. Derided as she has been by some traditional receptors, particularly Ficino, she has remained because Plato wrote her down and later recorders preserved Plato's writing. The oral texts of most ancient women rhetoricians were not preserved because they were not regarded as important. Nevertheless, women rhetors existed. Their spoken performances evanesced and disappeared; the devoicing of women occurs repeatedly in historical rhetoric. Women and the spoken word are inextricably linked in rhetorical history. As we rehistoricize, we must continue to search for non-erasures and to transmit to our students the subjectivities of these rhetors and the subjectivities that attempted to erase them.

The move that needs to be made is to use the theories such as those found in audience-response writers and to move back to the classical rhetorical emphasis on language as power out in the world and language as activity. In other words, Sophistic classical rhetoric offers important material for electric rhetoric and understanding our current, electrified time. However, it is insufficient merely to return to any historical period in a theory-unconscious way. A new way is called for. James Porter writes, "Audience represents a field of community out of which the writer arises. From this view, the audience can be said to 'write the writer.' "[44] In this construction, repositioning Diotima to become more important and making Waithe's interpretation more accessible can follow Porter's account. These moves will enable women students of rhetoric to represent ourselves, making it an aspect of our own rhetorical performance. We all, men and women interpreter/actors, become new logos users. However, that move is not enough. The next aspect, the issue so important in classical rhetoric, is to self-consciously link language with power and action and the new communication technologies of electric rhetoric. The beginning of that power and action lies in the production of discourse.

Articulation, particularly in writing and in speaking, is the central issue here. The problem with reader response theory and with other literary-theory schools is that they do not account for the production of discourse. The writing of standard academic essays and—if the students are

44. *Audience and Rhetoric*, p. xii.

fortunate—speaking in class discussions are very limited kinds of production of discourse. This production is not adequate. The students need more opportunities for the production of discourse and training in how to make it effective; they need rhetorical repertoires. The trivialization and erasure of specific women (whether historical constructions or wholly fictional constructions) is a topic that we need to address in classical-rhetoric seminars and at the undergraduate level as well. It is, simply, a topic that can no longer be suppressed. The case of Diotima provides rich resources for understanding the operations of receptions of classical rhetoric and for better enabling our students to understand the centrality of action and power in language and its remarkable formalistic suppression in the twentieth century. In this move, Diotima becomes a case history.

II

Logos Performers, Screen Sophism, and the Rhetorical Turn

4

The Next Rhetoric

The effect of speech upon the condition of the soul is comparable to the power of drugs over the nature of bodies. For just as different drugs dispel different secretions from the body, and some bring an end to disease and others to life, so also in the case of speeches, some distress, others delight, some cause fear, others make the hearers bold, and some drug and bewitch the soul with a kind of evil persuasion.

Gorgias, Encomium of Helen[1]

The memory market is in fluctuation.

Gateway 2000 Computer Print Advertisement[2]

We all reside in rhetorical HUTs, households using television (the demographer's term), and the machine's ubiquity has changed rhetoric. Ninety-eight percent of United States households have televisions; forty percent have personal computers.[3] In addition, television monitors have proliferated for forty years, imperceptibly changing consciousness/ mentalité and written and spoken articulation. The ear in particular has changed among HUT dwellers, partly because of the use of television as background sound and partly because of its fragmented, associative deployment of electronic logos.[4] It is no accident that the term "sound

1. Section 13. In Sprague, *The Older Sophists*, p. 53.

2. Brochure, 1995.

3. See Steve Lohr, "The Great Unplugged Masses Confront the Future."

4. The standard work on the sensorium, the arrangement of the five senses, is by Marshall McLuhan: "If a technology is introduced either from within or from without a culture, and if it gives new stress or ascendancy to one or another of our senses, the ratio among all of our senses is altered. We no longer feel the same, nor do our eyes and ears and other senses remain the same. The interplay among our senses is perpetual save in conditions of anesthesia. But any sense

bite," a central metaphor of television culture, is aural and not visual. At the same time that sound is emphasized in this ubiquitous and pejorative phrase, tactility, another of the five senses, dominates as well.[5] Television is more acoustic than visual, and so is attached strongly to oralism/ auralism. One can turn one's gaze away from the television, but one cannot turn one's ears from it without leaving the area where the monitor leaks its aural signals into every corner. Television sound—with its standard tinny speakers that tend to be far inferior to most radio sound—occurs more and more frequently in HUTs (people are buying more monitors so that more rooms are furnished with them) and in public spaces. The disjointedness, fragmentation, and nonlinear nature of this nearly ubiquitous sound continues to have a profound effect on rhetoric and culture.[6] This effect corresponds to Isocrates' oral/aural world; the *koinoi topoi* (commonplaces) he developed present striking historical correspondences for our own rhetorical situation because he both represented and moved forward a large change in the hegemony of alphabetic literacy.[7]

---

when stepped up to high intensity can act as an anesthetic for other senses. The dentist can now use the 'audiac'—induced noise—to remove tactility" (*The Gutenberg Galaxy*, p. 24).

5. Since the word "sound" stands in the adjectival position of this phrase, it could be argued that "bite" is stronger and so that the tactile sense is emphasized. In addition, biting includes the sense of taste for the biter. Although a literal bite is very negative because it hurts, it also has the characteristic of surprise; it interrupts the expected. It is also connected to the computer term "byte," a series of binary digits.

6. The ubiquity of electronically communicated oral/aural texts might be related to this century's preoccupation with print textuality. A deep desire to study printed material seems to be unrecognized by many text-dominant schools of theory.

7. For early work on television, see John Fiske and John Hartley, *Reading Television*; Horace Newcomb, *TV: The Most Popular Art*; David Marc, *Demographic Vistas: Television in American Culture*, 2nd ed.; and Daniel Czitrom, *Media and the American Mind: From Morse to McLuhan*. For more recent work, see John Fiske, *Television Culture*; Robert C. Allen, ed., *Channels of Discourse Reassembled: Television and Contemporary Criticism*; Gregory Ulmer, *Teletheory: Grammatology in the Age of Video*; Annabelle Sreberny-Mohammadi, "Media Integration in the Third World," and Roger Silverstone, "Television, Rhetoric, and the Return of the Unconscious in Secondary Oral Culture" (both in Bruce Gronbeck et al., eds., *Media, Consciousness and Culture*); and Kathleen Hall Jamieson, *Eloquence in an Electronic Age*.

We are all *logos* users in the sense that Isocrates explored in writing and that I explored in part I as an alternative paradigm to the Aristotelian paradigm that has dominated Western cultures. How we think depends on the native tongue that each one of us acquired and the communication technologies that we intersubjectively interact with, as well as on the caretakers we interacted with.[8] Because this is so, we need elaborate, complicated, multidisciplinary logos training and practice throughout life.[9] Because of the technological revolutions of the last fifty years, this training must include the oralism of video, a consciousness that is utterly dependent on writing and the consciousness that the written word brought about (in manuscript at first but then more profoundly in print).[10] The associative property of electrically transmitted speech continues to condition current literacy. As I developed it in chapter 2, "*logos*" now signifies the associative. It signifies more than the merely rational and recognizes social constructions of "reality" even as one simultaneously partakes of a particular "reality." It also strongly resists the corrosive *topos* (a line of inquiry) that thought is a container that holds meaning, an idea rejected by Isocrates and by postmodernist rhetoricians and compositionists. This whatness has been replaced with discourse communities, with collaborative constructions, and with a recognition of the necessarily unstable ethos (or unstable ethe) that, in ideological embeddedness, contributed to literacy activity. A new sophistic performance has emerged. Pre-Aristotelian rhetoric, particularly Isocratic rhetoric, resembles postmodernism.

To understand the enormous change in literacy brought about by HUT culture, we need to reject the Great Divide theory of orality and literacy, as we saw in chapter 2, and instead accept their merger and interdepen-

---

8. The basis of this argument is from Lev Vygotsky. See "The Problem and the Approach" and "The Genetic Roots of Thought and Language" in his *Thought and Language* and "Tool and Symbol in Child Development" in his *Mind in Society*.

9. In a book in progress on technology, rhetoric, and women's writing, I will offer a discussion of a proposed techno-liberal-arts that is gendered and that accounts for technology.

10. Television in its broadcast, cable, satellite, and other forms proceeds according to scripts, that is, to elaborately written down material. It cannot proceed in any other way.

dence; we need to reject the autonomous theory of literacy (represented so influentially by Jack Goody) and replace it with the ideological one (articulated especially by Brian V. Street);[11] and we need to get over the intellectual snobbery that discounts television listening/viewing as déclassé, an activity so shameful that the instruments need to be closeted.[12]

Electric rhetoric, an emergent consciousness or mentalité within discourse communities, is the new merger of the written and the oral, both now newly empowered and reconstructed by electricity and both dependent on print literacy. Electronic technologies have led to electronic consciousness, an awareness or mentalité that now changes literacy but in no way diminishes it. As we saw in chapter 1, the false and ubiquitous separation of literate consciousness from oral consciousness leads to dangerously simplistic ideas of literacy, which has entered a new phase after one hundred years of electric communication. *Logos* users need the powerful theorizing provided by rehistoricized Western rhetorics because they account for all language use, not just cordoned off Literary use (in the old-fashioned formalist sense that still holds much power) but all uses in all contexts, from a Shakespeare sonnet to a graffito to a television advertisement. At the same time, rhetorical theories, left unmodified, are inadequate. Isocrates, the representative here of a retheorized classical

---

11. See Street, *Literacy and Theory in Practice*, and chapter 2 above.

12. It is remarkable that television monitors tend to be hidden in built-in cabinets, free-standing cabinets, armoires, chests, bookcases with opaque doors, and other containers of various kinds; some spectators deploy carts with wheels so that the monitor can be rolled away to unseen rooms, rooms that are deemed inferior to the main living space. This shame characterizes much of HUT cultural activity and needs to be unveiled and explained by rhetoric/compositionists as well as others. While 98 percent of all people commune in varying ways with (usually a plural number of) monitors, denial of tuning in remains very high. The rhetoric of design and the shame attached to the monitor exist in another kind of hierarchy as well: rooms with television in many middle-class HUTs are designated the family room, the recreation room, etc. The room highest in the hierarchy of this kind of HUT is the livingroom, in which no monitor resides and in which no person goes. This discordance of monitor placement and its rhetorical significance for oralism/auralism and other *logos* habits need further study. Why, for example, do the 98 percent routinely deny that they ever watch television? How can we ever understand this powerful rhetorical device if intellectuals in particular deny ever engaging with it?

rhetoric that walks away from the linearity, rationality, and dualisms of the entrenched Socrates, Plato, and Aristotle, needs electric rhetoric. It is impossible for people now to understand Isocrates as disciplined by a Diotimic regendering of historicized rhetoric without the impact of electronic technology, because our own logos is electrified, a phenomenon that objectivists deny. There is no recapturing of Isocrates' rhetoric and culture without a thorough infusion of our own, which remains (especially for academics) print privileged.

Because of the slow absorption from oral dominance to literate-oral mergers, classical Greek rhetoric offers us a dynamic historical transition that corresponds in some ways to our own. Radical changes in communication technology bring about different ways of articulating; they also bring about different relationships between a discourse community and its native tongue.[13] However, this history of communication technology will be useless if it follows the modernist whatness of the form-content debate, that duality that appears almost everywhere, that dominates many educational systems, and that serves to mask the racism and misogyny of traditional histories.[14] Isocratic rhetoric enables us to retheorize classical rhetoric from the ossified canon and feel-good humanism of the Heritage School into a theory of informed performance. This action includes the recognition that most U.S. citizens live in rhetorical HUTs

13. In the United States currently and historically since the French and Indian Wars established the hegemony of the English language, the native tongue has been English. Most U.S. citizens articulate only in English (a radical failure of our *paideia* and one that reinforces isolationism and the form-content binary that dictates that ideas can go into any given container and not change). Rhetorical studies of bilingual Spanish-English speakers in North America are urgently needed. Obviously, writing instruction is significantly affected and needs to be taken account of in rhetoric/composition scholarship. In addition, work on Native American languages and English needs to be developed. See Womack, "A Creek National Literature."

14. As I wrote in previous chapters, other historical periods of rhetoric would work as well. Early modern western Europe is one example. See chapter 1. See Maurice Coutourier, *Textual Communication: A Print-Based Theory of the Novel* on literary production and the rise of print. See also Roger Chartier, *Cultural History*; *The Culture of Print*; *The Cultural Origins of the French Revolution*; and *Forms and Meanings*; also Ian Watt, *The Rise of the Novel*; Lucien Febvre and Henri-Jean Martin, *The Coming of the Book: The Impact of Printing, 1450–1800*; and Elizabeth Eisenstein, *The Printing Press as an Agent of Change*.

and that they conduct interior and exterior dialectic with the heavy influence of electronic consciousness.[15] Postmodern *logos* has an inevitable relationship to oralism: it is wired. Print-dominant academics have frequently offered powerful resistance to the new oral-literate technologies. Electric rhetoric enables fragmentation, nonlinear juxtaposition, and ironic appropriations of the past, as we can see in the Madonna video *Express Yourself*, in the MTV-influenced television advertisements that proliferate, and in selections from *The United States of Poetry*.[16] Intertextuality has particular resonance in our current state of oralism. Electric rhetoric is utterly associative, a defining feature of oralism, which has links and transitions that resonate more than they lineate.[17] The difference between traditional *logos* (which includes the cognate "logic") and postmodern Isocratic *logos* lies in the move away from the dominance of print literacy to the changes brought about through the electronic forms of discourse. It needs to be recognized that encoding through speaking is not merely acquired in some pipe-transfer mode but is interactively, intersubjectively performed.[18]

15. The term "transformation" needs to be problematized. It works well to depict radical change; it works less well if it carries the connotation that some instantaneous, nearly miraculous, and very rapid change takes place. Havelock reiterates the sudden, "revolutionary," and rapid change from spoken-dominant communication technology to alphabetic dominance. See, for example, *The Literate Revolution in Greece and Its Cultural Consequences*. Heim, in *Electric Language*, names Ong's theory "transformational technology" in a more persuasive way (see pp. 46–69).

16. *The United States of Poetry*, broadcast on many Public Broadcast Systems, blends the ancient oral features of poetry—public performance—with print-based alphabetic literacy (all these poems were drafted on computer and/or paper). It transcends both of these by being a postmodern, repeatable performance. Record the shows and watch it, splice it, imitate it. It is already fragmented and anti-objectivist. Its audience is potentially the 98 percent HUT dwellers because it appears on free TV. The alphabetic performance partakes of immediacy, word and image, and apparent contact of performer/poet to audience.

17. I do not refer, of course, to associationism, a kind of faculty psychology; instead, I refer to a nonlinear, nonhyperlogical means of inquiry that links according to aural/oral/print features and not through a rational line.

18. Similarly, hypertext electronic discourse is reader-dominant, or merges reading and writing, making the former much less passive. See George P. Landow, "Hypertext, Metatext, and the Electronic Canon" in Myron C. Tuman, ed., *Lit-*

There is no escaping the oral/aural. This is true in the main sense of form of consciousness, or mentalité, and in the sense of individual utterances, even as encoders are multiply constructed. The hegemony of form/content thinking makes oral texts detachable and not inherent. A dominant, assumed belief conveys the idea that spoken language (like knowledge, like writing) is escapable. It is thought to be escapable by people who tacitly view it as a convenient tool that can be owned and applied as necessary. Neither language/literary specialists nor the general population have been able to articulate strongly enough the fact that the spoken word is inescapable.[19]

The spoken word resides in the subjective memories of people who interact in various discourse communities that articulate in a particular language.[20] Memory, of course, has been the fourth canon or function (*ergon*) of rhetoric for 2,400 years, undulating, being rearranged in importance, and being reorganized according to various ideological constraints.[21] The language and memory changes that face us now are as great as those that confronted the Renaissance, as Gregory Ulmer writes in *Teletheory: Grammatology in the Age of Video*:

The failure of the Humanities disciplines to communicate with the public may be due in part to the fact that what separates specialized humanists from laymen

---

eracy Online: The Promise (and Peril) of Reading and Writing with Computers. At the same time, in its rapidity and informality, electronic mail resembles speaking. In this way, electronic mail—with all its unrevised exuberance—maintains strong affinities with writing pedagogy and the oral/aural features available in first drafts. See Welch, "Autobiography and Advanced College Writing."

19. In addition, we have not articulated why the written word is inescapable. Nevertheless, a strong public belief holds that language study is crucial.

20. I resist here the concept of "interpretive communities" from Stanley Fish and others because it is too passive, even though those critics do not intend it to be. Instead, I deploy the term "discourse communities" from rhetoric/composition studies, where informed performance is consistently privileged.

21. There is a common misperception that the five canons or functions of rhetoric go back to Aristotle. This interpretation fits into the mode of historicizing that begins all rhetoric with Aristotle. In fact, the canons go back much further and were highly developed in Greek rhetoric by the time Aristotle took them up. See Aldo Scaglione, *The Classical Theory of Composition from Its Origins to the Present*. The canons have ebbed and flowed in Western rhetoric during this period. See chapter 5.

[sic] is not only our conceptual apparatus and the discourses of the academy, but the very medium in which we work—the printed word. (P. viii)

Print rules. That is to say, print on paper rules. While it will not continue to rule, alphabetic literacy will appear nearly everywhere; alphabetic literacy currently and in the future will attain greater importance. This literacy is electronic and currently centered on television and computer, two communication machines that may merge so that one screen can perform numerous functions. Electric rhetoric will supplant print/paper hegemony.[22]

Electric rhetoric brings not merely a new idea. It brings a new performance, Sophistic performance, which is postmodern in its dispensing with unity (that buzzword of Aristotelian formalism), in its repetitive constructions, and in its commitment to mixing and fragmenting the images of mass and high modernist culture. Historicizing rhetoric and computers has been proceeding effectively. Jay David Bolter in *Writing Space: The Computer, Hypertext, and the History of Writing*; Richard Lanham in *The Electronic Word*; and Michael Heim in *Electric Language* have addressed the continuing changes in mind/language brought about by the proliferation of computers. Bolter, a classicist, Lanham, an English professor, and Heim, a philosophy professor, all deploy historicized rhetoric to great effect. In addition, computers and composition have been rigorously studied by rhetoric and composition scholars in English: for example, Cynthia L. Selfe in *Computer-Assisted Instruction in Composition: Create Your Own*; Selfe and Hilligoss in *Literacy and*

22. Although nearly every U.S. household has television, only 40 percent have computers. In addition, many universities, colleges, and schools not only have few or no computers; they do not have the ethernet or even the telephone lines to perform fully electric rhetoric and representative democracy. This situation has serious consequences for literacy education. While one solution might be the expected technology of computers merged with television monitors (as the Zenith corporation, for example, has developed and is now marketing), with signals arriving via coaxial cable and monitor, the only genuine solution is a massive federal- and state-government commitment to wiring every educational building, supplying monitors, and training everyone. At a "Communication and Institutional Change: Closing the Technology Gap" roundtable, Conference on College Composition and Communication, Cincinnati, March 1992, the unavailability of wired buildings and the consequences for literacy education were discussed extensively.

Computers: The Complications of Teaching and Learning with Technology; Myron C. Tuman, *Word Perfect: Literacy in the Computer Age* and *Literacy Online*; and many others have developed powerful new pedagogical theories based on computer-assisted instruction.[23] This kind of investigation has so far not taken place in the theorizing of video and rhetoric.

Next Rhetoric Requires a New Historiography

To understand our *logos* intersubjectivities in rhetorical HUTs, which is to say our new literacy, we need to historicize oralism, or the consciousness that merges electrified discourse from wired speaking and writing practices with the traditional print-based practices. One definition of rhetoric is what is there; what language situation is already in place. Our students perform habits of literacy that are substantially different from people born into a three-channel video world or before. For the first zapping generation (that is, those people who acquired language in cable-and-broadcast rhetorical HUTs beginning in 1981 with the widespread introduction of the technology in the United States[24]), the oralism of video contributes to their literacy as consciousness. For intellectuals to disdain these proliferating, chopped up, repetitive, formulaic video texts as untouchable means that we have lost contact with our students and our public. It means we have become the priests of Dead Culture, an Arnoldian world that replicates much of the worst that has been thought and said and that can offer up, as a feeble justification, only the bromide that it has always been this way.[25]

23. See also essays in the journals *Rhetoric Review* and *College Composition and Communication*, which have presented new theorizing on computers, rhetoric, and composition.

24. By 1996, 70 percent of U.S. dwellings were wired for cable (Lawrie Mifflin, "USA Strives for Network, Not Channel").

25. A situation long denied by traditional literary chronologists is that literature as we regard it now is an eighteenth-century construct. This situation does not recognize the centrality of rhetoric that dominated the West until that period. The power of print literacy had much to do with the change in status acquired by Literature. Its status now undergoes radical change for much the same reason: technological change. The word has become more richly amorphous and has been rigorously problematized.

The new life of the formula presents us with important material for this new historiography. John Miles Foley, in *The Theory of Oral Composition*, explicates the formula and its positioning in cultures with powerful oralisms. The formula enables a discourse community to empower memory (the fourth canon of rhetoric, which, along with delivery, is ignored as trivial by modern rhetoricians, who are print dominant). Far from being rote memorization, the formula contains linguistic markers that enable an encoder within a community to reconstruct a particular issue. Memory as a rhetorical/psychological function has changed radically with the repeatability offered by videotape, film on video, and silicon.[26] With these new technologies and the symbol systems they engender, memory is stored materially; decoders can, given the right circumstances, access the history stored in these wired forms, just as they can with writing. They are repeatable; they are reproducible; they remain the same. As inert texts they remain the same; as artifacts they remain the same; in a binary world of form versus content they remain the same. Nevertheless, they do not remain the same. In their very repeatability and reproducibility they are transformed as the decoder's desire for the text wanes. Repeatability is a double-edged sword: it offers immediate access but it brings about a loss of desire in the sense that Burke explains in *Counter-Statement*, where he defines form as the instilling and fulfilling of desire in writing, music, sex, and other expressive locations.[27] Repeatability kills desire. It also changes the nature of commodification. The proliferation of video HUTs has led to radical changes in discourse communities and makes audience-response theory in rhetoric and composition studies even more important.

The Oral-Formulaic Theory can be usefully applied to current texts and cultures. Texts as various as Isocrates' *Antidosis*, Walker's *The Color Purple*; a Diet Coke video advertisement, and *Origin Myth of Acoma* possess powerful oral features that can lead to dismissal by traditional formalists and video rejectors. Rather than denigrating such texts for being overblown, repetitive, redundant, and excessive, *logos*

26. See Aristotle, *On Memory*; anon., *Ad C. Herennium*; Frances Yates, *The Art of Memory*; and Mary Carruthers, *The Book of Memory*, for standard treatments of memory and its complicated history.

27. See "Psychology and Form," pp. 29–44.

users can identify with the power of the oral that continues to permeate literacy as consciousness and, in turn, the written texts produced by this consciousness. I return to the Oral-Formulaic Theory and its rhetorized incarnation in video in chapter 5.

The easiest way to preserve spoken texts during the last one hundred years or so is with electronic means.[28] Repeatability is one point of Walter Benjamin's "The Work of Art in the Age of Mechanical Reproduction," in which he explains that repeatable art, beginning with woodcuts, change the entire notion of art.[29] This change identified by Benjamin has everything to do with rhetoric and composition studies and how it will be made to develop in the coming decades of profound change—particularly technological change—in higher education. He thus historicizes rapidly reproducible art:

Theses about the art of a proletariat after its assumption of power or about the art of a classless society would have less bearing on these demands than theses about the developmental tendencies of art under present conditions of production. Their dialectic is no less noticeable in the superstructure than in the economy. It would therefore be wrong to underestimate the value of such theses as a weapon. They brush aside a number of outmoded concepts, such as creativity and genius, eternal value and mystery; concepts whose uncontrolled (and at present almost uncontrollable) application would lead to a processing of data in the Fascist sense. The concepts which are introduced into the theory of art in what follows differ from the more familiar terms in that they are completely useless for the purposes of Fascism. They are, on the other hand, useful for the formulation of revolutionary demands in the politics of art. (P. 218)

Benjamin predicted postmodernism and the centrality of instantly reproducible artifacts, with its changes in the nature of commodity. These artifacts can be cut, spliced, sampled, reconfigured, and usually fragmented in rapid appropriations.

Frequent reproducibility leads to familiarity, then overfamiliarity, and then often disdain. This reproducibility is one of the reasons that televi-

28. For histories of electrified communication, see, for example, Daniel Czitrom, *Media and the American Mind: From Morse to McLuhan*; Harold Innes, *Empire and Communication*; and Robert Sklar, *Movie-Made America*.

29. *Illuminations*, p. 218. He writes, "With the woodcut graphic art became mechanically reproducible for the first time, long before script became reproducible by print. The enormous changes which printing, the mechanical reproduction of writing, has brought about in literature are a familiar story. However, ... print is merely a special, though particularly important, case" (pp. 220–221).

sion is disdained even as 98 percent of the U.S. population are HUT dwellers. To use Benjamin's term, television routinely has no aura. It has no aura because it is so accessible, so repeatable.[30]

The Oral/Aural Formula and Televisual *Koinoi Topoi*

The oral formula finds remarkable longevity and power in the common topics (*koinoi topoi*), which have appeared in historical rhetoric from our first knowledge of it and have exerted substantial power in discursive practice and pedagogies.[31] *Koinoi topoi* and formulas in general are

30. It could be that student writing is held in disdain by many English faculty for the same reason that television is disdained: it is so available, so repeatable. The vast numbers of its frequent production—especially in process pedagogies, which depend on repeatability to enable students to learn how to perform their own writing—make it all too available for many teachers. Just as television monitors are frequently hidden in cabinet and closet, so student texts are often shunned even as they are always there. Students quickly learn to hide their own writing: the elaborate packaging in which many students present their work—plastic binders, for example—reveals the shamefulness of what is inside as it conceals what is there. The concealment of student texts also assures the concealment of the current-traditional teacher response, where red ink spilled over "errors" (another result of print-based alphabetic rules) resembles nothing so much as blood. Student writers are wise to hide these exsanguinations, which do not help them but instead make them fearful of their own language performance. See Chris Anson, *Writing and Response*, for an example of positive teacher responses to student writing. See Welch, *The Contemporary Reception of Classical Rhetoric*, pp. 79–87, for an analysis of a class system of texts in which student writing resides at the very lowest rung.

31. Any beginning of rhetoric is difficult to locate. Origin stories of rhetoric are, as in all fields, standard. A typical beginning for rhetoric is the Corax and Tisias narrative. In the fifth century B.C.E., litigative activity grew alongside increased power for selected groups of males, and legal matters involving property disputes acquired more importance. Corax of Syracuse (a hotbed of rhetoric), according to this strong narrative, wrote a handbook (a *techne*), now lost, that provided effective instruction in how to win a case. His most famous student was Tisias, also of Syracuse, and they have been twinned in traditional histories of rhetoric. They may also have been the same person. (See D. A. G. Hinks, "The First Rhetorical Handbooks.") The problem with the Corax and Tisias reception has been that they are made to be the first step in the progressive march of Western Civilization, in which a white, property-owning male (an exclusion that leaves out most men on the basis of class) is the universal, tacitly acknowledged subject. Others such as women and nonwhites are not allowed to be in this subject posi-

always oral in some respects. Consequently, they are highly retrievable, always at hand, and so susceptible to easy repetition. Before alphabetic literacy took hold by the fourth century B.C.E., the formulas were spoken. Since they were highly repeatable, they could last in the absence of a communication technology that could supply permanence through repetition. The reliance on epithets in the Homeric poems, for example, angry Achilles and clever Odysseus, illustrates one manifestation of formulaic language, an issue explicated by Foley and others. However, they are only deceptively simple. They serve partly as tags that enable the speaker (who was not merely repeating rote words)[32] to recollect (that is, to gather again) segments of culturally loaded stories. Small and probably large changes came about as a result of this kind of oral preservation. *Koinoi topoi* came to be particularly powerful with the increase in alphabetic literacy among the cognoscenti and their scribes (of a different social class) in the fourth century B.C.E. By the time of Aristotle, a very advanced stage of Western rhetorical history, they were fully codified, and they became one center of rhetoric until the most recent waning of rhetoric in the nineteenth century. Aristotle became a primal source for *koinoi topoi*,[33] and he codified two types: the special topics (*eide*) and the common topics (*koinoi topoi*).[34] *Eide* apply to specialized fields, while

---

tion, and so are suspect. See Bernal, *Black Athena*, vol. 1, and below for explications of racist historiography. See Joan Wallach Scott, *Gender and the Politics of History*, and Cheryl Glenn, *Rhetoric Retold*, for explications of sexist historiography.

32. See Foley, *A Theory of Oral Composition*.

33. Just as Aristotle became a primal source for so much of twentieth-century language study, much of it unconscious. Further research on pre-Aristotelian development of the topics is needed. Currently, Aristotle is regarded as the fount of the *topoi*, part of a more general Aristotle love that dominates much of rhetorical studies.

34. The standard English translation of Aristotle's *Rhetoric* is George A. Kennedy's (see Aristotle, *On Rhetoric: A Theory of Civic Discourse*), a text that supplants Freeses 1926 translation, with its now-jarring archaisms, Rhys Roberts's 1924 translation, and Lane Cooper's 1932 translation, which is more readable (for our period) but is also problematically interpolated. Kennedy's lucid translation is a crucial event in current historicizing of rhetoric for many reasons, one of which is his retranslation of formerly standard sexist English translations. See Aristotle, *On Rhetoric* (Kennedy trans.), p. xii.

koinoi topoi apply generally. In the first book of the *Rhetoric* Aristotle states,

> I am saying that dialectical and rhetorical syllogisms are those in which we state *topoi*, and these are applicable in common [*koinei*] to questions of justice and physics and politics and many different species [of knowledge]; for example, the *topos* of the more and the less; for to form syllogisms or speak enthymemes from this about justice will be just as possible as about physics or anything else, although these subjects differ in species. But there are "specifics" that come from the premises of each species and genus [of knowledge]; for example, in physics there are premises from which there is neither an enthymeme nor a syllogism applicable to ethics; and in ethics [there are] others not useful in physics. It is the same in all cases. The former [the common *topoi*] will not make one understand any genus; for they are not concerned with any underlying subject. As to the latter [the specifics], to the degree that someone makes better choice of the premises, he will have created knowledge different from dialectic and rhetoric without its being recognized; for if he succeeds in hitting on first principles [*arkhai*], the knowledge will no longer be dialectic or rhetoric but the science of which [the speaker] grasps the first principles. (1358a[35])

By the time Aristotle codified the *topoi*, they had been in wide circulation. A *topos* is not a *what* Greek keyword; rather, it is a *how* keyword. It enables us to efficiently escape the form/content binary of modern (post-seventeenth-century) language study.[36] "*Topos*" in postmodern rhetoric and composition does not fall under the content cate-

35. Kennedy trans., p. 46.

36. As I discussed in chapter 3, this binary poisons the well of humanities education in school and after because articulation as written or spoken text (or written or spoken performance) automatically becomes secondary and inferior to content, which corresponds to thought. Thinking is deemed to be prior and superior to any kind of articulation. In this view, if writing is a mere second-hand articulation, then it is a comparatively weak representation of the real stuff of the mind. From this assumed belief comes the organization of writing programs as instrumentalist (skills and drills): writing programs then are located in basements or in less-desirable buildings, removed from the important buildings that house content. When this organization is interiorized as reality by writing instructors— as it frequently is—two major issues come about: (1) profound boredom (who wants to produce these weak imitations of the real stuff in the mind?) not only for the writing students but for their teachers as well and (2) a disdain for one's own writing. For more on the writers-in-the-basement metaphor, see Susan Miller, "The Feminization of Composition" and the "sad women in the basement" who teach writing with almost no support because the system within which they labor designates writing as a weak representation best served by current traditional pedagogy.

gory or the form category. Instead, it is part of informed performance. *"Topos"* in Greek signifies place; it is a location where one takes oneself in order to develop an issue (as in the Latin *locus*). The current-traditional paradigm of *topos* misconstrued as a thesis (as in "topic sentences," for example) erases the sense of place, a move that in turn erases context, location, situation, and eventually ideology. It is not difficult to see why "the windless closures of the formalisms" represented by the current-traditional paradigm and the U.S. New Critics would conform so easily to the conversion of "topic" to a disembodied issue that cannot resonate because it is not attached to the writer and is not attached to any discourse community (because the audience is a blob of universality; the audience is everyone for all time).[37] It is also not difficult to see why the humanities so defined as this nowhere-topic, non-*topos* writing instruction on the composition side and as the unsituated glowing over Literature on the other side have frequently dropped out of the discussion of educational reform. Language study is frequently not even mentioned in current discussions of educational revision.

We need *topoi*, both common and special, in our newly oral/aural/script-based era of electric rhetoric.[38] We do not need the devolved *topos* of topic-sentence instruction, which kills students' interest in language.[39]

37. I assume here a multiply constructed writer and not the faux romantic writer posited and celebrated by individualism and some early expressionist process pedagogy such as those of James Moffett, Peter Elbow, and William Coles. The windless metaphor is Jameson's, *The Political Unconscious*.

38. Although it goes beyond the scope of this book, it is notable that the special topics and the common topics offer a way to understand part of the culture wars, particularly as they are manifested in the discipline of English. Much hue and cry has been voiced and written about the opacity of some critical writing. There is an assumption on the part of such respondents that everything written by humanities scholars should be with a common topic so that virtually any educated person can understand it. There is resistance in this view to the notion that the discipline of English would have its own special topics, just as, for example, microbiology has.

39. A recent examination of 15 random textbooks indicated that 14 were overtly or covertly current-traditional; included the sentence-paragraph-theme progression that is intended in some mysterious way to enable students to write; relied on the truncated canons with no acknowledged historical source; and, of course, included the numbingly dull principles of exposition, description, narration, and argument (with "process" frequently tacked on).

The common topics need to be retheorized and redeployed to aid in gaining control of the overload of screen and print texts produced in electric rhetoric. In the era of print/paper dominance (which we remain in but are fast departing in an unknown direction), when the artifact of the text overwhelms us with its importance, permanence, and authority, *topoi* appear to be cliched, superficial, and incapable of providing the kind of depth that has been prized.[40] *Koinoi topoi* were in the ancient period places to locate lines of inquiry; they were regions. In *Rhetoric*, book 2, chapters 2 and 19, Aristotle sets up the *koinoi topoi*. In chapter 19 he emphasizes these *koinoi topoi*: possible and impossible, past fact and future fact, greatness and smallness, and amplification and depreciation.[41] In book 2 of *Rhetoric*, Aristotle digresses with 28 common topics. Topic 6 has to do with turning a verbal attack against oneself to the speaker:

Another [topos] is from [turning] what has been said against oneself upon the one who said it, but the way of doing it differs [with the context]. . . . In general, it is out of place [*atopos*] when someone reproaches others for [failing to do] what he does not do—or would not do—himself. (1398a[42])

Aristotle's examples derive from written texts and spoken texts. The common topics are found in both situations and easily cross and recross the changing borders between the written and the spoken. As with the common topics throughout Western antiquity, Aristotle's are highly memorable and highly teachable. After they have been learned and practiced, the encoder can turn to them to devise written or spoken texts; in addition, trained audiences will be able to understand them and to follow the text.

The common and special topics take on new importance in an era of print/television and print/computer-screen dominance, where the artifact goes away with great ease: one can press "power" on the remote control and end the aural and visual stimulation of television or one can close

40. The word "authority," of course, shows its origin in print/paper dominance by its first six letters.

41. This list is Edward P. J. Corbett's in "The *Topoi* Revisited." See also William M. A. Grimaldi, "The Aristotelian *Topics*."

42. Kennedy translation, pp. 194–195.

icons on a personal computer.[43] Why did *koinoi topoi* disappear at some point in the modern period and, for most of the twentieth century, appear to be quaint relics of a dead rhetorical tradition? One part of the answer lies in the fact that they did not provide adequate assistance in working with print literacy; they were no longer needed because different kinds of memory storage were available. Instead, they seemed to supply only the obvious; they appeared not to be subtle. The repeatability of a common topic, which became so offputting for the permanence of print/paper, has now become desirable. Rhetoric/composition theories need to analyze and relegitimize these newly powerful topics and to identify new ones.[44]

Koinoi topoi are memorable and amenable to speaking and hearing in particular. They can be accessed readily. In electric rhetoric, they are no longer symptoms of undeveloped language; rather, they are powerful communication issues. Next Rhetoric requires them as part of its theorized electrification. However, as they are redeployed, they need to be retheorized with recent theory.

Constructing Whiteness and Constructing Classical Rhetoric in Televisual Culture

History of any kind cannot be usefully written without addressing racial construction. Electric rhetoric must take account of the racism of much of traditional historiography and its strong continuation in new communication technologies. U.S. rhetoric must account for the embedded, unquestioned racism that infects the culture through all its texts in all symbol systems and that has existed as a defining part of the dominant culture for its entire history. Part of the persistent erasure of African-Americans has been through the hegemony of one version of print literacy that automatically, unthinkingly discounts the strong oralism/auralism of many African-American communities. A pointed example of

43. Icons, of course, were a hallmark of nonliteracy. Public houses in England, for example, were marked by representations of objects, such as the Lion and the Rose, as well as by the writing of those words. Those who could not read could understand the icon.

44. See also Dudley Bailey, "A Plea for a Modern Set of Topoi." Bailey sees the new importance of the topoi.

this erasure is represented in "Black Petitions for Freedom," a text written by white-enslaved African-Americans who had partial access to print literacy. Its request for rights that resembled the requests of whites, especially white males, stands as a monument in U.S. culture.[45] The recognition of the power of writing in asserting rights is compelling here. Nonprint oral/aural texts used to disappear; they have been discounted by print hegemonists for hundreds of years. Historiography has been print-dominant. Now that oral texts can be preserved electronically, they have acquired many of the properties of print texts. Discounted oral production can now be redeployed with the new recognition that they are as important in kind as print production; this new recognition will change the nature of the historiography of rhetoric and composition.

One aspect of the nonexistent golden past of classical Greek culture that continues to blight classical rhetoric and other classical fields has been exposed by Martin Bernal in *Black Athena: The Afroasiatic Roots of Classical Civilization*, vol. 1: *The Fabrication of Ancient Greece, 1785–1985*. This exposure can be particularly helpful in the rehistoricizing of classical rhetoric and current rhetoric, composition, and literacy studies. Philologists and historians from the nineteenth century (and before) continue to exert enormous control over language studies in the Untied States and, of course, elsewhere. Bernal explicates the situation:

By the middle of the 18th century, however, a number of Christian apologists were using the emerging paradigm of "progress," with its presupposition that "later is better," to promote the Greeks at the expense of the Egyptians. These strands of thought soon merged with two others that were becoming dominant at the same time: racism and Romanticism. Thus chapter IV also outlines the development of racism based on skin colour in late-17th century England, alongside the increasing importance of the American colonies, with their twin policies of extermination of the Native Americans and enslavement of African Blacks. This

45. See Donald McQuade et al., eds., *Harper American Literature*, vol. 1, pp. 491–493, for the texts, which come from *Collections of the Massachusetts Historical Society*, 5th series, 3 (1877): 490. "At the same time as Samuel Adams was drafting polemic essays condemning Parliament's suppression of the colonists' 'natural rights' and Thomas Paine was urging them to take up arms 'to reap the blessings of freedom,' an anonymous group of black slaves petitioned the Massachusetts governor and assembly to recognize their legal claims to freedom. The petitioners asserted that they too were a 'freeborn Pepel and have never forfeited this Blessing by aney compact or agreement whatever.' "

racism pervaded the thought of Locke, Hume and other English thinkers. Their influence—and that of the new European explorers of other continents—was important at the university of Göttingen, founded in 1734 by George II, Elector of Hanover and King of England, and forming a cultural bridge between Britain and Germany. It is not surprising, therefore, that the first "academic" work on human racial classification—which naturally put Whites, or to use his new term, "Caucasians," at the head of the hierarchy—was written in the 1770s by Johann Friedrich Blumenbach, a professor at Göttingen. (Pp. 27–28)

This racist past will be replicated in electric rhetoric unless the racial construction of objectivist historiography is interrogated and reinscribed. The energizing and important resurgence of historicized rhetoric and composition—part of Next Rhetoric—must not imitate objectivist historicizing, a way of constructing the past that has been too easily absorbed in schools and universities as normal, natural, and inevitable, that is, as *physis* and not as the *nomos* it is. The resistance to this project is, of course, enormous.

Classical Greek rhetoric arose and became powerful as a cultural practice in a context dominated by the triad of slavery, rape, and imperialism, all three of which not only informed the culture but enabled the culture to exist at all. No study of classical rhetoric should take place without a thorough study of these three related systems, just as the study of, say, U.S. writing or Literature should also be thoroughly grounded in this triad. It might be said that the main rhetorical legacy of ancient Greece translated to the United States is not knowledge but the continuation of slave culture, rape culture, and a crass imperialism that is not only economic but, of course, cultural. The powerful ideology of nostalgia operates to validate our own slave/rape/imperialist culture, to excuse it, and to perpetuate it.

Bernal's Revised Ancient Model provides a way of historicizing that offers unusual potential in overcoming tacitly racist constructions in many areas of language studies, including rhetoric and composition studies. Bernal helps us in Next Rhetoric to resist the familiar fount metaphor of classical Greece as the originator of "Western civilization" and imbricated in, specifically, the moribund liberal-arts tradition. The fount metaphor of historiography is as common in our end-of-the-millenninm cultures as the air we breathe, and it is just as invisible and powerful. Bernal's Revised Ancient Model allows us to rehistoricize classical "Western" cultures by deconstructing the "fount," the dead metaphor of choice whose literal level is rarely interrogated.

Bernal dives deeply into "pre-Golden Age" Greek history (2100–1100 B.C.E.) and the reception of narratives already very old for Athenians of the dominant culture in, say, fifth- and fourth-century-B.C.E. Athens. Bernal, who comes at this material as a scholar in Chinese studies working in a department of government (in other words, as a disciplinary outsider, a point he emphasizes) establishes two models (he resists the word "paradigm") for the construction of the sanctified Greece that many of us learned to base interpretations on, or have been conditioned to accept as "factual," even if we resisted it as "truth." The first model he names "the Ancient Model," the one that fifth- and fourth-century-B.C.E. people relied on for their own construction. Bernal writes,

Black Athena is essentially concerned with the Egyptian and Semitic roles in the formation of Greece in the Middle and Late Bronze Age.... The first volume of *Black Athena* is concerned with the development of the Ancient and Aryan Models, and the first chapter, "The Ancient Model in Antiquity," treats the attitudes of Greeks in the Classical and Hellenistic periods to their distant past. It considers the writings of authors who affirmed the Ancient Model, referred to Egyptian colonies in Thebes and Athens, and gave details of the Egyptian conquest of the Argolid and the Phoenician foundation of Thebes. I discuss the claims made by various 19th- and 20th-century 'source critics' that the Ancient Model was concocted only in the 5th century BC, and I cite iconographic evidence and a number of earlier references to demonstrate the scheme existed several centuries earlier. (P. 22)

Bernal's second model, the Aryan Model, appeared in the eighteenth century and gained particular power in the nineteenth. Bernal writes,

Since the 1840s Indo-European philology, or study of the relationships between languages, has been at the heart of the Aryan Model. Then, as now, Indo-Europeanists and Greek philologists have been extraordinarily reluctant to see any connections between Greek—on the one hand—and Egyptian and semitic, the two major non-Indo-European languages of the Ancient East Mediterranean, on the other. (P. 4)

Bernal sets forth as "plausible" the idea that Egyptian and Semitic aspects of pre-"Golden Age" Greece were suppressed because of ideological agendas that connected to a kind of academic-pop-faux-anthropologic-scientific stance among the historians who, according to Bernal, dispensed with the Ancient Model and bequeathed truth on the

Aryan Model. Bernal contends that the "fundamental bases of "Western civilization" have been formed by what he calls "racism" and "continental chauvinism" (p. 2). He finds that the two hundred years of the presentation of "Western civilization" from 1775 to 1985 came about because of the reluctance to see the "mixture of native Europeans and colonizing Africans and Semites" (p. 2).

For those readers conditioned to accept the liberalism of academic writers since the U.S. domestic revolutions of the 1960s and before, Bernal's assertion and his subsequent laborious setting forth of the thesis of racism in familiar constructions of Western civilization promote discomfort and frequently resistance. Matthew Arnold has, of course, been the frequently unacknowledged source of the arid "best that has been produced in literature" and the famous touchstone metaphor. Bernal, who devotes an entire section to "The Arnolds,"[46] shows that Matthew Arnold's own "sweetness and light" rest partly on racist assumptions. Bernal, citing texts that frequently do not appear in curricula in English departments (units that continue to revere specific texts in Arnold's "best ever" category) writes,

The contrasts between Thomas and Matthew Arnold provide an instructive example of the changes that were taking place in English racism in the 19th century. Dr. Thomas Arnold was preoccupied in the 1820s and 30s with the conflicts between Teuton and Gael—including Gall-Roman—and notably those between the English and the French and Irish. He was proud to be known as "that Teuton of Teutons, the Celt-hating Dr Arnold." His son Matthew in the 1850s, 60s, and 70s favoured both the Irish and the French, believing that he had transcended his father's narrow-mindedness. Fully aware of the new linguistic advances, he was a systematic supporter of Indo-Europeans and Aryans. He loved them all. (P. 347)

Bernal recasts characters familiar to people trained in literary chronology. According to Victor J. Vitanza's construction in " 'Notes' Towards Historiographies of Rhetorics," Bernal would appear in the sub/versive category because he reconstructs the bases of traditional and revisionary rhetorics, the other two categories Vitanza establishes for the historicizing of rhetoric.

Bernal subverts partly in the ways we have come to expect, by looking at suppressed ideological/rhetorical stances. In addition, he examines the ancient reception and the 1775–1985 reception of the one thousand

46. Pp. 347–350.

years from 2100 to 1100 B.C.E. He analyzes "Greek cultural borrowings from Egypt and the Levant in the 2nd millennium B.C." (p. 17).

It is useful for Next Rhetoric and its electrified state to focus on Bernal's analysis of the Arnolds, particularly Matthew Arnold, whose pedagogical influence in the discipline of English continues unabated.[47] "On the Study of Celtic Literature" is one text where Arnold establishes cause-and-effect relationships between racial characteristics and national literatures. For example, the Germans are said to be great poets who have no "style." Similarly, the Celts, which includes more than the Irish, have a lot of "style."

Another strategy for enacting electric rhetoric lies in the inclusion of so-called non-Western material in the work of classical rhetoric and composition studies. This strategy involves examining the presentation of classical studies historically; in other words, rhetoric and composition scholars and teachers require more intensive and extensive examination of how we in the late twentieth and early twenty-first centuries have been conditioned to receive ideas about classical culture (including the word "classical"). Bernal offers a radical understanding of the formation of current Euro-American attitudes toward ancient Greek culture, and he sees two models that have been used for the construction of classical culture: the Aryan Model and the Ancient Model.

Most people are surprised to learn that the Aryan Model, *which most of us have been brought up to believe*, developed only during the first half of the 19th century. In its earlier or "Broad" form, the new model denied the truth of the Egyptian settlements and questioned those of the Phoenicians. What I call the "Extreme" Aryan Model, which flourished during the twin peaks of anti-Semitism in the 1880s and again in the 1920s and 30s, denied even the Phoenician cultural influence. According to the Aryan Model, there had been an invasion from the north—unreported in ancient tradition—which had overwhelmed the local "aegean" or "Pre-Hellenic" Culture. Greek civilization is seen as the result of the mixture of the Indo-European-speaking Hellenes and their indigenous subjects. It is from the construction of this Aryan model that I call this volume *The Fabrication of Ancient Greece, 1785–1985*." (Pp. 1–2; my emphasis)

47. Matthew Arnold and Aristotle have largely constructed English studies in the United States and elsewhere and both have been exhausted in many ways. Arnold has been interrogated in literary studies; Aristotle has been interrogated in rhetoric/composition studies.

Bernal provides one kind of response for rhetoric and composition scholars and teachers who have asked the question, is classical rhetoric/composition not only useless but dangerous as well? The question, as we have seen, was posed strongly by C. H. Knoblauch and Lil Brannon in *Rhetorical Traditions and the Teaching of Writing* and by Stephen North in *The Making of Knowledge in Composition.*[48] Bernal offers an unusually compelling understanding of why critics such as Knoblauch and Brannon and North (and, of course, many other writers and/or teachers) have reacted so unhappily to the Heritage School presentation of classical rhetoric and composition.

The understanding that most of us have of classical culture derives, Bernal demonstrates, from a construction of the classics of so-called Western civilization based on political, ideological, and cultural stances assumed by German scholars in the rather new field of philology as it took form in the first part of the nineteenth century. All of us who study classical cultures—whether from the rhetorical stance of Knoblauch and Brannon or the new historicist stance represented by Swearingen, Glenn, Jarratt, Vitanza, and Berlin—were educated in standard forms of presentation of the ancient world. Bernal explains:

> If I am right in urging the overthrow of the Aryan Model and its replacement by the Revised Ancient one, it will be necessary not only to rethink the fundamental bases of "Western Civilization" but also to recognize the penetration of racism and "continental chauvinism" into all our historiography, or philosophy of writing history. The Ancient Model had no major "internal" deficiencies, or weaknesses in explanatory power. It was overthrown for external reasons. For 18th- and 19th-century Romantics and racists it was simply intolerable for Greece, which was seen not merely as the epitome of Europe but also as its pure childhood, to have been the result of the mixture of native Europeans and colonizing Africans and Semites. Therefore the Ancient Model had to be overthrown and replaced by something more acceptable. (P. 2)

If Bernal's elaborately documented case is accurate, then the need for classical rhetoric and composition scholars and teachers to change their own constructions of classical cultures is urgent. From this perspective, Knoblauch and Brannon and North are right in promoting the abandonment of classical rhetoric and composition as a useful system. Those

---

48. The response by historicists to Knoblauch and Brannon's book was striking. See, for example, Welch, "A Manifesto."

of us with these different strategies in mind will be compelled to persuade our students and our colleagues to change their ways of thinking. (They, after all, are the products of largely the same educational structures that we emerged from.) If Bernal is right when he claims—with elaborate evidence[49]—that racism formed one major basis of the taken-for-granted status of classical studies in various fields (for example, classics, English, and speech communication), then our reasons for reconstructing classical rhetoric/composition, classical literature, classical politics, classical economics, and so on, are utterly compelling. The kairic moment for change has arrived.

Bernal, as the outsider he declares himself to be,[50] deploys his knowledge of philology, languages, dialects, and the disciplines that have transmitted this knowledge. Few people in any discipline have the training with which Bernal works. He blasts open the prison bars of insular disciplines from within. Whether or not traditional objectivist classicists or philologists (the latter frequently found among traditionalists in departments of English, usually cordoned off into their own groups) will be changed by Bernal is discussed below. My focus is the reception that Bernal's work will receive in what is arguably the most powerful subdiscipline in the discipline of English: rhetoric and composition studies. Bernal compels people working in the humanities to take the pulse of the liberal-arts tradition that declares the "source" or "fount" of European culture to be a "purified" Greek and Roman ancient beauty and light. He has changed the nature of the dialogue/dialectic that rhetoric and composition writers and teachers have with this weighty past, whether it is mentioned explicitly or more powerfully maintained as an invisible presence.[51]

If Bernal's thesis is taken up by enough writers and teachers, if radical pedagogy will actually treat it, then the cloying wholesomeness of the

49. See, for example, pp. 75–120, 189–206, and 233–237.

50. It is important to note that Bernal has explicitly acknowledged the power he receives as a white male academic, particularly one with an Oxbridge English accent. See "*Black Athena* and the APA."

51. *Black Athena* has been canonized in rhetoric and composition studies by its excerpting in *The Rhetorical Tradition*, ed. Patricia Bizzell and Bruce Herzberg, the first anthology in the current era of Next Rhetoric.

Heritage School of classical rhetoric and of other disciplines and sub-disciplines can become part of inert history (texts treated as valuable commodities, attractive antiques, or religious relics), rather than a part of its formative present, which acknowledges racism, sexism, technology, and other issues that used to be ignored as irrelevant. The problem with wholesome historicizing is that no one really takes it seriously. Pablum is dull and does not make any difference to many people.

The reception of Bernal's *Black Athena* warrants attention because it displays the deep emotional investment held by many scholars in maintaining a tacit whiteness (not to mention whatness) at the center of ancient Greek history (even as white hegemony is denied in the name of modernist universality). *Black Athena Revisited*, edited by Mary R. Lefkowitz and Guy MacLean Rogers, is remarkable for its sustained anger, its outraged indignation, which indicate that Bernal has struck a chord.[52] Much of the critical response from classicists has been so passionately angry at Bernal (including the use of argumentum ad hominem to a surprising degree) that one concludes that Bernal's work threatens their very identities.[53] In the Introduction to *Black Athena Revisited*, Lefkowitz closely links Bernal to the Afrocentrist movement represented by Molefi Kete Asante and others—a move that serves her strategy of discrediting Bernal as a scholar but that is not in accord with the sources with which Bernal works. The sense of territoriality in her essay and in her Internet response is quite strong. Bernal is regarded as the uninitiated interloper who should stay away from this topic. The territoriality of *Black Athena Revisited* brings with it a sustained defensiveness; Bernal has touched on something deep, and it hurts a number of the territorialists. In particular, Lefkowitz resists addressing the issues of race construction and the construction of history. For her and most (not all) of

52. See the continuation of this dialogue on the Internet: http://www.cite/com/ascac/news.html, April 22 to May 31, 1996.

53. It is illuminating to compare classicists' response to Eric A. Havelock's *Preface to Plato* to the response of many to Bernal. Havelock similarly evoked and continues to evoke much hostility. However, the response to Havelock seems to have been more measured, less ad hominem. Both Bernal and Havelock seem to have touched some issues of identity. Bernal in particular appears to have threatened the power bases of some traditional classicists, most of whom equally resist current theory.

the contributors to the volume, being raced—particularly as readers operating in various discursive formations—is not to be mentioned; it interferes with their objectivist stance.

A more moderate response occurred in a special issue of *Arethusa*. In "The Challenge of *Black Athena*," scholars from classics and related fields analyze Bernal's book from different points of view and from different disciplinary stances. Molly Meyerowitz Levine, the editor of the issue, writes,

> This special volume of *Arethusa* is both a record and an extension of "The Challenge of *Black Athena*: The Classicists' Response," an interdisciplinary dialogue which was first presented as the presidential panel of the 120th meeting of the American Philological Association in Baltimore, 1989.... This volume offers a preliminary response to the case against classics and classicists set forth in Martin Bernal's *Black Athena* ... [in which] Professor Bernal, scholar of Chinese history and government, professor of New Eastern Studies, and self-avowed "outsider," lays serious and sweeping charges against what he sees as the "classics establishment," the "insiders," i.e., the natural constituency of both the APA and this journal. We, it is claimed, owing to residual racism, anti-Semitism, sheer scholarly inertia, and/or exaggerated respect for authority, have suppressed or ignored the weight of what Professor Bernal considers to be overwhelming evidence of substantial semitic and Egyptian roles in the development of Greek language and civilization. (21 [1989]: 7)

Some traditional classicists are responding, and responding with great persuasive power, as this volume indicates repeatedly. The effect that Bernal's challenge will have on pedagogy will take longer to gage.

Two current historicizers, one in rhetoric and composition studies and the other in literary studies, respond in the inclusive spirit that Bernal presents as a rhetorical stance toward the not-too-golden age of Greece. They are James N. Comas in "The Presence of Theory/Theorizing the Present" and Edward Said in *Orientalism*. Comas writes on a topic closely related to issues in historiography, "It might be best to take *theory* as referring, today, not only to the epistemological emphasis of traditional theory or to the challenges of the new 'theory,' but to the site of a struggle between the two attitudes toward knowledge (and the political values behind them)" (p. 4). Said writes, "Ideas, cultures, and histories cannot seriously be understood or studied without their force, or more precisely their configurations of power, also being studied" (p. 5). Both Comas and Said recognize and acknowledge, as Bernal does, that historicizing must act as a force in shaping general perceptions, and not only professional perceptions within the academy. They recognize and acknowledge the centrality of power formations. Lefkowitz denies these power issues in her rigorous, emphatic, and reactionary responses to Bernal.[54] The inclusion of Africans in the construction of ancient Greece changes the conceptual bases that the liberal-arts tradition frequently works under and through.

As the United States undergoes self-scrutiny about the failures and successes of education, the integration of Bernal's shattering but constructive presentations offers all of us in the academy a powerful new way to attack racism where it may be least suspected of residing: in the disciplines that have transmitted what we know and how we know. The discipline of English continues to thrive on elitism, nostalgia for various pasts that never existed, the professor as priest, and the crusty Arnoldian stance that holds at every turn that we, the holders of the keys to the gates of the kingdom of Culture with a capital "C," are necessarily superior to everyone else. When the majority of the people working in English can say to ourselves that we are not a priestly caste preoccupied with the guardianship of preserving Culture, then we can continue the project that Bernal has promoted so effectively.

As we race classical rhetoric, that is, acknowledge that race has been a *nomos* and not a *physis*,[55] that it has been constructed to make non-whites (and white women) invisible, that it partakes of the nonunity and

---

54. As Bernal points out in the Internet debate between Lefkowitz and him, she understands well the institutional wavelengths of power, as is evidenced by the elaborate support she has received from very conservative think tanks. See http://www.city/com.com/ascac/news.html, 3 May 1996, pp. 1–5.

55. *Nomos* and *physis* were definitive theoretical and pedagogical issues for the older Sophists. *Nomos*—custom, more, formal or informal law—is human-made and so is susceptible to human change. *Physis*, usually translated as nature and so proliferating in meaning for English and other speakers, signifies the inherent and what cannot be changed. Tracing the undulations of *nomos/physis* in the historicizing of the ancient Sophists is an important *logos* activity, as it indicates the kinds of verbal performances that were around and performed in their usually movable schools and speeches. One of the best discussions of this distinction is in W. K. C. Guthrie, *The Sophists*, pp. 55–134. See also G. B. Kerferd, *The Sophistic Movement*, pp. 111–130; Swearingen, *Rhetoric and Irony*, pp. 29–30 and 98–99; and Jarratt, *Rereading the Sophists*, pp. 41–42.

fragmentation of postmodernist tendencies, it is helpful to turn to investigations of racial construction. In addition to Bernal, we can turn to *Before Color Prejudice: The Ancient View of Blacks*, in which Frank M. Snowden examines the possibilities of race by tracing amicable relations between blacks and whites from Egyptian to Roman times. He writes, "There was clear-cut respect among Mediterranean peoples for Ethiopians and their way of life. And, above all, the ancients did not stereotype all blacks as primitives defective in religion and culture" (p. 59). Snowden makes the equally important point that slaves were not chosen according to race: "In antiquity slavery was independent of race or class, and by far the vast majority of the thousands of slaves was white, not black. The identification of blackness with slavery did not develop. No single ethnic group was associated with slave status or with the descendants of slaves" (p. 70). The development of race hatred as it has characterized the United States, for example, did not occur in classical Greece. Other hatreds predominated. Although difference was noted, as Snowden and others illustrate, group hatred based on Black features did not exist. Snowden's argument acts as a corrective to the Aryan Model and its tacit, virulent assumption of whiteness as part of the fount metaphor of Western civilization.[56]

Oralism/Auralism, Women, and Classical Communication Technology

It was in the depths of her house that a Greek woman was supposed to live out her existence as young girl, as wife, and as mother; and it was shut up in her houses, far from the gaze of others, that she had to end her life.

Nicole Loraux, *Tragic Ways of Killing a Woman*[57]

---

56. Snowden's assumption of an objectivist stance provides some difficulty, as it does in his earlier *Blacks in Antiquity*. He writes, for example, "Those scholars who have allowed ancient art *to speak for itself* argue that the so-called ugliness or comic exists primarily in the minds of the modern beholders, not in the eyes of the ancient artists, and that Negro subjects are among some of the finest and most sympathetically executed pieces to have come from the workshops of ancient artists" (p. 64; my emphasis). A postmodernist stance disputes the idea that any text or art can "speak for itself." This positivistic stance enables that status quo to reproduce itself. However, as we have seen with traditional histories of rhetoric, other traditional histories (or, as in this case, semitraditional, since placing Blacks in the subject position has been rare) can offer important material for appropriation.

Just as Next Rhetoric, the era of electric rhetoric, must race itself, so it must be gendered. Race and gender issues need to be worked into the very fabric of the education of *logos* users in electric rhetoric. We do not know much about the education of girls and women in the fourth century B.C.E. Their daily activities and traditions are now being explored by many classicists, but the absence of evidence remains an impediment. However, we know that an infant female, then toddler, and then an older girl acquired language through interaction with others, that she learned (developed) and spoke a dialect of Greek, that she conveyed learning for her segregated spheres through conventions (*nomoi*) of language, and that she was for the most part deprived of the formal and informal educations, the *paideia*, of boys and men. The consciousness changes that Eric A. Havelock argues for cannot be assumed to apply to females.[58] Havelock's literate revolution has much to teach us, but his ideological positioning on gender makes his arguments even more problematic (although this problem is not the reason that most classicists respond so

---

57. P. ix.

58. Havelock occupies a world in which woman is merged into man, so his entire theory of revolutionary changes in consciousness brought about by the alphabetization of ancient Greece is suspect. He universalizes an unacknowledged white male subject. It is important to note on this point that Walter J. Ong, so frequently linked with Havelock as if they were twins, does not operate from this world; his investigations into the different kinds of consciousness acknowledge and address the formative gender issue: "Not only were all of the teachers of Learned Latin males for well over a millennium, but all its learners were males as well, with exceptions so few as to be negligible. By the nineteenth century, academic education opened up more and more to girls (who earlier had often had impressive nonacademic education, particularly if they were of the aristocracy or gentry, such as enabled them to manage formidable households of sixty or seventy persons or more not only with efficiency but often also with grace and charm).... Communication in Latin for the programmatically agonistic, disputatious, Latin-writing and Latin-speaking world of the West, from Cassiodorus through Erasmus and Milton and beyond, the only academic world the West had ever known at all until three centuries ago, was never anything other than an all-male enterprise" ("Transformations of the Word," in *Interfaces of the Word*, pp. 25–27). Grace and charm aside, Ong has long recognized and addressed gender difference. See also C. Jan Swearingen's explication of Ong and gender in "Discourse, Difference, and Gender: Walter J. Ong's Contributions to Feminist Language Studies."

negatively to his work). The false binary of orality and literacy, dismissed in chapter 2,[59] can easily turn into a second false binary of writing men and speaking women. This binary must be rejected also because it ignores the central issue that kinds of consciousness changed regardless of one's level of functional literacy.

If Lev Vygotsky is correct, that the infant acquires language in linguistic, physical, and social interactions, particularly with primary caretakers, then this phenomenon would hold true for fourth century B.C.E. females as well as for early twentieth-century Soviet females and males. Two immediate questions arise: Can we legitimately apply Vygotsky's findings in this way? How do we study pre-Aristotelian Greek rhetoric without identifying whether or not we are working phylogenetically or ontogenetically? The pressing problem with phylogenetic analysis—the kind performed by Havelock, for example—is that it supposedly merges female with male but actually continues the tradition of making women into broken-down men. Vygotsky was working ontogenetically. Recent feminisms are working on both.

Although universalizing is a risky trend and seems to drag us back to the modern domination of the privileged white male property owner, with woman disappearing into that construction in name and identity, I believe that it is useful in fact to apply Vygotsky to language-acquisition issues in the fourth century B.C.E. Many classical rhetoricians, particularly Isocrates and Quintilian, deployed rhetoric partly as a way to address language acquisition.

The question of whether one is working phylogenetically or ontogenetically needs to be addressed so that different starting places are not confused. Vygotsky, working on individual language acquisition, worked ontogenetically; Ong works phylogenetically.[60] As the Loraux epigraph indicates, women (as a group) occupied interior spaces that were set apart from men. The social classes of fourth-century-B.C.E. Greece dif-

---

59. Brian Street, in *Literacy in Theory and Practice*, has done the same, finding two kinds of literacy/orality positionings, one "autonomous" and one "ideological." The latter is assumed here.

60. Ong's work on large groups is probably one source of the antagonism he receives. It is easy to decode generalization in this kind of analysis; the generalization is moved over to another issue. This slipperiness is the reason that Ong can be appropriated as privileging the oral or privileging the literate. See chapter 2.

fered, of course, radically from our own.[61] As I discussed in chapter 3, the great advancements in Greek culture of the fifth and fourth centuries B.C.E. were damaging to women. A new kind of silence was accorded women, who mostly could not speak in the constructed public spheres and who were not allowed to participate in government.

As we account for oralism/auralism, or consciousness, as it has been changed in the last one hundred years of the electronic forms of discourse, we must account as well for the silent ones, as Cheryl Glenn and others have begun to do.

Rhetorical HUTs and Their Discontents

Our HUTs, households using television, need to be theorized from the point of view of the humanities in general and of rhetoric and composition studies in particular. The focus in *Electric Rhetoric* has been rhetoric and composition studies, which have provided rich, ample, proliferating studies of diverse kinds that need to be applied to our domiciles, which are mostly aurally filled at least part of the time with the signals emanating from television. The ubiquity of televisual machines accounts for part of the consciousness, or mentality, changes that characterize our end-of-the-millennium era of radical change and that reconstruct the nature of literacy into something that it has never been before.

The hegemony of mechanical print now concludes after four centuries. Alphabetic literacy, however, remains entrenched, crucial, and even more important than it used to be. However, print now coexists with other communication forms, all of which are rhetorically as well as electrically charged. In addition, the number of screen and print signals proliferates so that much of the world has become rather noisy. While the reign of formalisms and their aesthetic loveliness that leads nowhere slowly concludes with, in some quarters, anguish,[62] new studies reveal the profound

61. See also Jean-Pierre Vernant, "Marriage," in his *Myth and Society in Ancient Greece*, pp. 55–77.

62. The profound resistance of traditionalist formalists to adapting to the episteme should not be understated. Formalism in rhetoric/composition studies (think of the Lazarus-like condition of the five-paragraph theme in all its dull-witted boredom; it will not go away) and the continuing reign of poetry, drama, and fiction at the top of the strong-text hierarchy in literary studies continue to drive much of humanistic study in a direction of decay.

opportunity offered by our period of rhetorical transformation in electronic communication.

How do we articulate differently, especially in writing and speaking,[63] as a result of HUT rhetorical living? I have already offered some analyses of television and its rhetoricity. I offer another line here.

We can further our understanding of televisual aurality and the changes in oralism by deploying the common topics, the *koinoi topoi*, discussed above. Some of the *koinoi topoi* newly available to us are the contrasting of opposites. With its absence of print-literate depth, the *topos* of contrasting opposites in television is especially relevant because broader issues are dealt with. Television tends to be more two-dimensional than dominant print texts (for example, a novel, either high art, such as George Eliot's *Middlemarch*, or low art, such as Stephen King's *Carrie*; a George Bernard Shaw play that depends heavily on set directions, such as *Major Barbara*; and a business report[64]). The time constraints of individual video texts, coupled with the rapid movement of images and spoken words, has led so far to the two-dimensional dominance of television. This phenomenon is in contrast to radio, which can achieve depth through greater time periods and the absence of moving images.[65] Television loves opposition. Black and white refers to more than the absence of color. In particular, commercials in the United States are highly two-dimensional unless they choose to emphasize visual art, in which case there is another kind of depth.

A second common topic newly applicable to television is praising some things on the air while privately praising other things.[66] Again, television

---

63. Clearly, other forms of articulation could be and should be analyzed. These studies would examine what it means to be an encoder of photographs or an encoder of video. For a rather pejorative stance on photographs, see Susan Sontag's *On Photography*; for a positive appropriation of videography, see Ulmer, *Teletheory*, especially his merger of theory and pedagogy.

64. See a sample text in Information in Action by M. Jimmie Killingsworth. The study of business reports as texts is quite active in technical-writing courses, which proliferate in English departments across the country.

65. For an analysis of radio and its modernist possibilities, see Elissa S. Guralnick, *Sight Unseen*.

66. For both these common topics, see Aristotle, *On Rhetoric*, book 2, 1399a (p. 198 in the Kennedy translation); anon., *Ad C. Herennium*; and Edward P. J.

commercials deploy this *topos* regularly in the pursuit of instilling spectator desire, which leads to increased sales. In these commodity situations, claims are made that are known to be untrue or exaggerated. Frequently a true claim is made, but the fact that it applies to competitive brands is not mentioned, thus suggesting that the feature belongs only to the advertised product. In its emphasis on two-dimensionality, television resembles the mode of literary allegory, which shares many of the same properties. Soap operas in particular are highly allegorical.

Look, for example, at these two exemplary *koinoi topoi* from texts of the *NBC Nightly News* (an anchorperson reads the spoken text from a teleprompter, where the printed text appears and where a version of subvocalization occurs when a news producer speaks to the anchorperson through an earpiece and the audience hears the nearly ventriloquized voice of the anchorperson). The first common topic, that of opposition, lies at the center of television news. Two-way conflict, which provides narrative interest, lies at the heart of this kind of televisual presentation. In particular, the political process in the United States has been the recipient of the common topic of opposition when broadcasters seek contrast among candidates, again to fuel a narrative.[67] In the 1996 presidential election, for example, a dangerous lull in opposition was said to endanger the whole political process. In fact, what was missing was narrative conflict and therefore narrative momentum.

The second of many possible video common topics is praising something publicly (on the air) while privately wishing for something else. The ownership of the *NBC Nightly News* by General Electric makes this *topos* apparent and powerful. Self-censorship is one result of this topos. A limitation in what can be broadcast is more likely to derive from a unit than from the leaders of the company. This kind of self-enforcement calls into question, of course, the idea of a free press. The owners of the electronic and print presses determine, one way or the other, what is disseminated and how it is disseminated. They determine who is voiced

---

Corbett, *Classical Rhetoric for the Modern Student*, pp. 97–132. See also Janice M. Lauer, "Issues in Rhetorical Invention," in *Essays on Classical Rhetoric and Modern Discourse*, pp. 127–139.

67. See, for example, "food-fight" political television shows, where unreflected common topics are automatically dispensed without apparent thought.

and who is unvoiced. They determine what is important and what is not important.

The Urgent Need for Rhetorical Television Pedagogy

These and many other oral/aural rhetorical features are so pervasive and overwhelming that we need a new televisual pedagogy that accounts for their actual and potential effects. This kind of inquiry and analysis needs to be incorporated into the techno-liberal-arts.[68] Television is so heavily implicated in children's acquisition of language that they require school training in how to be effective decoders of television. Adults as well need training in the grammar, vocabulary, and ideology of this pervasive symbol system. Although some communication departments teach television (as do some other disciplines), rigorous, required training in it remains absent in most curricula, which are consigned to the land of whatness and have become a Cliffs Notes rendition of content that reinforces the form/content universe that continues to imprison us. The freshman writing course is an excellent location for teaching articulation and power, as well as the repertoire of historicized writing strategies that exist in the best programs. This course—still embedded in the majority of universities and colleges—remains one of the few locations for privileging student articulation. This power needs to be reinforced and redeployed. We can then train our freshmen how to be *logos* users as they negotiate their discourse communities in their rhetorical HUTs and beyond.

Next Rhetoric differs radically from other oralisms: it is mechanically repeatable. With electricity and machines we can preserve the spoken word. Before electric rhetoric, oral discourse resisted transcription (the rhapsodies, for example, had elaborate formulas to make the fourth rhetorical canon, memory, reproduce—not exactly, not verbatim—their spoken texts).[69] In our own era of Next Rhetoric, repeatability, and banality, inheres in the machines that provide us with artifactuality.

68. The techno-liberal-arts would help to define the era that will follow postmodernism.

69. Plato's Ion remains a striking—and of course negative—rendition of a rhapsode. The oral, inexact repetitions of rhapsodes provoked Plato, but Ion nonetheless remains a winning example of the rhapsode.

Eschewing Sussman's dismissal of television as kitsch, Next Rhetoric recognizes that television is powerfully present and requires the full power of historicized rhetorical theory to understand it, resist it, and deploy it differently.[70]

There are strong claims that the technology of television, computer, telephone, and so on, is changing so rapidly that we cannot understand what is happening in the current cultural moment and that we cannot predict, much less analyze and deploy, the dimly foreseeable technofuture. Perhaps. But what humanities scholars and teachers, particularly those in rhetoric and composition, need to do is to join in the fray and analyze the half century of broadcast television, fifteen years of cable, and few years of satellite and other forms, just as we have led the discipline of English in computer literacy and theorizing. Generations of people have already been seriously affected by this technology and the ideological forces that led to its placement in 98 percent of U.S. domiciles. We cannot refrain from engaging electric rhetoric simply because the technology is changing rapidly. A lot of the technology is in place, and we need to analyze it from a rhetorical point of view.

We can then define literacy at this end of the millennium in the following way: it constitutes intersubjective activity in encoding and decoding screen and alphabetic texts within specific cultural practices and recognizes the inevitable deployment of power and the control that larger entities have over these media. Literacy in this sense resists widespread devotion to individualism and recognizes how individualism operates to maintain a particular Enlightenment ideology; collaboration then becomes primary. While literacy now and historically is conditioned by communication technology, it is not determined by it; changes in

70. Street via Raymond Williams reminds us of how technology is no neutral machine: "The requirements of profit, he [Williams] argues, directed technological inquiry in the early part of this century into efforts to produce individual viewing units for sale to each household rather than large screens for use in communal halls. He would maintain that it is false, then, to dwell on the 'influence' or 'consequences' of television as though it were a neutral technology that had just appeared due to the disinterested work of scientists. Rather, the 'influence' of television depends upon the particular form its development has taken and thus on the commercial practices involved in the production and distribution of the form—in this instance, the nature and context of the individual 'set'" (Street, *Literacy in Theory and Practice*, p. 96).

consciousness bring about social constructions in which some writing and speaking activities are privileged and others devalued.[71]

HUT behavior has been secret, hidden, and frequently associated with shame. In spite of these conventions, it has constructed new kinds of discourse communities and their relationships to the spoken word, which inevitably connects to aurality. We need to acquire more *logos* sophistication in our rhetorical HUTs, where so much cultural activity now takes place. This cultural activity takes place in a new public, with a new kind of disembodied audience, with new discourse communities, all of which then contribute to reconstructing literacy. A primary strategy for acquiring power in commodified rhetorical HUTs is to become a Diotimic/Isocratic Sophist, whose features are highly applicable to our era of electric rhetoric: fragmentation, teachability (including the strong desire to perform teaching), the power of Isocratic *logos*, Otherness, and relativism apply as easily to the older Sophists as they do to rhetorical HUT dwellers.

Writing instruction in the United States has been sophistic for quite some time, as Jasper Neel, Sharon Crowley, Susan Jarratt, and others have pointed out. Teachers of expressive-process writing were performing with their students a fragmented, highly open-ended rhetoric, developing *logos* users whose power gave them informed performance. Next Rhetoric and its technology need to be embraced by the academy so that *logos* users in rhetorical HUTs have the opportunity to walk outside the prison of the modernist form/content universe and enter a world in which informed performance is a new community action. Electric rhetoric, Next Rhetoric, is the third Sophistic. It is what will come after postmodernism.

71. The last phrase is Street's idea.

5

Technologies of Electric Rhetoric

Video—I see. I am seeing. I do see.[1]

In the past decade, the changes in the intellectual identity and cultural impact of the computer have taken place in a culture still deeply attached to the quest for a modernist understanding of the mechanisms of life.

Sherry Turkle, *Life on the Screen*[2]

The Sophistic performance of electric rhetoric has arrived. We are immersed in a new *logos* performance that is in part anti-Platonic and Isocratic/Diotimic. It is on computers, which now dominate most workplaces and appear in many schools and universities, and it is on television, which proliferates in rhetorical HUTs, or Households Using Television. Whereas the charged rhetorical performances of a fourth-century-B.C.E. Sophist such as Gorgias burst forth as he spoke to live Athenian audiences and as these previously written speeches then inevitably disappeared aurally into the memories of the constructed audiences (memories so different from our own), the Sophistic performances of current *logos* users possess, in high contrast, the oral/aural technology of computer, television, and video camera. Nearly endless repeatability (permanent storage) of verbal and graphic texts now exists, together with

1. English translations of the Latin word "video." See also *Cassell's New Latin Dictionary*: "In general, LIT., to see with the eyes. TRANS., not with the eyes: to perceive; with the mind, to perceive, notice, observe, see" (p. 641). See also *Oxford English Dictionary*, 2nd ed., where definitions and examples of the word take up five and one-half columns. The first definition is, "That which is displayed or to be displayed on a television screen or other cathode-ray tube; the signal corresponding to this" (p. 614).

2. P. 25.

the attendant possibilities and problems. So while one can look at the past hoping for correspondences to our own *logos*-using condition as one strategy for trying to interact with the new logos machines of electric rhetoric, one has to realize that the Sophistic past, so rich in alternatives to Aristotelian receptions, offers more difference than correspondence. One of the most significant of the many technological differences is that Gorgias's *Encomium on Helen* could be repeated inexactly through the figure of speech prosopopoeia—the words he deployed could be repeated by others in a form of ventriloquism—but his performance could not be exactly replayed.[3] The replication of Gorgianic speeches was inexact (because they were spoken) until some were written down. In our own era we have technologies that can repeat endlessly. However, as we saw in the Next Rhetoric of chapter 4, repeatability, attractive as it is, leads to the loss of aura, to overfamiliarity, and frequently to banality.[4] The very repeatability of electric rhetoric can dull the vision and hearing of its spectators, thereby making the electronic texts—computer or televisual—vividless. Rhetorical HUTs, with their endless repeatability, dominate the household landscape so thoroughly now that *logos* users are dulled to the oralist/auralist possibilities of television, one of the central oralist technologies that now conditions literacy. In addition, they are oblivious to the rhetorical beauty that television pours into HUTs—beauty delivered by broadcast waves, cable wires, fiber optic (glass) wires, satellite dishes, video cassettes, and now merged computer/television monitors. Raymond Williams, in *Television: Technology and Cultural Form*, observes this televisual spectator response and writes,

So many uses of the medium have been the transmission ... of received forms ... that it is often difficult to respond to some of its intrinsic visual experiences, for which no convention and no mode of description have been prepared or offered. Yet there are moments in my kinds of programme when we can find ourselves looking in what seem quite new ways. *To get this kind of attention it is often*

3. See, for example, Plato's *Phaedrus*, where putting speeches in the mouths of others, prosopopoeia, constitutes the very structure of the three-speech dialogue. The presentation of all this oralism is, of course, the writing on which Plato relied and the writing to which Plato demonstrated that he was so committed. For an important disussion of prosopopoeia, see William J. Kennedy, "Voice as Frame: Longinus, Kant, Ong, and Deconstruction in Literary Studies," pp. 80–81.
4. See Benjamin, "The Work of Art in the Age of Mechanical Reproduction."

necessary to turn off the sound.... What can then happen, in some surprising ways, is an experience of visual mobility, of contrast and angle, of variation of focus, which is often very beautiful.... I see it as one of the primary processes of the technology itself..., [but when] I have tried to describe and explain this, I have found it significant that the only people who ever agreed with me were painters. (P. 77; my emphasis)

The colleagues with whom Williams shared his visual interpretation of television—with the telling exception of painters—saw no striking visual rhetoric, no random beauty of televisual construction that calls attention to the technology itself in all its relative newness. For William's non-painterly colleagues, television was so bad that it did not merit their attention. And its loss of aura through repeatability made it too banal to study. Nevertheless, the painters with their particular nonverbal visual dominance could see; the scales had fallen from their eyes. Studying television by turning down the sound is, in fact, one of the most important ways to study it. This is so because when you remove the sound and quiet the ear, the most familiar (aurally verbal) *koinoi topoi* disappear. One is then left to study the visual *koinoi topoi*, and they are far less familiar and so less available for analysis by humanists and other verbally based inquirers. Almost no standard training in visual rhetoric occurs, with the exception of some aspects of art history and, of course, film and video studies.

In chapter 4, I suggested deploying the freshman writing course partly as a study and performance of technology and communication forms. In this kind of writing class, students can learn the grammar of television (an operation that can introduce them to the ideology of the technology) as well as functional computer literacy.[5] Two writing assignments can derive from such a grammar: an exegesis of the video text in writing (which we can juxtapose with and analogize to the exegesis of, for example, a sonnet in a traditional English class or a contract in a law class),

---

5. I reiterate that all courses in the teaching of writing should include the historicizing of ideas, partly as a way of treating situatedness and partly as a way of unveiling ideologies that appear to be part of *physis* but are deeply part of *nomos*. Incorporating the historicizing of ideas into all writing courses helps students enter more easily the Burkean parlor of cultural conversation and, of course, works against the content/form binary that inheres in the current-traditional paradigm.

and then the writing of a script for a commercial (or the actual production of one), a text that can be used to develop a number of verbal/visual abilities.

Students who are trained in electric rhetoric, that is, to perform and interpret electronic texts in Sophistic ways (ways that are situated, raced, fragmented, self-consciously performative, gendered, relative) will be more likely and able to decode other texts that constitute their lives. Look, for example, at the text of a university (how the discursive practices of the university determine who we are, in the Foucauldian sense): if a student cannot read the text of her or his university, to understand its discursive practices, then it is less likely, of course, that the student will succeed in it and other institutions that control our lives.[6] A second example of decoding to gain partial control of our lives lies in reading the text of a presidential campaign, in the way that Kathleen Hall Jamieson has in print (see, for example, *Eloquence in an Electronic Age*) and that she has performed on video.[7]

Digital literacy is now required for citizens to get and maintain jobs in the new information-based economy. Just as important, digital literacy is now required for citizens to partake of a new identity, as the Turkle epigraph illustrates. Consequently, the universal freshman writing course needs to become a site for the advancement of digital literacy and for explorations of what happens to subjectivity and ethics when we commune with our relatively new machines.

Jamieson consistently argues (in the technologies of print and television) that citizens in a representative democracy need more complex verbal and visual relationships with their leaders. It is important to add that the computer screens require more sophisticated attention as well. Although her rhetorical stance differs, she is in concert with *High Reso-*

6. For an important analysis of the challenges that face student writers, see David Bartholomae, "Inventing the University." See also "Facts, Artifacts, and Counterfacts: A Basic Reading and Writing Course for the College Curriculum" by Bartholomae and Petrosky.

7. See, for example, Jamieson, "Inside Politics," Cable News Network, July 1996, 7:23 p.m.–7:26 p.m. Mountain Daylight Time. The fact that Jamieson in print longs for a "golden age" of oratory (*Eloquence in an Electronic Age*, pp. 3–31) and so for a moment enters the Heritage School of classical rhetoric, does not obviate her point that speech training is needed to produce an informed citizenry.

lution, where Henry Sussman contends, "The greatest extension of literacy involves the very careful reading of the relationships that configure all organized systems, not only the linguistic and imagistic codes or artworks but also systems of production, distribution, management, communication, education, law enforcement, and social services" (p. 224). However, Sussman, as we saw earlier, does not push the issue far enough. Reading alone is not sufficient. His hyperliterate commitment to Literary formalism blocks the screen literacy that his book needs. Writing, encoding, and other kinds of performing are required to adequately understand how texts operate in an oralist/auralist era such as our own. Students need to know how to recognize manipulative texts as well as straightforward ones. They need to know how to write what Jasper Neel has named "antiwriting,"[8] written compositions in which a student hides out altogether, not making a human connection but fulfilling a requirement (for example, a meaningless assignment in a course or a meaningless task in an office).[9]

Students from orally/aurally-dominant cultures—many Native American dual citizens, for example—can especially benefit from applications of oralist/auralist theory in the classroom.[10] These students have fre-

8. See *Plato, Derrida, and Writing*, pp. 84, 93, 131, 149, and 168, for this important concept.

9. As we know from much of the composition research of the last thirty years, antiwriting (a reasonable response to the current-traditional paradigm) has dominated student writing and school literacy. This phenomenon has led, of course, to students and citizens who either detest their own writing or are afraid of it. These responses form a major location of the literacy problems in the United States. Students know (or have some awareness) that they occupy multiple (and frequently conflicting) subject positions. When standard, boring writing assignments force students into only one subject position (which is not even recognized as such), they recognize the disjunction, they understand the phoniness. The traditional universal narrator of an objective current-traditional theme can be deployed as *one* strategy, *one* subject position, available to a student in her writing repertoire. If it is taught as some form of Truth, it is debilitating.

10. I have had success with this pedagogical strategy in working with Native American students at the University of Oklahoma. Oklahoma, of course, has more Native Americans who are born in the state than any other state, though California has the highest Native American population (many of whom relocated from other states). The Oklahoma number increased in the 1990 census since many citizens assumed their Native American identity instead of suppressing it.

quently faced enormous White cultural resistance to the oralism/auralism that partly defines their cultures and does so in ways that differ radically from the presence of the spoken in dominant White culture. In addition, a number of Native American professors have faced enormous resistance from students who actively resist the study of Native American writing and that of other marginalized Others; they claim that this is not "Literature" and that they are not being trained in real Literature. Of course, these students and some of their White professors mean that "American Literature" is a White set of texts, as we saw with Morrison's exegesis of that adjective. For alternatives, look at the written or spoken texts from Native North American literatures; look, for example, at the *Origin Myth of Acoma* from the Acoma tribe located in what is now western New Mexico, a complex, rich, spiralling genesis story that is especially formulaic, repetitive, additive, situational, and so on, in highly complex, important ways that most Western, print-based eyes can easily misinterpret. (See the appendix for a partial script of this story.) Many monocultural White people might regard the *Origin Myth of Acoma* as merely straightforward and simple; oralism shows us that the story is highly abstract, deep, and sophisticated. Such stories also resemble the still-canonical Homeric poems and the texts of electronic discourse.

Digital literacy and Native American studies have more in common than many have been willing to admit. It is the oralism/auralism of the two that partly accounts for their strong connections.

By examining the dynamism of the spoken word and the unspoken word (compare the idea of White people as chatterboxes), we can better include non-White, non-European groups that have been historically excluded and marginalized, left to face the fact that they are not understood by the dominant print-based university culture.[11] The oralist/auralist theory of electric rhetoric offers us one of many ways of including and empowering students from these cultures. It should go without saying but does not, U.S. Euroculture needs the wisdom and *logos* performances of these other groups. The need is almost desperate.

11. Note also the tradition in many, though not all, Native American cultures of males' not making eye contact with females and the rudeness of interrupting many Native Americans when they speak, a mode of speaking quite common among Euro-American intellectuals, who tend to vie for space to speak.

For many groups—for example, Native Americans, Whites, African-Americans—literacy empowerment in writing takes place with the deployment of electric rhetoric. Literacy empowerment can derive from making writing courses locations for the training of Sophistic *logos* performers who understand the power, pressures, and possibilities of the fifth rhetorical canon of delivery in its newly revivified manifestations in electric rhetoric.[12] Writing courses can show students how to produce and evaluate texts of many kinds. Theories of oralism/auralism can comprise one critical part of this urgent project. However, writing textbooks must account for delivery as it exists in oralism/auralism. They must cease their erasure of electronic discourse from the domain of school rhetoric. Should they do so, the tedium that comprises so much writing instruction might very well convert to thrilling intellectual energy. Our writing students need theory; they need to learn electric rhetoric, including how to decode life in HUTs. Our rhetorical HUTs have remained rhetorically untheorized and so useless. Spectator-auditors cannot do anything with these endless signals without theories that convey underlying, connective issues. *Logos* users in our era of electric rhetoric are now numb. To stir responses, to arouse logos users from their absence of Sophistic affect, the textbooks need to teach televisual rhetoric, a project that will promote alphabetic literacy, partly because all the forms of electric rhetoric depend on written literacy. The aversion of the traditional humanities to engaging television (and, to a lesser extent, computers and communication with the public) has contributed to their irrelevance, which grows daily, as the form-content universe of language-as-a-container-that-holds-meaning proceeds along its unexamined way, tacitly reinforced by the timidity of many (but certainly not all) humanities endeavors.

The Ideological Suppression of the Rhetorical Canons of Memory and Delivery

As we saw in chapter 2, the five canons (*erga* in Greek, *officii* in Latin) or functions of classical rhetoric have maintained a remarkably long life in

12. I use the term "empowerment" here in the sense deployed by Patti Lather in *Getting Smart: Feminist Research and Pedagogy with/in the Postmodern*, p. 167, n. 5.

different guises, a life that I have examined elsewhere as having exerted an enormous and largely unrecognized claim on the issues that drive the teaching of writing in North America and the positioning of Plato in current rhetoric and composition theory.[13] Invention, arrangement, style, memory, and delivery (the standard and powerful English translations of the canons) have recurred in different forms and with different emphases in varying historical eras. We can partly historicize Western rhetoric and writing practices by charting their movements.[14] The completeness, interaction, and interdependence of the canons in both Greek and Roman classical rhetoric provided one of the sources of the power of rhetoric in those eras and cultures. Later, however, individual canons were frequently incorporated, according to one particular ideology or another, into other canons and then seemed to disappear. U.S. pedagogy remains firmly in the grip of one wizened version of the canons. In the twentieth century, the canons' enormous and largely unacknowledged power was reflected in the reliance of writing pedagogy on textbooks that truncate the five canons from five to three, so that invention, structure, and "style"[15] repeatedly colonize the last two, memory and delivery, and then eradicate them.

It is crucial to an understanding of Western literacy at the newly electrified turn of the millennium to recognize that the disappearance of memory and delivery is not a benign removal. Rather, it is part of a larger movement in the United States to pablumize the humanities in general, and to vitiate writing in particular, by behaving (especially in

13. See my "Ideology and Freshman Textbook Production: The Place of Theory in Writing Pedagogy," in which I analyze the canons of rhetoric as they are repeated in textbook after textbook on writing, and my *Contemporary Reception of Classical Rhetoric*, pp. 95–100, in which I examine some of the consequences of removing memory and delivery from Plato's highly performative and utterly visual (written) rhetoric. In both places I attempt to show what happens to an unacknowledged theory and how this absence of recognition leads to major interpretive problems, in the first place for theory-unconscious textbooks and in the second place for understanding Plato's rhetoric in current rhetoric and composition studies.

14. This historicizing would be a useful one. For another rhetorical stance, see Barbara Warnick's *The Sixth Canon*.

15. I resort to scare quotations to indicate the ethical and rhetorical bankruptcy of this nearly ruined term.

our educational institutions) as if it were a mere skill, craft, or useful tool. The colonizing of memory and delivery reproduces the form/content binary that drives the movement to relegate writing to skills and drills and perpetuates the status quo of racism and sexism, as I explored in chapter 4 with the historiographies of rhetoric and what they tacitly incorporate and reproduce. The writing-as-tool metaphor, in fact, recurs in composition textbooks, in many discussions of writing, and in many generally held assumptions about why writing is "good for you." It occurs even in discussions among some writing specialists in the discipline of English. If writing is a tool, then it is part of the Cartesian dualistic reality in which we all continue to live. A tool is a thing out there in the world, a palpable object that one can store in the garage and retrieve as necessary. A tool can be put aside; language cannot. A tool does not partake of intersubjectivity, one of the hallmarks of current literacy. The persistence of the tool metaphor reveals a great deal about how language is regarded; it is a metaphor that needs to be examined and replaced.

In the functions of memory and delivery reside many issues of culture, ideology, society, and the construction of public and private lives, the last of which is routinely and tacitly regarded not as a construction at all but palpably, "obviously" as two separate entities. The elimination of memory and delivery in the majority of student writing textbooks constitutes the removal of student-written language from the larger public arena. The removal reinforces the common, dualistic idea that students live outside ideology if they choose to do so, just as they live outside language if they choose to do so. The memory and delivery excision fits well, as I wrote in previous chapters, with the formalist appeal of dominant twentieth-century writing instruction, especially current-traditional writing. In addition, it accommodates well the formalist approaches to the study of Literature (with a capital "L"), removing Great Books from the taint of "real life" and the murkiness that exists there in the formation of power relations and in other ways. The come-let-us-glow-together school, the Truth and Beauty School, of formalist literary interpretation cannot allow hotly contested issues, the political realm, to enter the study of the assumed Great Books, except insofar as those issues appear as dead (that is, resolved) conflicts. This school's proponents claim that the study of literary texts is apolitical. While traditionalists in literary studies do not, as far as I know, explicitly treat the canons of rhetoric (truncated or otherwise), they too tend to suppress questions of ideology and how all writers and readers are entwined in it.

In a persistent call to the aim of the moment, in the revision-is-good-for-you rhetorical stance, and in the other features of skill-bound writing instruction (in its current-traditional manifestation and in some, but not all, of the more powerful and helpful process schools), the still-dominant current-traditional teachers lead their student writers outside of language, outside of ideology, and outside of history. The suppression of ideology and the attempt to stand outside of language provide two of the connections between the traditional study of writing and the traditional study of literature. To the extent that memory and delivery interfere with the writing process and its privileging of invention and the thoughts and feelings of the writer, they are dangerous to the status quo of two parts of the process movement: the expressivist and the cognitivist.

A standard explanation for the removal of memory and delivery from the five canons relies on the simplistic idea that the burgeoning power of writing made memory and delivery less relevant because those two canons are said to be more powerful in orally/aurally-dominant cultures. This is not the case. Memory and delivery do not wither with the encroachment of writing; rather, they change form, as they do many times historically. While the interiorizing of writing did in fact have profound effects (although not in Havelock's ungendered sense), there is no split between the oral and the written, as many of the commentators analyzed in chapter 2 would have it. With the increasing empowerment of writing, memory and delivery acquired different attributes. Elsewhere I have connected memory to psychology and delivery to medium.[16] A crucial point is that memory and delivery were not afterthoughts as they gradually developed in Greek rhetoric and found fuller expression in, for example, Hermagoras' lost work and in Cicero, particularly in *On the Character of the Orator*.[17]

However, beyond the hegemonic texts of the West, such as Cicero, lie a multitude of texts from many groups—including Native American

16. See, for example, my *Contemporary Reception of Classical Rhetoric*, pp. 98–100. See also John Frederick Reynolds, "Introduction," in his *Rhetorical Memory and Delivery*, pp. 7–12.

17. Hermagoras' work can be construed from later references to it. See George A. Kennedy, *The Art of Persuasion in Greece*, p. 304.

groups, nations, bands, and tribes—that are utterly intertwined with the two rhetorical canons of memory and delivery. Many Native Americans are bicultural in that they live in Western civilization but live as well in a Native American culture that is indigenous.[18] The canon of memory accounts for the depth and resonance and cultural centrality of the *Origin Myth of Acoma*, a genesis story. It was until rather recently transmitted orally/aurally, though it is now transmitted in part through the written word, as many Native American articulations are.

Both the memory and delivery of works such as the *Origin Myth of Acoma* will be reconfigured as they become available on the Internet and reassume the instability (the nontextuality) of digital literacy. These works will occupy a new kind of oralism/auralism, different from the Isocratic/Diotimic kind but with many attributes in common. Human, in-person articulations of spoken texts involve one kind of memory and delivery; printed articulations have another kind; and digital versions yet another. In each kind of transmission, there is a change and a sameness. One looming digital problem is the recolonizing of, for example, the Acoma people by "digerati" who may want to digitalize their articulations and construct the canons of memory and delivery in ways that obliterate the power of the tribe. The previous colonizing of the Acoma and other Pueblo tribes continues unabated, of course, as the imperialism of the U.S. government and Whites continue to place the Acoma today in very difficult circumstances.

Digital literacy for any group does and will include reconfigurations of the canons of memory and delivery. Perhaps the recognition of all five canons and the definitive twentieth-century erasure of memory and delivery will lead to the obliteration of the current-traditional paradigm and its twin the false binary opposition of content and form.

The Death of Sophistic *Logos* in Writing Textbooks

Every academic year, students are compelled to spend millions of dollars for textbooks that purport to teach writing. While exact figures are unavailable (publishers guard these particular revenue numbers care-

18. In many curricula, stabilized Native American texts are regarded as "non-Western," a term used as a distribution category in many degree programs.

fully), it is not difficult to conclude that writing textbooks provide an important source of money for most nonuniversity publishers, most of which underwent a series of mergers into conglomerates during the 1980s and later. Most of these writing textbooks continue to maintain a destructive commitment to three of the five canons partly through connection and repetition; the books frequently repeat material that has occurred in other books, partly because new textbooks are contracted according to the publishing genres of the rhetoric textbook, the reader, and the argument textbook. (Handbooks that provide rules for the writing of dominant-culture English constitute a separate issue.[19]) As with other genres, these publishing genres have conventions, constraints, and "rules." They operate in the world of textbook production and consumption, but they do not operate outside of it; in fact, they appear to be hermetically sealed, as other genres can be. Most writing textbooks are based not on new, energizing, and important writing theory but simply on other textbooks in the genres. One successful textbook leads to many competitors, each vying for a portion of an already proven market. These markets are based on tried material, on issues that have already worked, according to the number of sales they have generated.[20] The room for

19. No history of handbooks has yet been written, but that history would do a great deal to contribute to our understanding of historical rhetoric and writing practices. Of course, Plato and Aristotle complained bitterly, frequently, and justifiably against the *technai*, usually translated into English as "handbooks." They differed from mechanical-print-era handbooks, which stipulate rules. This kind of book provides a useful and important reference, since the apparent (although not the actual) stabilization of rules in the mechanical-print era leads to dominant-culture English (usually called standard English). Handbooks remain useful for students who need to refer to the dominant-culture dialect. The ones that insist on "standard written English" remain a problem because there is no "standard English." Rather, there is a dominant dialect of English. All dialects are created equal. My own approach to this issue in the always-theorized writing classroom relies on framing the matter as an issue of social class and the deployment of power. As for learning dominant usages, Mina Shaughnessy's method of detecting patterns of errors, and not concentrating on a proliferation of individual errors (which may follow only a few patterns) works well for writers at all levels, not only those at the basic level (formerly called "remedial writing").

20. See W. Ross Winterowd, "Composition Textbooks: Publisher-Author Relationships," for one of the most trenchant denunciations of the deals struck by textbook publishers.

newness, particularly for newness of writing theories, is small. As I have argued elsewhere, composition textbooks appear to be driven by publishers who believe that writing teachers desire constructions such as the three canons (or modes of discourse or the expressivist-process-is-terrific stance). However, as Arthur Applebee has pointed out in *Tradition and Reform in the Teaching of English*, the textbooks teach the writing teachers first (p. 127). The putative "desires" of imagined writing teachers are in fact the desires inculcated by theory-unconscious textbooks that too often trivialize writing into a tool marketed to large numbers of paying students, many of whom are taught by instructors with little or no training in writing theory that would lead them away from the dominant notion of writing as a mere skill. Indeed, many of these teachers believe—really believe—that the teaching of writing occupies a place on the hierarchy that is low, very low.[21]

In these ways and others, the repetition of the truncated canons has taken on a life of its own. Dozens of textbooks present the first three canons—invention, arrangement, and "style"—as the center of writing concern, a center presented as just "there" and not susceptible to examination. The continuing reliance of these textbooks on the truncated structure speaks to the tenacity of the canons as a way of producing discourse, and to the mesmerizing effect that theory-unconsciousness continues to have on the textbook industry.[22] Other reasons can be found to explain the tenacity of the first three canons. The rigorous suppression of memory and delivery (to provide one historical example) also connects to the cordoning off of rhetoric enacted by Peter Ramus in the sixteenth century, when he constructed rhetoric in a way that made invention,

21. These teachers—some of them teaching assistants—remind one of a familiar joke: I would not be a member of any club that would stoop so low as to have me as a member.

22. Fortunately, many excellent textbooks have been published in recent years, textbooks that acknowledge the theory that always operates. The problem I treat here lies in the continuation of the truncated canons in many of the theory-unconscious textbooks, a symptom of the desire to deprive students and their teachers of the dynamic theory that is taking shape now, and to replace it with formulaic guidelines that are boring and that teach student writers to distance themselves from their own writing.

arrangement, and memory central parts of dialectic and not of rhetoric.[23] With the removal of these functions from rhetoric, "style" and a narrow idea of delivery then received more emphasis and, I would argue, a more imbalanced emphasis than they had. The long journey of rhetoric as attenuated style or language decoration gathered great power that continues today.[24] In Ramus's powerfully influential construction, rhetoric was diminished by removing canons that were central to it. We continue to work with the results of this dangerous legacy.[25]

What will the writing textbook of the electric future (and/or present) look like? In all likelihood, we will continue to have ten percent or so of theorized, up-to-date writing textbooks, while the other ninety percent will continue to reproduce the scourge of the two-hundred-year-old current-traditional paradigm with its faculty associationist psychology, its gridlike boredom-inducing formulas, its commitment to obsessive error correction, and, worst of all, its project of making student writers develop great negativity toward their own writing—a result that leads to an

---

23. See chapter 2 for an elaboration on Peter Ramus. Ong's analysis of Ramus has a great deal to teach us about the rearrangement of power between dialectic (Ramus's version of "logic") and rhetoric. Ong writes, "Ramus' influence is in school or university textbooks and is perpetuated as part of that great deposit of textbook literature dealing with the most familiar of our ideas which is rewritten in every generation, while remaining so much a part of the universal heritage that no one can believe it has ever changed or even derived from a particular source" (*Ramus*, p. 9). See also Frances Johnson, "Historicizing Peter Ramus: Current-Traditional Rhetoric Reconfigured."

24. Nearly daily in midcult locations such as the *New York Times* or on *The Newshour with Jim Lehrer* one hears, frequently from politicians, the derogatory connotation of "rhetoric." While the modern connotation is essentially Ramistic, the derogatory connotation can be found as well in Plato's *Gorgias*, where the character Socrates discusses, in a seven-part crescendo, rhetorical questions that peak with the unveiling of rhetoric (459). This connotation of "rhetoric" also suits the form/content binary universe of discourse (to adapt James Moffett's phrase) so favored by Western politicians at this end of the millennium. Rhetoric as putrid decoration (or even sweet decoration) remains a powerful, tacit constructor of all language for U.S. and other citizens.

25. A full investigation of this persistent problem in advancing literacy in the United Sates lies outside the scope of this book. Much more research needs to be conducted on these influences so that we can teach writing and reading more effectively and, most important of all, so that we can leave behind the current status quo in which students are taught to hate their native tongue(s).

uninformed citizenry bereft of rhetorical strategies, bereft of the understanding that the native tongue drives meaning (language speaks us; we
do not speak language), and bereft of the ability to change the dominant
culture. The current-traditional paradigm transmits easily to the technology of CD-ROM. The reproducibility and teachability of the current-
traditional paradigm, as we have seen, are its strongest features. And so
transferring it on a disk is quite simple.

The writing textbooks of electric rhetoric will be based not so much on
CD-ROMs as the World Wide Web, where the electronic issues of interactivity, bistable decorum, and textual instability will reign, as will, of
course, the primacy of the image. It is entirely possible that writing textbooks could appear on Web-TV or other video forms, since video is, of
course, so amenable to the image. But it is far more likely, partly because
of humanities intellectuals' low public regard for television, that the
computer will take over much of the work of print writing textbooks,
while television continues to occupy its category of shame that I presented in earlier chapters. Unless these CD-ROMs theorize oralism, they
will merely be transferring print oralism (Chartier's mentalité, Ong's
orality) without accounting for the enormous changes in articulation/
thought that electric rhetoric allows as it interacts with the forces of
ideology, economics, and so on.

CD-ROMs are best understood, as is all of electric rhetoric, by rehistoricized (including regendered and reraced) rhetoric. CD-ROMs have
many possibilities and limitations. They are finite. Since they do not
provide access to the World Wide Web, they do not provide the nearly
endless material of the Web. However, the finiteness of this computer
technology also means that material can be referred to and constructed in
ways that maintain quality (or otherwise) to which we are accustomed.
CD-ROMs can provide material supplementary to print books and to
teachers. They will probably have significant marketplace influence because textbook publishers can maintain their profit margins with the
stable writers of the CDs. Over the long period, however, the finiteness of
CDs will probably put them on the path of Betamax videotaping.

Intellectual property and the way that it is constructed in the near
future will determine to a large extent the kind of technology available to
students and other citizens. In other words, copyright law enacted at the

federal level in the United States will determine the access and literacy critical for representative democracy.[26] If websites, which will become the next generation of writing textbooks, do not bring a monetary return, then textbook publishers will not be able to publish them. Given the financial windfalls provided by some writing textbooks, there could be a strong rear-guard action to maintain the hegemony of the print book or at least the dominance of CD-ROMs. If students are charged tolls to log onto particular websites, then the library without walls will become the department store without walls. The basis of the library, of course, is that it is, for the most part, free for its users. When Benjamin Franklin established one of the early lending libraries in Philadelphia, he realized the crucial role that an educated citizenry would play in the representative democracy envisioned by men and women of that period. That situation remains essentially the same.

Rerhetoricizing Memory and Delivery as Definitive Functions of Electric Rhetoric

Some discussions of the five canons link memory and delivery, but a great deal of the research (probably most of it) exists separately. The historical situation of rhetorical memory has received powerful new interpretations by, among others, Mary Carruthers in *The Book of Memory*, and Jody Enders in "Memory and the Psychology of the Interior Monologue in Chrétien's *Cliges*" and "Music, Delivery, and the Rhetoric of Memory in Guillaume de Machaut's *Remède de Fortune*," in addition to Frances A. Yates's definitive *Art of Memory*. These writers have worked to revise some of the standard arguments about the nature of parts of medieval thought by analyzing the pivotal role of memory in epistemology, and so have taught us a great deal about this frequently neglected canon. Sharon Crowley, in *The Methodical Memory: Invention in Current-Traditional Rhetoric*, has, among others moves, analyzed

26. Given current campaign finance law, it is highly likely that more power will flow to the telecommunications monopolies that pay for votes favorable to their desire to make more money. The connection between rhetoric/composition studies (and its definitive connection to pedagogy) and federal law has never been clearer.

systems of invention and how constructions of memory enabled those systems to operate forcefully. Work on memory and writing in our own era needs this and more rhetorical attention. The idea of memory as shards of consciousness, or mentalité, and the connection of memory to psychology (cognitive and depth, to name two kinds) continues to be an important area in the historicizing and production of discourses. Memory has been forgotten. One site of the erasure of memory has been in most of the writing textbooks that remain so powerful in our culture. I will not forget memory here but will instead go on to treat delivery (Latin *actio*, Greek *hypokrisis*) and its status as medium.

To explore delivery here, I will center on how it has been reconstructed through electronic forms of discourse. Delivery, in its life as medium, has acquired enormous power in the twentieth century. I want to suggest connections between the Great Books and the (mostly unconscious) theory of representative writing textbooks and how they replicate the form/content status quo and its attendant racism and sexism. In addition, I hope to offer some suggestions about one strategy for reorganizing the humanities—one that is dangerous in many ways—rather than perpetuating its current life as a toothless sage that is acknowledged as important and then sharply ignored as irrelevant. In other words, I hope to draw the connection between the crucial placement of writing as a central form of articulation in our time and dominant culture and its placement as a center for the reinvention of the humanities away from the pablumized, weekend diversion that it now appears to be in the dominant culture.

Delivery is weakened if it refers only to the gesture, physical movement, and expression that many commentators have dismissed it as limited to. The fifth canon of rhetoric includes this aspect of visual communication in person, but it includes much more as well.[27] This issue is central to understanding the striking revivification of classical rhetoric in the second half of the twentieth century, part of Next Rhetoric.

Just as there is no point in arguing about the human need for eating, breathing, and sleeping, so there is no point in arguing about the pres-

---

27. Following Patrick Mahony's explication of Marshall McLuhan in "Marshall McLuhan in the Light of Classical Rhetoric," I have elsewhere elaborated on the canon of delivery as medium (see "Ideology and Freshman Textbook Production").

ence of electronic forms of discourse, including their relationship to writing. The familiar cries about illiteracy (children will not read books!) and the attendant proclamations that Western civilization is about to collapse under the weight of television (and similar regrets about the use of the telephone as a replacement for letter writing) reveal a profound sense of loss. Not infrequently this loss converts to anger.

I suggest here—and I want to carry the suggestion over to writing pedagogy, a cultural practice that needs to reflect culture as well as change it or offer possibilities for subverting it—that there is not so much a loss as there is a change, including an addition. We now have many ways of communicating. Literacy—the reading and writing of texts and the partial formation of consciousness based on written communication—has not been displaced by anything; rather, it has grown even more powerful, as the growing number of published books indicates. Writing has irrevocably changed because of oralism/auralism. Composition and rhetoric need to take account of this metamorphosis with more thorough theories and more emphasis on dissemination of those theories. These agendas include theories that will inform composition textbooks on an explicit level, and not on their usually implicit level, where they now so commonly reside.

Our classroom performances and other institutional practices have been profoundly conditioned by the new oral/aural world of television and computers. However, these performances, based on a changed consciousness/mentalité/subjectivity, have not been analyzed or incorporated into new curricula.

It is essential that the humanities, posthumanities, and literacies develop working criteria for what constitutes functional computer literacy and critical computer literacy. The former can now be said to be the ability to send and receive electronic mail and to access the World Wide Web. The latter, critical computer literacy, is, of course, much more difficult to define. What appears to be clear, however, is that each discipline will determine its own critical computer literacy. This process is going on in a haphazard way now. It needs to take place in a large way, including the publication of manifestos by professional lobbying groups in the humanities, posthumanities, and literacies. Of these groups (for example, the National Council of Teachers of English, the Modern Language Association, the American Historical Association, and the American Philological Association, to name some) only one is engaged in decades-long work on computers, pedagogy, and research. That is a branch of the NCTE, the Conference on College Composition and Communication. In addition, the study of computers and composition is now twenty years old, with journals, conferences, websites, chat rooms, and so on. If there is lobbying conducted by the NCTE, I am not aware of it. The lobbying conducted by the MLA consists of tepid letters to congresspeople and occasional articles in national newspapers such as the *New York Times*.[28]

HUT Dwelling in Oralism/Auralism

Oralism/auralism as it occurs in U.S. HUTs requires radical new theories. Both British and U.S. cultural studies offer powerful ways of explicating the deluge of electronic signals.[29] Reconstructed Sophistic classical rhetoric offers different theories that are distinguished by an emphasis on performance not only by the collaborative encoders of televisual texts but also by the discourse communities that reperform these texts in ways that have been uncharted by humanists. Let us return to the nine characteristics of oral texts set out by Ong (again, this is not a complete list of characteristics but lists some central ones). Oral texts are

- "additive rather than subordinative,"
- "aggregative rather than analytic,"
- "redundant or 'copious',"
- "conservative or traditionalist,"

28. Compare the digital exhibits at the annual meetings of the MLA and the CCCC. The former, which has not even a division on computers and English, has actually decreased the presence of digital work. The latter is online, interactive, and grows more digital by the year, offering extensive conference sessions devoted to computer literacy. This tale of two conferences, to paraphrase John Schilb, tells us the future: the traditional humanities are nearly dead, moribund in their commitment to not looking toward the future.

29. See for example, *Technoculture*, ed. by Constance Penley and Andrew Ross.

- "close to the human lifeworld,"
- "agonistically toned,"
- "empathetic and participatory rather than objectively distanced,"
- "homeostatic," and
- "situational rather than abstract."

In addition to these characteristics, primarily oral cultures are complexly formulaic, not simplistically formulaic. It is crucial to remember, in reviewing these characteristics, that our only access to primarily oral cultures is utterly imaginative. Because of print dominance and its infiltration around the globe (in Western cultures since at least the eighteenth century), the oral/aural cultures of, say, Homer and his predecessors cannot be experienced. So it is only the residue of these characteristics that we can examine to help us with the surplus of texts in electric rhetoric. These characteristics can be applied to television texts because electric rhetoric may share many properties with primary orality even though it differs substantially.

Rhetorical HUTs and Rhetorical Digital Households

Our rhetorical HUTs have, for less than one-half of the U.S. population, been changed by digitally literate households, where computer screen and television screen coexist as centers of familial activity. In this kind of private space, the household member can delve into the computer screen by visiting websites, by associatively surfing locations, by shopping, by entering a synchronous chat room or MUD (a multi-user domain, in which the digitally literate person can assume various personae), by reading and/or posting to an asynchronous listserve (or by reading only, a move that has been named "lurking"), and by many other activities with CD-ROMs. Many people have reported the experience in their digital households and HUTs (or their offices or cyberhall cafes) of subjectively going elsewhere on the computer, of interacting subjectively with the machine in a way that increases and/or complicates human interaction with technology, a kind of interaction that we have seen elaborately played out in the fifth, fourth, and third centuries B.C.E. with other kinds of technology.

New Literacy and Electric Rhetoric

Electric rhetoric as a form of consciousness (mentalité) and as a definitive part of the new literacy is not many things, and it is important to rehearse these negatives, which dominate so many public and academic discussions of the condition of literacy in the United States. First of all, electric rhetoric is not a destroyer of literacy, as is commonly thought. It is, instead, an extension of literacy, a thrilling extension. Although one can understand the sense of loss for those committed deeply to the printed book (for example, perhaps most of the humanities professoriat), this sense of loss often drives literacy research and teaching in the wrong direction. Electric rhetoric resists this stance (while understanding it); electric rhetoric is an extension of literacy that will bring about many important changes and may bring about good changes. The direction of emerging technologies has proceeded with little influence from those working in the humanities. The fact that many intelligent and sensitive humanists believe—really believe—that electric rhetoric threatens print-based literacy is a phenomenon that needs more investigation. Henry Sussman, in *High Resolution: Critical Theory and the Problem of Literacy*, expresses this sadness about the low quality of the televisual part of electric rhetoric, which he automatically dismisses as kitsch (a term he does not probe), as we have seen.

Second, literacy and electric rhetoric are not in opposition. Rather, they are merged. Conventionally, in the public and academic imaginations, literacy and the televisual part of electric rhetoric are held to be opponents. This false opposition leads to the formulation that reading is good and viewing is bad.

Electric rhetoric requires rigorous participation and training in the humanities/posthumanities if our HUT behavior is to go beyond the passive viewing and random hearing that characterizes televisual decoding now. In our present situation, spectators constituted by and in discourse communities lose themselves to a certain extent. Likely, little reflection takes place during these habitual, sometimes occasional absorptions of televisual texts. The video response that stops with passive reading typifies not only general spectatorship but the spectatorship of many intellectuals as well. People are simply not in the intellectual habit of critiquing a video text. A knowledge of the grammar, syntax, and vocabulary of video and the histories of communication technologies among humanists and their students is now essential. However, as I have traced it in previous chapters, the nearly habitual intellectual response to television is that the televised text (its "content") is not worthy of this kind of investigation. In this way, the airwaves, cables, telephone lines, and new technologies are left to corporate capitalists, who rush in not only to sell goods but to consume our psyches as well.[30] The sophisticated explication of U.S. televisual texts—which to a large extent promote, defend, and extend corporate capitalism, sexism, racism, and other aspects of the status quo—is not only necessary but crucial. Electric rhetoric abounds; refraining from analyzing their operations as powerful sources of delivery, the fifth canon of rhetoric, means that decoders are going to be less sophisticated in dealing with the powerful forms of the newly powerful delivery systems of electric rhetoric.

The Canon of Delivery in Retro-Writing Textbooks

In spite of the centrality of rhetorical delivery and its reconfiguration in electric rhetoric, a strange erasure of the forms of electric rhetoric has taken place in writing textbooks, an erasure that makes them retro. I have examined 45 recently published first-year writing textbooks to determine the extent to which these powerful sources account for the forms of electric rhetoric. While a number of textbooks now on the market are theoretically sensitive, pedagogically sound, and attractive in many other ways, the vast majority of them (writing textbook genres are called readers, rhetorics, argument textbooks, and hybrids) do not substantially account for the powerful new kinds of delivery. Rather, they treat the forms of electronic discourse not as *issues that affect consciousness* but as *new sources of content*. They reinforce the stale, useless, and harmful content/form binary opposition in which rhetoric, writing, and all the humanities become a fortiori the deprived term. Textbook excerpts from professionally produced writing now regularly include essays or parts of

30. The 1996 Communications Act removed decades of public control over these technologies, favoring instead the laissez-faire capitalism that flourishes in a culture whose political discourse operates according to sound and sight bites.

longer works "about" some aspect of television or film. Students are even shown how to cite electronic forms of discourse.[31] However, they are not taught anything about the new forms of consciousness. In fact, a distressingly high number of the books continue to repeat the modes of discourse, the truncated canons, and an attenuated version of "process" (as opposed to the important and intellectually challenging kinds of process pedagogy). The highly oral/aural features of many of our students' discourse—the repetition, the formulism, the additive qualities, the absence of subordination (what Westerners call depth), for example—are not accounted for. Students enter a world in most of these textbooks that assumes that enormous changes in delivery have not happened at all, or if there is some minor acknowledgment, most of the textbooks teach that the new delivery has nothing to do with student writing and their own lives lived with an excess of electric rhetoric. These textbooks, with rare exceptions, act as if electric rhetoric has not changed delivery and as if we all are not conditioned by these forms. A duality then develops. Electronic discourse is for "real" life. Print discourse, including students' own writing, is for school culture (which, it goes without saying, is a central site for the promulgation of official culture). In this duality, school discourse is not a place to pour out one's passions, to engage one's life force. It is something to get through or something to get by with. Real life and school life are disconnected, and students are not shown what they need: how the discourses of real life and school life partake of the same thing. When we fail to make these connections in our writing courses, we give up the most powerful of the available means of persuasion in the particular case of wising up our students and ourselves, to vaguely echo Aristotle.

When we, driven by the endless supply of retrogressive writing textbooks, deny electric rhetoric in the classroom, we erase what we know is there. A pretense therefore takes place. The uncritical reception of electronic texts is promoted. Students are implicitly instructed not to inter-

---

31. Examples of two important electronic texts are *The Norton Anthology of African-American Literature*, ed. Henry Louis Gates and Nellie Y. McCay, which has appeared in print and on compact disk (the latter is an innovation but one with a finite amount of possibilities; since it does not connect to the web, its interactivity is limited) and Linda Hogan's *Everything Has a Spirit*, a videotape of a broadcast.

pret texts outside of school and outside of print. The television- and computer-dominated world they inhabit is denied by their educational training. This need not and will not continue if electric rhetoric develops in appropriate ways.

The Canon of Delivery in Textbooks That Acknowledge the Electric

In a writing class that acknowledges the existence of electric rhetoric, students and teachers can move in a number of directions, two of which are working in webbed environments (in a classroom with interactive computers that connect to the Internet) and studying changes in consciousness (mentalité) that have been brought about by electric rhetoric. Such study necessarily includes excavating the strong Western bias toward print/paper literacy that has existed in various ways for five hundred years and that drives schools and universities.[32] The first I explored in chapter 3. The second I pursue here. A number of pedagogical strategies can be worked through. One move, a form of bricolage, lies in interpreting an apparently ordinary visual electronic text, such as a Coca-Cola advertisement, and probing its ideological positioning as it emerges from the rhetorical canon of delivery. Nine (or more) issues could be addressed in class discussion and used as a basis for students to script their own soft drink commercials (in a different rhetoric class, students could and should, as part of the techno-liberal-arts, videotape their own commercials): (1) Where are the cameras? (2) What is the nature of the fifth canon, or the medium (is it videotape or film, black and white or color or both; what kind of monitor is being watched)? (3) What is the *mise en scène*? For example, what is the placement of the people in the frame, the space taken up by various people or objects, the interaction of color, light and shade, line and form? (4) How does editing influence the message (self-conscious editing, the use of wipes, the length of takes, and so on)? (5) How are light and shadow manipulated? (6) What are the production values (the relationship of television advertisements to the high Hollywood gloss that we expect from classic Hollywood cinema)?

32. For an analysis of the relationship between the rise of publishing and the rise of the western European universities, see Lucien Febvre and Henri-Jean Martin, *The Coming of the Book: The Impact of Printing, 1450–1800*, pp. 248–332.

(7) What are the anonymous encoders' subject positions? (8) How does this ubiquitous version of electric rhetoric compel discourse communities to occupy a particular subjectivity? (9) How does intertextuality operate in the text? These questions are central to our televisually immersed culture in which even highly educated citizens frequently are not even close to being televisually literate, much less televisually eloquent.

Both the computer-assisted writing class, which grows in number and develops and advances yearly (as a glance at the programs of the annual meetings of the Conference on College Composition and Communication attests), and the theorized writing classroom, which enacts and interprets various electronic technologies, are central to Next Rhetoric.

These classrooms and the cultural practices that they include and influence (including the familiar "libraries without walls," which describes the new computer access to many libraries in the world) enact the new Sophistic outlined in chapter 1, where I set up three strands: (1) the redeployment of Sophistic classical rhetoric (including recognizing and dismantling the hegemony of Aristotle in the twentieth-century twin formalisms of the current-traditional paradigm in writing pedagogy and theory and the New Criticism in literary pedagogy); (2) the broader establishment of literacy studies within rhetoric/composition studies so that historicized rhetoric and writing practices are more fully accounted for; and (3) the recognition that video is inherently rhetorical and written and possesses great power in the history of literacy, a power that remains ignored and reviled by the majority of humanists and understudied by posthumanists and literacy scholar/teachers.[33]

Electric Rhetoric and a Text of the NBC Nightly News

As we have seen with Aspasia, Diotima, Plato, and Isocrates, logos occurs in households as well as in other venues, households that, like other bodily spaces, are constructed differently in various historical situations. Our own end-of-the-millennium private spaces of the household are now changing rapidly because of communication technology. Human logos interaction with television has reconfigured the nature of private

33. See pp. 13–14.

space. Subjectivities are now undergoing rapid change. The proliferation of channels, household monitors, and public monitors has made the surplus of televisual texts into a Niagara Falls of rhetorical artifacts, written, graphic, and spoken. As Isocrates wrote in the central *Antidosis* passage, a skilled person can deliberate issues outwardly; a wise one can deliberate effectively within oneself. HUT dwellers (again, 98 percent of the U.S. population, cutting across lines of social class, genders, races, and ethnicities) tend to be awash in tidal waves of aural and visual signals, whether they intend them to be absorbed or not.

What has happened to the interior and exterior logos performances as a result of these tidal waves? In this section I will deploy and adapt selected rhetorical theories to a text of *The NBC Nightly News with Tom Brokaw*. I do so not only because electric rhetoric (like all rhetoric) is inherently political but also because television news shows now constitute the dominant source of political information and analysis for most U.S. citizens. HUT dwellers tend to interact more with their TVs for news than they do with their newspapers. The randomly selected text is from November 13, 1996.[34]

Rhetorical HUT analysis must begin with textualizing and then reducing the surplus of texts, particularly for those intellectuals and others who are printbound and so unconsciously resistant to mass-produced, highly repeatable graphics. One strategy for reduction resides in soundless screening analysis. The main rationale for soundless analysis lies in its conformity to the print bias common among (and required of) intellectuals and its enabling readings that are closer than those that include the ear. (I exclude intellectuals and music.) In addition, the spectator can experience the aesthetic beauty of the painterly images described by Raymond Williams above. I concentrate on soundless analysis rather than the aesthetic properties, while acknowledging that the aesthetic is deeply important.

Postmodernism and its hallmark symbol system, video, are characterized by a surplus of texts. The rapidly moving visual representations supply so many verbal and visual texts that they cannot readily be ana-

34. Broadcast from 5:30 p.m. to 6 p.m. Central Standard Time and videotaped in a HUT in Norman, Oklahoma, via Oklahoma City KFOR, Channel 4.

lyzed. To remove the sound portion of the texts provides one strategy to decrease text supply; this move leads to more effective analysis. In a section below, I analyze the sound portion without the visual representations, working toward the same goal of decreasing the surplus so as to expose the manipulations and the unintended effects.

This 1996 televisual text follows the genre of broadcast news with 21 minutes of news, 9 minutes of commercial advertising, and 20 commodities advertised. The visual *koinoi topoi*, a category of analysis elaborately developed in classical rhetoric, provide a strategic way of decoding this text.[35] These *koinoi topoi* appear to be automatic and natural, or even banal, and so first need to be defamiliarized.

Four visual *koinoi topoi* are of particular relevance in the electric rhetoric of news made soundless: (1) editing, (2) mise-en-scène, (3) the presentation of faux computers, and (4) talking heads. Many other visual *koinoi topoi* could and should be deployed as well; I present four here.

The editing of the text, or the switch (frequently a cut) from one image to another is a *koinos topos* so familiar that it tends to reside firmly in the land of *physis*, the Sophistic division where the natural, obvious, and divinely given resides without undue notice. In addition, editing forms a major aspect of the third canon of rhetoric, style. The first five minutes of the text has 46 edits. The frequent editing accounts for much of the surplus of text. Even as Brokaw supplies a narrative line for the 30 minutes (including the carefully led-into and led-out-of commercials), the speed of the editing helps to supply a surplus of material that frequently buries the narrative line, although that line reappears orally/aurally in the Brokaw-read narrative.

Sight Bites and *Koinoi Topoi*

The surplus becomes sight bites that are highlighted by soundless analysis. The sight bites are fragmentary; they are visual shards that lead nowhere except to the visual similarity of the commercials. They have the psychological effect (via the fourth canon of rhetoric, memory) of reduc-

---

35. See Chapter Four, where I elaborate on the *koinoi topoi*, the common topics, and the *eide*, the special topics, as they relate to electric rhetoric.

ing the ability of any decoder in any discourse community to absorb and assess what is going on. Look, for example, at the first full minute of narration read out loud from written documents (scripts). Minute one:

Another suspected spy in the CIA said to be working for the Russians—and this was no low-level clerk. The final terrifying moments inside the ValuJet cabin, fire and panic, then a steep deadly dive into the Everglades. And the fleecing of America—tonight the government as banker for the Indian tribes, but billions may be missing.

[*Voiceover male narration*]   From NBC News world headquarters in New York, this is NBC Nightly News with Tom Brokaw.

[*Return to Brokaw reading aloud*]   Good evening. The cold war may be over but tonight the FBI says the spy business is alive and well in this country, and the latest suspect once again comes from within the heart of the American intelligence community, the CIA. He was a former station chief up for a major post overseas. More now from NBC's Andrea Mitchell.

[*Mitchell voiceover*]   The suspected CIA mole was whisked into court today charged with spying for Russia for at least two years, possibly longer. [Conclusion of one minute from visual/verbal lead-in.] Harold James Nicholson, a sixteen-year veteran on the fast track at the spy agency.

[*Caption: John Deutch, CIA Director*] [*Spoken by Deutch*]   He [Nicholson] revealed a significant amount of classified information which we are still analyzing.

[*Return to Mitchell voiceover*]   Sensing trouble, the CIA transferred Nicholson last July to the agency's counterterrorism center to keep a close eye on him. It was there, prosecutors say, only six days ago that Nicholson photographed sensitive documents under his desk. A hidden camera caught him in the act. The FBI also found classified documents in his home. And in a twist worthy of Hollywood, in mailboxes near the CIA they intercepted two postcards allegedly from Nicholson to his Russian handlers. [One minute from Brokaw's postintroductory reading.][36]

The second visual *koinos topos* mise-en-scène can be understood by the study of one freeze frame; in this case, the frame is replete with information, even without the sound. An anchorperson occupies a position that differs from earlier anchor locations; a multiplicity of screens appears; and combinations of vivid colors, mostly from monitors on the set (television within television), characterize the frame. The visual ethos of the serious, credible, earnest, attractive White male anchor contrasts strongly with this plethora of machinery. From another point of view, Brokaw simply joins the machine as another talking head. So much visually takes

---

36. Lead-in read aloud by Tom Brokaw.

place that the spectator—depending always, of course, on her or his discourse community and subjectivity while watching—must ignore part of this material. The habit of familiarization operates strongly here as well.

An analysis of this mise-en-scène reveals an illusion of no borders. Using Neal Burch's idea that the spectator can read what is above the screen, below the screen, on the two sides of the screen, in back of the screen, and in front of the screen, we can see that this visual *koinos topos* is intended to serve several functions. A representation of a television studio works here, and five sides of the freeze frame include the work space of the studio (above, the two sides, and behind). The established space of the traditional news anchor as a seated talking head with a single graphic in the background is gone.[37] The visual dynamics supplied by actual digital graphics (as opposed to the faux digital graphics, discussed below) have downsized the anchor. Consequently, the rhetoric of the show has changed significantly because the space viewed in the monitor contains more nonhuman representation than human representation.

The third (still soundless) visual *koinos topos* is the presentation of faux computers, by which I mean computers that do not compute, that have no function other than to decorate and entice and reinforce the ethos of the show. Computers are represented as decorative objects, more like paintings on the wall than functional computers. The wall computers in this frame resemble nothing so much as Coca-Cola and Pepsi soft-drink dispensing machines that glow and entice with their exceptional color and design. Both the soft-drink machine and the *NBC Nightly News* set are beautiful, carefully crafted *objets d'art*.[38] The interactivity of the digital *logos* user, who can sophisticately perform through, for ex-

37. This space dominated by the seated White male talking head characterized broadcast news until fairly recently. Its residue appears on the *Saturday Night Live* "Weekend News Update," which relies on a seated White male talking head with a graphic in the background.

38. On CNN and HNN news shows, two other apparently faux computers are used as decoration and ethos reinforcement: (1) A laptop computer near the anchor is never used by the anchor but is there as additional set decoration, as a prop. (2) A computer menu fills the screen and one item among many is "selected." Of course, there is no selection possible by the spectator in this traditional televisual configuration with coaxial cable, broadcast waves, or satellite waves.

ample, electronic mail and the Internet and who, through hypertext, can construct new text by putting together material from the faraway sources of libraries without walls as well as other sites, remains utterly absent and voiceless from this text of *The NBC Nightly News with Tom Brokaw*. Instead, the *Nightly News* encoders have painted a picture, a representation of a computer on a noninteractive television.[39] The only interactivity lies in zapping, turning the sound higher or lower, and turning the monitor on and off. On these nonvirtual and unworkable "menus," the encoders display pointing but provide no clicking sound and certainly no hourglass icon (because too much money is involved). Strikingly, the indispensable real work of computers and the production of the news is made invisible. Just as this televisual text, like all televisual texts, depends for its very existence on print and alphabetic literacy (for example, in the second-by-second scripting of the thirty minutes), so the show totally relies on alphabetic and numeric literacy provided by computers in word processing, generation and presentation of graphics, communication on the set and beyond, computers on satellites that provide instantaneous visuals, and so on. But these computers that do real work are hidden from view. The computers in view, the faux computers, decorate the screen, boosting the ethos of the entire show.

The fourth soundless *koinos topos* is the peripatetic Brokaw. While the very metaphor "anchor" suggests a stationary quality, a hard-to-move weightiness, the anchor of this show has a body that is more visible because he is precisely scripted (he follows written directions) to walk around the set in various ways. Once again, this is material for textual analysis, as a critical spectator has to analyze the forms of persuasion that are taking place.

As the peripatetic Brokaw, a now oxymoronic anchor, an anchor who is not stationary—walks around the Manhattan studio, he resembles the Sophists, most of whom also walked from teaching location to teaching

39. Other broadcast and cable television news shows place laptop computers at the sides of the talking-head news anchor. See, for example, CNN's *Headline News*. These material computers appear never to be used and so become a prop that improves the show's ethos, the general idea of its character. The display of a laptop as nearly an extension of the anchor's body and as a prop lends gravitas to the show.

location and who, before Isocrates, the zenith of classical Greek male Sophism, got into a lot of trouble for their movement. The traveling of the Sophists was thought to decrease their authority, to devalue their *ethe*. The peripatetic Brokaw resembles Sophists such as Protagoras and Gorgias in other ways: he is very close to power (remember Protagoras's great friendship with Pericles), he makes a lot of money, and he is charismatic. However, Brokaw is in addition the target of much criticism, also similar to that leveled against Protagoras and Gorgias: Brokaw is regarded as untrustworthy insofar as he is perceived to be part of the same social stratum that high-ranking politicians occupy and his ethos is fused with the general complaints about television and its deficiences. He is regarded as untrustworthy insofar as representations of him are emitted from a medium that so many citizens regard as deeply suspect, as suspect as any of the older Sophists, including Diotima, Socrates' teacher, who has only recently been elevated to the rank of Sophist. More than any other Sophistic feature, the *NBC Nightly News with Tom Brokaw* functions as the drug that Gorgias describes in the epigraph of chapter 4; *logos* is so very much like a drug that it can bewitch the bewitchable, heal the sick, and sicken the well. The narcotizing of the United States by the *logos* drug of television news remains a central rhetorical, political issue that has barely been examined, as intellectuals run from the drug and back to their books and computers. Think for a moment of a now ubiquitous facial appearance: the televisual trance. Watch the watchers of television and see the druglike state, the zoned-out features, that characterize so much (but not all) of spectator response to television. This rhetorically induced trance is now a central aspect of U.S. communication. Like Gorgias's *logos*, it is a drug. Is it healing or is it sickening? Watch the watchers to see how Sophism continues to operate in electric rhetoric.

In addition to these four soundless televisual *koinoi topoi*, there are the nine features of electric rhetoric that I outlined above and offered as starting places for the more critical scrutiny of video that should be taught in our schools as regularly as mathematics and the sciences and the humanities/posthumanities/literacies.

Before the analysis of the nine orally dominant features, it is necessary to describe the material presented in the selected television text. The narrative line of the November 18, 1996, text of *The NBC Nightly News with Tom Brokaw* unfolds in 7 news stories in 22 minutes and around 20 commercials. While many spectators distinguish between these two televisual genres (which dominate television in the United States but not necessarily in other similar democracies), electric rhetoric compels us to regard the entire 30-mintute slot as a single entity. The narrative sequence of 16 units is as follows: (1) opening crane shot to a stationary Brokaw (long shot to medium shot); (2) segue to the voiceover reading (by reporter Andrea Mitchell) of a narrative of a CIA spy (a mole), Harold James Nicholson, concluding with a head-and-shoulders shot of Mitchell placed in front of an anonymous public Washington, D.C., building; (3) segue to Army sexual-harassment/rape allegations; (4) segue to four commercials (for Royal Caribbean cruises, a Moen faucet, J. C. Penney's Dockers trousers for men, and Immodium AD antidiarrheal medication); (5) segue to a story about a ValuJet-flight-recorder transcript; (6) segue to Richard Nixon tape story; (7) lead-in to "Who Cares?" a narrative about Thomas Cannon;[40] (8) segue to four commercials (Toshiba desktop computer, Total cereal, Primatene Mist asthma medication, and Green Giant Pasta Primavera); (9) segue to a resumption of "Who Cares?" narrative; (10) segue to six commercials (Schwab mutual funds, Mailboxes Etc., Aleve pain reliever, Panasonic men's razor, Grand Prix Pontiac automobile, and a promotion for the news by the local NBC affiliate);[41] (11) segue to Teen Tragedy, alleged infanticide in New Jersey; (12) segue to Alger Hiss addendum (correction) to a narrative presented during the previous week; (13) segue to six commercials (Merrill Lynch reitrement planning, Caltrate Plus calcium supplement, Braun Oral B plaque remover, J. C. Penney's Dockers trousers for men, Eldorado Cadillac automobile, and a promotion for *NBC Dateline*); (14) segue to the fleecing of America (federal Bureau of Indian

40. This "in-depth" narrative, a subgenre whose existence is emphasized by *NBC Nightly News* via repetition, establishes the story of Thomas Cannon, a citizen, moves to commercials, returns with the editor of *Forbes* magazine and a story on Marta Drury, who provides scholarships for young women of color, and a short interview with Martha Lopez, whose family members labor as agricultural workers and are compelled to move frequently to follow crop growth.

41. Owned by The New York Times Company.

Affairs mishandling of Blackfeet Tribal funds); (15) segue to closure and helicopter shot of Rockefeller Center with GE (General Electric, the owner of NBC News) display; and (16) segue to NBC News website address and copyright claim.

All 7 narrative strands (news stories) and 20 commercials conform to the Oral Formulaic Theory discussed in chapter 2. In addition, the news stories and the commercials are characterized by the features of the Classic Hollywood Cinema (CHC), a standard film term for the glossy, beautiful, absorbing, highly controlled, escape-producing films that developed in the 1930s and that continue to dominate much of U.S. cultural exports and domestic ideology.[42] Examples of CHC include Busby Berkeley musicals, John Ford westerns, and texts made recognizable by a Hollywood studio.[43] The CHC features of glossiness, beauty, and escape via high production values drive every minute of this text of *The NBC Nightly News with Tom Brokaw* and account for much of the ritualistic pleasure felt by so many spectators.

Let us now return to the nine Ongian features of oral dominance as they were introduced in chapter 2 and set up above in this chapter (being additive, aggregative, redundant, conservative, close to the human life-world, agonistic, empathetic and not distanced, homeostatic, and situational rather than abstract).

The first feature is the additive nature of the November 13, 1996, text of the *NBC Nightly News with Tom Brokaw*. The entire 30-minute text

42. Film and video are discrete symbol systems, each characterized by its own grammar, syntax, ideologies, conditions of production and reception, and so on. Just as symbol systems overlap and cross boundaries (for example, performance art by Meredith Monk or Laurie Anderson in which dance, video, electronics, photography, and other symbol systems are put together to create a collage text), so film and television share some characteristics, such as CHC features. However, in the general public as well as in the academy, the two tend to be regarded as almost the same. They are not the same; they are radically different. A film screened on video loses as much material as a Cliff's Notes pamphlet loses in summarizing a book. The difference is that the video presentation loses massive quantities of visual material.

43. See Thomas Schatz, *The Genius of the System: Hollywood Filmmaking in the Studio Era*, for an analysis of the auteur theory as it applies to Hollywood films.

consists of additions rather than subordination, a condition that compels an absence of depth. The addition strongly resembles the *Odyssey*, which consists of a series of events strung together (without the depth, for example, of the much later epic the *Aeneid*, where the title character develops and is presented with decidedly unheroic psychological problems that help to drive the narrative). Another additive feature lies in the fact that a television station can stay on the air for 16 hours, 20 hours, or 24 hours a day; it need only add material, usually material that has been previously transmitted.

The second oral/aural feature is that events are aggregative rather than analytic. Epithets are applied to many people and entities; while maintaining the guise of journalistic neutrality, the text uses verbal and visual epithets to a remarkable degree.

The third oral feature, the redundant capacity of television, is a relatively new thing in the world. Televised texts can be screened endlessly. The phenomena of the sound bite and the sight bite depend for their existence on the repeatability provided by the technology of videotape, video cassette recorders, and television sets, as well as on the manipulation of electromagnetic waves with antennae and satellites and coaxial cable. In fact, its essence can be said to lie in its repetition. Televised advertising, obviously, depends on repetition for part of its persuasive power. Redundancy significantly occurs in announcing the same story repeatedly, so as to maintain viewers and decrease zapping. Consequently, the "Who Cares?" human-interest story was introduced three times to persuade spectators to stay with the network.

The fourth oral feature is the traditionalist/conservative one, and it defines the show. It replicates the status quo and reinforces the power of the corporation that owns the news, in this case General Electric. This ownership arrangement leads, of course, to self-censorship by NBC News and to multiple conflicts of interest. One goal of the news organization is partly, like that of other bureaucracies, self-preservation. Another goal is the desire/need for profits. Being strongly conservative goes hand in hand with being literally owned by a multinational corporation whose raison d'etre is to earn profits for executives and shareholders, not to present news.

A Digression on the Second Rhetorical Canon: Structure

If we turn for a moment to the second canon of classical and subsequent rhetorics, arrangement (*taxis* in Greek, *dispositio* in Latin) or structure, we can understand more fully the nature of some spectators' responses to the televisual borrowing of the features of the Classic Hollywood Cinema (for some discourse communities). Almost all spectators—one imagines most of the citizenry—have now been conditioned by 60 years of filmic beauty and allure in movies such as *Double Indemnity* (to cite a classic film noir shot in black and white) and *Carefree* (to cite a classic Hollywood musical with Ginger Rogers and Fred Astaire) to respond deeply to CHC features. Predictability, repetition, narrative resolution, expensive sets, cameras, cranes, dollies, and, crucially, editing computers all contribute to the second canon of rhetoric as it is performed on *The NBC Nightly News with Tom Brokaw*.

Kenneth Burke offers us a strategy for further understanding the electric rhetoric of the selected text of *The NBC Nightly News with Tom Brokaw*. In his first book, *Counter-Statement*, he defines "form" (a synonym for the second canon of arrangement) as the instilling of desire and the fulfilling of desire. In discussing psychology and form in the chapter of that name, he writes,

The psychology here [*Hamlet* I, 4] is not the psychology of the *hero*, but the psychology of the *audience*. And by that distinction, form would be the psychology of the audience. Or, seen from another angle, form is the creation of *an appetite* in the mind of the auditor, and the adequate satisfying of that appetite. This satisfaction—so complicated is the human mechanism—at times involves a temporary set of frustrations, but in the end these frustrations prove to be simply a more involved kind of satisfaction, and furthermore serve to make the satisfaction of fulfillment more intense. (P. 31)

Most HUT spectators (again, 98 percent of U.S. houses are HUTs) have been conditioned to respond strongly and positively to the visual features of Classic Hollywood Cinema. The glossiness of the evening news show, including the commercials, now resonates with filmgoing spectatorship. And as the network news organizations reconstruct their long competition in light of the encroachment of cable and satellite news organizations, the glossiness, the high production values of their shows, increase accordingly.

Continuation of Televisual Oral Features

The fifth oral characteristic, closeness to the human lifeworld, also applies to the text because small narratives are constructed around human-interest stories. In each of the news segments, individuals' stories are told; that is, the larger issue—the CIA mole, Army sexual harassment, and so on—is attached to a person. The mole is a man televisually presented as a bad person (through lighting and extreme closeups, for example); the sexual-harassment case is a group of Army recruits who are presented as being deeply flawed. The close-to-the-human-lifeworld characteristic becomes even stronger when the "Who Cares?" episode occurs. Particular people—Thomas Cannon, Marta Drury, Paul Newman, and Martha Lopez—are highlighted in treacly tone. Television news here appears to be working hard to be close to the human lifeworld and, one supposes, the human lifeworlds of the spectators, who are seen, of course, as consumers of goods and services so that profits can be made.

The sixth oral/aural characteristic, being agonistically toned, is perhaps the least evident in this text of the *NBC Nightly News with Tom Brokaw*. Nonetheless, it is there: the CIA's story versus the mole's story, Richard Nixon's hand-from-the-grave manipulation of his secret documents versus the public's right to have access to them, and so on.

Traditional journalism relies on the standard Western practice of two-sided debate, a practice that historically reaches all the way back to Protagoras. Consequently, news stories continue a tradition of reporting two sides, as opposed to, say, ten sides. Television news derives from print news in this respect.

Yet the apparent agonism in the *Nightly News* is tepid, particularly when one compares it to the agonism of a print-news source such as the *New York Times*, where investigative journalism flourishes on many fronts. In fact, the *NBC Nightly News* is so calm, is so unchallenging, so promotes the status quo (again, recall that the owner is General Electric and that television functions as a drug in Gorgias's sense) that real critique, critique of the kind that a representative democracy requires, is virtually absent. Very short narratives are presented, narrated, and resolved, frequently with a small facial gesture by the peripatetic anchor.

The increasingly frequent human-interest stories, exemplified in this text by the "Who Cares?" narrative, do not adhere to journalistic traditions of investigating two sides; instead, the "Who Cares?" report presents a story of a good African-American man, a story with which no one can disagree but whose saccharine sweetness condescends to the person covered and to many spectators.

The subgenre of the news fits well with the seventh characteristic of the oral/aural, being empathetic and participatory rather than objectively distanced. Subtextual pleas for empathy characterize both hard news and human-interest stories. This pathos, or appeal to emotion, one of the *entechnic pisteis*, results in a 30-minute text that is treacly in tone.

The eighth characteristic, homeostasis, fits well with the post-Fordist move to maintain equilibrium.

The ninth characteristic, situationalism rather than abstraction, is emphasized by the inherent characteristics of television. The pictures are of definite situations (in this case, for example, the CIA mole, the New Jersey infanticide, the Nixon tapes). Abstraction occurs mostly in the pathos of the often repeated treacly tone.

Moving beyond these nine oral characteristics, we can see that they are transcended by the subtle reinforcement of cultural, rhetorical situations. One of the most important of these is the presentation of race.

Televising Racial *Koinoi Topoi*

The appearance of African-American citizens in this televisual text tells a strong story itself. A total of 6 African-American citizens are represented in this text, 3 in news stories (1 hard news, the other 2 in the human-interest story) and 3 in the commercials. The African-Americans in the new stories are anonymous African-American drill sergeants, Thomas Cannon, and anonymous citizens in background shots of "bad" neighborhoods during voiceovers of the "Who Cares" segment. The African Americans in the commercials are in those for Immodium AD, Schwab, and Aleve. The commercial appearances are all secondary.

In this randomly selected text, 2 African-American men are presented in familiar ways. The first appearance occurs in the second hard news narrative, the Army sexual-harassment/rape allegations. To illustrate the story, the visual provided is that of an African-American male drill instructor standing over and yelling at (in Army-boot-camp style), a White woman recruit. The narration of rape that constitutes the aural portion serves to align the African-American male with the U.S. mythos/lie that Black men tend to commit rape more than men in other groups. In its merger of the visual and the aural (that is, the reading out loud of a script written by someone other than the reporter) the story serves strongly to reinforce half-held beliefs or murky ideas about the essence of African-American men. In the two shots of the drill instructor menacingly standing over the prone woman recruit (prone because she is performing pushups), a connection with this central U.S. mythos is made once again. The telling of the mythos is not overt; it is visual and aural; it is brief. It fits many of the nine oral characteristics in that it reinforces a strongly and widely held cultural belief. Fear of African-American males and their putative sexual behavior is thus reinforced for viewers, who may be only dimly aware of the ideological move that is here made. The visual *koinos topos* requires no explication; its redundance, its repetition, tells the tale, a tale that lies so strongly about the behavior of African-American males. It is a tale told and reinforced without words. It is a drug.

The second appearance of an African-American male in this televisual text forms the center of the human-interest story, Thomas Cannon in the "Who Cares?" segment. The immediate, almost full shot (head to knees in profile) of Thomas Cannon, represented holding a rake and sweeping leaves at a residence, overwhelms the verbal narrative read from a script written by a semianonymous person or persons. Just as the representation of the African-American male drill sergeant appears to graphically represent a menacing sexual aggressor, so the familiar image of an African American citizen performing menial labor represents a crucial racist stereotype. Even though Cannon is actually just taking care of his own property, the action of raking has no overt connection to the segment. Rather, it appears to exist as a reinforcement of engrained stereotypes of what African-American males do and how they function in the United States. Much of the history of U.S. television and film represents African-Americans who perform menial tasks as they laugh and sing. This text of the *NBC Nightly News with Tom Brokaw* thus reinforces two powerful, damaging cultural stereotypes, strong ideologies whose repetition through the forms of electric rhetoric lead to the continuing oppression of African-Americans. The fact that this electronic repetition occurs in a randomly selected text is, in fact, chilling. It appears to reveal the unconscious racist biases of the multiple authors of the text: the camerapersons, producers, directors, script writers, research writers, and others. It is not overt, but it is easy to expose when one analyzes supposedly objective news with electric rhetoric and the historical antecedents that partly compose it. The condescension of the second story quantitatively rivals the fear engendered in the first story.[44]

From one rhetorical stance, we can see that the conservative, traditionalist, homeostatic, additive, and repetitive characteristics of oralism all occur strongly in this text. These characteristics of one text of a long-running broadcast television news show remain deeply conservative in the sense that they covertly reinforce the status quo. The same features occur in the two Homeric poems and in the *Origin Myth of Acoma*.

By going beyond these nine oral/aural features and analyzing the *koinoi topoi* of the presentation of Whiteness and Blackness, electric rhetoric reclaims the powerful aspects of some parts of classical rhetoric and redeploys them to unmask a virulent cultural stereotype that operates within the lives of nearly every African-American person and that remains invisible in the lives of most White Americans. The cultural reinforcement of racist ideology, a defining aspect of the United States from its inception, is therefore exposed.

According to three of the characteristics of oralism, the forms of electric rhetoric are like the forms of the *Odyssey* and the forms of the *Origin Myth of Acoma*. The texts from both technologies rely on formula, repetition, addition, and so on. More significant, perhaps, the ancient poems and the modern news show, because of these characteristics, appear to be simple, elementary, and not really sophisticated to print-bound Westerners. They seem to literate minds to be superficial. The depth that we get from, say, a novel such as George Eliot's *The Mill on the Floss* does not seem to be there. Texts constructed in primary orality

---

44. I taught this text in an advanced undergraduate course, Rhetoric/Orality/ Video, on November 14, 1996. After I pointed out this racist pattern embedded in the visual and aural rhetoric, the class responded with audible gasps. After being instructed in these rhetorical issues, they were immediately persuaded.

and oralism appear to be centered on big events.[45] In the *Odyssey*, the journey of Odysseus obviously orders the big events. On the journey occur such big events as the encounters of Circe, the Cyclops, the Sirens, and so on; the storyteller (recreater/performer/speaker) could remember the poem by stringing together the big events, as we saw in chapter 2. Similarly, big events order the *Origin Myth of Acoma*. The births of the first two human beings, who are sisters; their creation of the first animals; the human and female emergence from underground through the aid of Badger and Locust; and so on.[46] Similarly, on the *NBC Nightly News*, the 30-minute text is constructed in a similar way. Parallel big events provide the form: disasters, assassinations, hurricanes, floods, Mideast tensions, battles in ongoing wars, and so on. Woven into the narrative fabric of these big events are the commercials (which have changed radically in the last decade because of the formal demands of cable technology, the proliferation of channels, and the phenomenon of spectator zapping and the consequent shortening of time devoted to the airing of commercials). Homer (or the Homeric poets) provided contrast between the big events of the Cyclops, Circe, the Sirens, the Lotus Eaters, and other big figures by providing relief (the development of Telemachus without a father and with only his mother, Penelope's manipulation of the suitors, and so on). The lulls in the *Origin Myth of Acoma* occur in the quieting of movement (for example, the returns to the darkness of the underground) as the world is created. Similarly, the evening broadcast news provides lulls or breaks from the big events by giving us a beautiful, kinetic graphic of stock market movement (with accompanying music as sedative) or a fast weather map with the following day's high and low temperatures represented on a map of the continental United States, and so on. In other words, in the collaboratively spoken (and then written) *Odyssey*, in the collaboratively spoken (and then translated and written) *Origin Myth of Acoma*, and in the collaboratively written visual and verbal *NBC Nightly News with Tom Brokaw* text, the formula requires

45. Again, "oralism" and "literacy" do not refer, as is so commonly thought, to individual utterances or texts. Rather, they refer to *mentalités* or two kinds of consciousness within which articulators encode. See chapter 2.

46. See an excerpt of the *Origin Myth of Acoma*, translated into English, in the Appendix.

some contrast between the presentation of big events. Otherwise, readers/ spectators would be exhausted by the sameness of very important events. The Homeric text, the Acoma text, and the television text have an extraordinary amount of common material. They are repetitive, formulaic, and additive. In fact, television producers refer to "segments" in their ordinary discussions. Segments are easily added or subtracted according to various demands; they differ substantially from addition through depth, or staying with one story and digging deeply (a presentation that requires time).

Recall here the dramatic change that Isocrates brought about in his advancement of Greek prose (which, again, had to contend with the hegemony of poetry in the fourth-century-B.C.E. context). Isocrates wrote with strong subordinate clauses that qualify and provide illuminating detail and nuance; he also wrote with *kai* (and), stringing phrases together in a way that is closer to Homeric poetry.[47]

Electric Rhetoric and the Text of a Website That Merges Research and Teaching

Just as I have deployed the theories of electric rhetoric to interrogate the oralism of one 30-minute text of *The NBC Nightly News with Tom Brokaw*, so we can deploy them to analyze a particular website, which can, of course, be accessed in any physical location in the world if a computer with sufficient memory, a person with sufficient digital functional literacy, and suitable electricity are available. I have chosen the website *Histories of Feminist Rhetorics and Writing Practices* (http://rossby.ou.edu/~femrhets), a site constructed collaboratively for an experimental graduate English course in rhetoric and composition studies at Ohio State University, Pennsylvania State University, and the University of Oklahoma interactively taught by Andrea A. Lunsford, Cheryl

---

47. See George A. Kennedy, *Classical Rhetoric and Its Christian and Secular Tradition from Ancient to Modern Times*, pp. 35–36, for an analysis of an Isocratic sentence, an analysis that focuses on the Gorgianic figures and that also illustrates the subordination so well deployed by Isocrates, who, in his move away from poetry and its hegemony, wrote prose that was very additive and very subordinative.

Glenn, and me respectively.[48] The course, Histories of Feminist Rhetorics and Writing Practices, taught during the fall of 1997, announced four aims, all available on the referred website as well as on paper: (1) "to further a new paradigm of the scholar/teacher whose research and pedagogy merge"; (2) "to improve the profession of English with recent feminist theories of rhetoric and writing by providing a course model for other scholar/teachers to use or adapt"; (3) "to enact multiple technologies that increase student access to scholar/teachers and students at other universities"; and (4) "to integrate women's rhetoric and writing practices into traditional receptions of historical rhetoric, not only by reading women's work into this history but also by exploring how various constructions of gender, race, and technology have worked to make women and all people of color invisible within the tradition."[49] The website functioned as both a primary text and secondary text for each geographical location of the course.[50]

Like television and intersubjective life in rhetorical HUTs, computers and life in all the many locations of computers (including HUTs) have reconfigured private space in dramatic ways. Human *logos* interaction, of the kind explored in regendered, reraced classical rhetoric (that is, Isocratic/Diotimic rhetoric) has changed the nature of intersubjectivity.

48. Devised at a series of meetings of the former presidents of the Coalition of Women Scholars in the History of Rhetoric and Composition, a feminist scholarly/political organization begun in Chicago in 1990 at the annual meeting of the Conference on College Composition and Communication.

49. Welch, Glenn, and Lunsford, *Histories of Feminist Rhetorics and Writing Practices*, 20 February 1998. Available online at http://rossby.ou.edu/ ~ femrhets/.

50. The professors and students at each site reported very different uses of the website, which underwent construction during and after the course. For example, at the Pennsylvania State University site, the website acted as a series of verbal/ visual texts used to initiate discussion in Cheryl Glenn's office; at the Ohio State University site, the website provoked some resistance that productively led to a highly innovative contribution named "quilting"; at the University of Oklahoma site, the website provided unusually high amounts of rhetorical invention and a site for learning technology, what to do with it, and how it can function negatively. As to the last, when the website was transmitted in a traditional classroom (wired and with a video monitor) from a Toshiba laptop to a Sony video monitor (which thus produced very beautiful graphics), the class stayed with the dialectic of class discussion and refrained from falling into the televisual gaze often produced by the presence of video screens.

The relationship between humans and our relatively new computing machines has changed intersubjectivity.[51]

The surplus of digital texts, a characteristic of postmodernism, is, at this technological moment, even greater than the televisual surplus. If television offers a Niagara Falls of rhetorical artifacts, both graphic and spoken (and both based on writing), then the digital world offers an Atlantic Ocean of rhetorical artifacts and performances, also written, graphic, and spoken. As explored in an earlier chapter, the demographics of television users and computer users are very different. The saturation of television in United States houses is complete, with 98 percent of householders owning one or more televisions, and so television interaction crosses lines of class, gender, race, ethnicity, and so on. In a starkly different rhetorical situation, only 46 percent of households have computers. These households are strongly differentiated by social class. Current household owners of computers tend to be more highly educated and more affluent across race and ethnic lines. Their users also tend to be male. A gender distinction exists in computer use: a number of studies indicate that the most frequent computer users are men and boys.[52]

As we asked in the case of television, so we must ask in the case of the computer: What has happened and what might happen to exterior/interior *logos* performances (merged in the Vygotskyan sense explored in chapter 2) as a result of this mighty surplus of computer texts? In addition, what happens to Sophistic *logos* performance with the much greater interactivity offered by the computer in contrast to that historically and currently offered by television?

The oralism of electric rhetoric (retheorized as in previous chapters) offers us ways to perform Sophistically with computers. As was argued in Part I, this *logos* performance includes interpretation but goes well beyond that to activity. Just as there are televisual *koinoi topoi*, so there are digital *koinoi topoi*. Performance of the retheorized, regendered, reraced common topics of the computer offers highly useful ways of furthering not only our understanding of the intersubjectivity of literacy in an electronic age but of merging encoding and decoding.

51. See Sherry Turkle, *Life on the Screen*, passim.

52. Some studies indicate a 75 versus 25 percent difference between the sexes. Others indicate a 70 versus to 30 percent difference.

I will offer here four possibilities, all based on reducing the surplus of text, as I did with the televisual common topics in chapters 4 and 5. Again, as in those previous chapters, the *topoi* do not refer to a form or to a content, that hallmark binary of the current-traditional paradigm in composition/rhetoric. As in my textual analysis of the *NBC Nightly News with Tom Brokaw*, I offer only a few illustrative cases of the new common topics of electric rhetoric. Dozens more need to be generated to achieve adequate understanding of television and our lives in HUTs and in digitally literate households. Here are four possible common topics for our new intersubjective computer literacies as applied to the website for the experimental course Histories of Feminist Rhetorics and Writing Practices: surfing, screening racial *koinoi topoi*, the *koinos topos* of the sight bite, and the narcotizing effect of words and images in computer-screen interactivity.[53]

Surfing as a *Koinos Topos*

A defining *koinos topos* of the World Wide Web is the construction of lines of inquiry or circles of inquiry by the computer encoder/decoder. While television spectatorship is partly determined by the *koinos topos* of the sight bite, computer activity is determined by other *koinoi topoi*, of which surfing is a primary feature. Accessing bites is less controlled by large corporations. In U.S. television culture access is much more controlled by large corporations. The computer user can remain on an image until her battery runs out or his time disappears. Digital gazing, like televisual gazing, is much more in control of the computer user, but the computer retains some of the addictive properties of television (many anecdotal reports exist of computer users who resist logging off or cannot log off). Nevertheless, striking similarities exist, and I will examine one here: the breathtaking beauty of many computer graphics. Raymond Williams wrote in the quotation toward the beginning of this chapter of the beautiful aesthetic properties of a silenced television set (and his

53. Again, although Aristotle did not invent the common or special topics, he did offer his typical, highly organized listing of them for his particular imperialist, misogynist, elitist Greek culture. See Lauer, "Issues in Rhetorical Invention" and Ochs, "Cicero's *Topica*."

frustration that the only people who would listen to him were painters). Similarly, many digital images are aesthetically fabulous, breathtakingly beautiful, and provide the computer spectator with the opportunity to stare, to inquire, to languish, to glow, over the beauty of a digital image. The three-dimensionality of the Femrhets home page, for example, in which icons twirl and glisten, can provide hours of digital pleasure and learning for the digital gazer. The sheer gorgeousness can be captivating.[54]

Racial *Koinoi Topoi* and the Femrhets Website

The Website Histories of Feminist Rhetorics and Writing Practices self-consciously set out to interrogate standard constructions of race as it appears in the so-called tradition of rhetoric and/or the history of rhetoric, which tend, as we have seen, to assume Whiteness and Maleness in the standard ways that those two features are represented and that continue to hold power over us even as challenges to it continue unabated. Realizing that the many constructions of race and ethnicity could lead to a lack of depth, the three professors of the course chose to focus on Blackness and Whiteness of women rhetors/writers. The three sections of the course were: (1) "Women and Writing in Classical Rhetoric: Situating Ourselves and Situating Our Histories," (2) "Unsettling the Nineteenth Century: African American and White Women Rhetors/Writers in Nineteenth-Century America," and (3) "Contemporary Women's Rhetorics/Writings: The Electronic Present." African-American and White American issues were dominant in pods 2 and 3.[55] The rhetorical force of the pod 2 rhetors and/or writers, particularly Sojourner Truth and Ida B. Wells, took over the rest of the course, informing all subsequent listserve discussions and class discussions at the three sites. In particular, the reader pain inevitably produced by Ida B. Wells's *Southern Horrors and Other Writers* conditioned all the reading and writing for the course, including our retrospective writings/discussions of Sappho, Aspasia, and Diotima. Wells's rhetorical crusade against the nomos (the Jim Crow law) of the habitual and unpunished lynching of African-American men

54. The URL of the Femrhets website is http://rossby.ou.edu/ ~ femrhets/.

55. The term "pod" derives from *Invasion of the Body Snatchers*, a novel by Jack Finney and two films directed by Don Siegel and Philip Kaufman.

had civic success because the number of lynchings decreased (but, of course, did not disappear). In addition, Wells's writing provided and provides a powerful exemplar of courage.

The Whiteness of the three professors and many of the students signaled difficulties. The definitive presence of African-American women rhetors/writers tended to be undermined by the absence of African-American women class participants. (This situation, of course, has characterized English studies in its entire 100-year existence). Not all the students were WASPs, however. As a number of students chose to indicate on the website, the class was composed of students now characterized as Others: a Philipina student, a Chinese student, and a White Latina student.[56]

The *Koinos Topos* of the Sight Bite

The text of the Femrhets website produces sight bites that differ substantially from those of the selected text of *The NBC Nightly News with Tom Brokaw*. The difference lies mostly in the greater degree of interactivity available in computing than in television; with the computer, the encoder/decoder currently has more power. This is so because the computer promotes activity; television almost demands passivity, unless one applies the technology of the videotape and remote control to achieve a repeated televisual text that can then be endlessly analyzed with more activity performed by the decoder. In contrast, a surfer can go to the Femrhets home page (a strongly resonant metaphor, of course, particularly in view of the preceding analyses of rhetorical HUTs) and reflect on

---

56. The continuing overwhelming Whiteness (especially WASPness) of English departments continues to damage all the work we do in literacy studies. We have failed so far to persuade sufficient numbers of African-Americans to study English. Who, we might ask, would want to, when premodern Whiteness constructions tend not to be seen as constructed (see, for example, Paul Gilroy, *The Black Atlantic*)? It is also useful to remember here the Toni Morrison quotation in chapter 4: the word "American" signifies "White." Frequently African-American and Native American scholars are asked to teach what are still essentially White American literature courses; when they attempt de-whitify the courses, some students have been known to respond with great anger. See *Understanding Others: Cultural and Cross-Cultural Studies and the Teaching of English*, edited by Joseph Trimmer and Tilliy Warnock.

the movement of the icons that lead the way to more materials within each of their categories: the icon for "Bibliography of Texts" represents, in a rectangle typical of many icons now, an open codex book with a quill pen moving from left to right down the page and back again. The image merges a number of episodes in the history of communication technology (a codex book that is carefully bound by machine would not have had its print provided by a quill pen), and so is a new thing, as Sherry Turkle describes much of digital presentation. Nevertheless, its very newness at the same time appears to be so technologically old (the representation is a quill pen with ink); and this suggests worlds of readerly possibility; it represents part of the history of writing technology.

Most striking of all, the icon's representation of the codex book with the handless pen (there is no representation of a hand, which must, of course, hold and move the pen) is nonreferential. It constitutes a representation of writing that cannot exist except as an image. It is kinetic, repeating the motion of the handless quill pen rewriting the already inscribed codex book. The aesthetically rewarding icon exists as a clickable gateway to the readings of the course. Print books do not have this kinesis, even if they are pop-up books or other three-dimensional books. By clicking and pointing, the decoder can go many places, backward and forward. Surfing, unlike most reading, is highly associative; in fact, I might go so far as to say that it is definitively associative.[57] The sight-bite example offered here displays that associativeness on a number of levels, as we have seen.

The *Koinos Topos* of the Narcotizing Effect of the Computer Screen

Just as we noted the televisual gaze, the trancelike state that numerous television and video spectators assume as they decode that kind of elec-

---

57. Obviously, much writing is highly associative, for example, many portions of Virginia Woolf's novels, such as *Mrs. Dalloway* and *To the Lighthouse*; James Joyce's *Ulysses*; and other stream-of-consciousness writers; Emerson in his major essays, such as "Circles"; much of the poetry of Allen Ginsberg, such as *Howl*; and most of Walt Whitman's poetry and most of Emily Dickinson's poetry. Sappho's poetry provides an ancient Western example of highly associative writing. For a hypertextual analysis of this, see http://sappho.car.ou.edu/akbolman/~project/html.

tronic screen, so we must identify and try to understand the computer gaze.

Many users of both television and computer screens report states such as passivity, the perceived inability to turn off the machine in question, and, quite important, the sense of addiction. The story of the number of hours that HUT dwellers have their sets on has been told here and elsewhere. But the story of computer "addiction" has not been adequately analyzed by social scientists and posthumanists/literacy-workers. A narcotizing effect comes over many computer users and may account for the transformational experience described by many former technophobes who end up staying on the connected screen and then cannot seem to get off.[58]

This condition is Gorgias' *logos* as drug, which provided the epigraph for chapter 4. The Sophistic *logos* performance required by computing is related to previous kinds of *pharmaka*. It is also profoundly different. The "on" and "off" states required by electricity accounts for part of this drug. And as Derrida points out in his own drug store ("Plato's Pharmacy"), like any drug, the computer screen can cure, heal, soothe, sicken, and kill. The computer screen is, then, one of the most powerful forms of *logos* ever devised.

The Nine Oral Features of the Computer Drug

The selected oral features delineated by Ong and read across the text of *The NBC Nightly News with Tom Brokaw* are also relevant, in very different ways, to the website Histories of Feminist Rhetorics and Writing Practices. The characteristics are the following:

Additive rather than subordinative
The website is both, as is Isocrates' prose and no doubt many other texts. But adding to the website is remarkably easy if one has enough machine memory and computer literacy. At this rather early, largely free stage, websites tend to be more additive than subordinative. They do not

58. This transformation from technophobia to seminarcotized screen love provides an important means of persuading luddite faculty members to engage the new digital technologies.

yet have the kind of depth that critically literate decoders enjoy and require. However, the surfer can provide depth by interacting in various deep ways.

Aggregative rather than analytic

Even though many people regard the computer as the most logical machine in the world, a website tends, as we saw above, to be highly associative. In our continuing Aristotelian world dominated by Aristotelian logic and the rigid categories of modernism, which retain their tenacious grips, such computer associativeness is regarded as suspect and nonrigorous. Alternatively, the continuing idea of the computer as an advanced calculator can scare away associative-dominant people.[59]

Redundant or copious

Both these characteristics abound on the Femrhets website. There is such a surplus of text on the site, with its many links (for example, to the parts of Perseus 1.0 that have been placed on the Internet), that a surfer can stay on the site for extended periods of time. By returning (clicking "Back," for example), the surfer finds not only redundance but relief at remembering where she is.

Conservative or traditionalist

The World Wide Web replicates, of course, much of the conservatism of the world; in some ways, the Web just extends it. But in other ways it profoundly undermines the status quo. Femrhets enacts one opposition to the status quo by challenging—with the copiousness offered by hypertext and its surplus of text opportunities—the traditional misogynist, racist construction of Western rhetoric.

Close to the human lifeworld

The selected website does appear at first glance not to be close to the human lifeworld. But in fact it is for those surfers who search, learn, and interact with the radical claims made on the site and for those who already possess a close relationship with the personal computer.

59. Turkle covers these styles extensively in *Life on the Screen*.

Agonistically toned

The intersubjective relationships described above focus on collaboration and mutual inquiry (including strong disagreements). Since the primary surfers of the Femrhets website, both female and male, agree on the reality of patriarchy, the sexism of traditional Western rhetoric, and the privileging of White males, agonism tended to occur in the clash of ideas. This occurred more strongly on the three-campus listserve, where students articulated many strong emotions in response to texts, for example, the sexism identified in *Wired*. The oralistic agonism that occurs on the Internet is perhaps best exemplified by the culture of flaming, or using insulting language in *argumentum ad feminam et hominem*.[60]

Empathetic and participatory rather than objectively distanced

Since the course was constructed according to a number of versions of feminism, we encouraged participation and collaboration, and in fact achieved it. In addition, the course at all three sites chose to interrogate the objective, which was viewed as a patriarchal construct to a large extent.

Homeostatic

The site was homeostatic in that it maintained dynamic equilibrium. It was not in that each class, the website contact, and the listserving frequently led to unpredicted consequences, almost all of them positive.

Situational rather than abstract

New forms of abstraction took place, not the traditional patriarchal, objective, distanced kind. Instead, the telling of stories, the quilting contribution from the Ohio State University site, for example, enabled us to explore and advance alternative ideas of abstraction, ideas that are similar to the abstraction of some Native North Americans.[61]

60. An example of flaming was the exchange in response to a listserve mailing of Martin Bernal's and Mary Lefkowitz's strongly different positions on Blackness in the ancient world. While Bernal and Lefkowitz did not flame, their respondents filled many hard drives with race-based flaming.

61. See Womack, "A Creek National Literature."

Abstraction and the Status Quo

As we saw in chapter 2, one of the most serious criticisms lodged against Ong has been his privileging of abstraction, illustrated by his ninth suggested oral characteristic. In these critical moves, he is linked with other researchers, especially Jack Goody and David Olson and Eric Havelock, all in different configurations as interpreted by various scholars. As we saw, however, these interpretations are based on a false binary opposition between the terms "orality" and "literacy" (reinforced by Ong himself in one of his book titles). As we also saw, Ong can be linked to Roger Chartier and reinterpreted in ways that displace the binary. In our end-of-the-millennium culture, and for at least two hundred years, the abstract has signified the superior, the learned, the advanced. Consequently, to declare a group to be not abstract is to demean it. For example, to declare that the Acoma band of Pueblo Native Americans are not abstract in the *Origin Myth of Acoma* is to declare them, in Western cultures, to be inferior. Goody, as we have seen, has proven especially resistant to charges of primitivism, a cultural stance of which he approves. Many kinds of abstraction exist, and Native American cultures participate in this complex mental process in ways that are just as or more sophisticated than the familiar Western ways of abstracting.[62]

In chapter 2, I moved away from this familiar false binary distinction of "orality" and "literacy" to discuss a third category, oralism, or the intersubjective activities of minds performing within a specific dominant culture. With this Sophistic performance, intertwined with Vygotsky in chapter 3 so as to establish the inherently social, interactive aspect of language/mind/articulation, we can enact the new paradigm of electric rhetoric, which includes the performance, and therefore the understanding, of literacy as it depends on *logos* in the pre-Aristotelian, Isocratic/Diotimic sense. Isocrates' Sophistic contribution, while essential, remains inadequate unless his misogyny and bigotry are addressed.

62. The issue of Western alphabetic (that is, formalistic) abstraction has been dealt with in numerous disciplines. It has not been adequately studied in the cultures of Native North Americans and other groups that have been colonized by colonialist and postcolonialist Westerners.

Oralism as a constitutive part of literacy demands to be heard. Oralism saturates our electrified communication culture and subcultures in a dizzying number of ways. We have entered Next Rhetoric almost without realizing it. It is time that we began the institutionalized training of citizen students in a rehistoricized (including regendered and reraced) rhetoric.

The book is dead. Long live the book. The five hundred years of print/book dominance now draws slowly to a close. From Gutenberg in the fifteenth century to Nicholas Tesla in the twentieth, the word, *logos*, in printed form has dominated cultures so thoroughly that those of us immersed in it could not even apprehend it. With the rapid changes in technology that occur now on a weekly basis, the familiar printed book—the book that so many of us have a profound emotional attachment to, that material object that stimulates, soothes, instructs, and delights—gives way to largely misunderstood new technologies.

As the familiar printed book continues its long decline (a decline that will last for perhaps another one hundred years and so not concern the bibliophiles who populate our universities and other institutions), literacy will become increasingly important. As this change continues, growing in speed, the intertwined decline of the humanities and the modern will continue. The humanities, so filled with intellectual and spiritual richness and depth of thought for so many hundreds of years, have become weakened, wizened, and utterly ineffectual in the public realm. The humanities could, should, and must be replaced by the literacies, which could, fortunately, absorb the great strengths of the humanities as they have been so strongly established since the early modern period of western Europe. Rhetoric, writing, and technology, all radically revised, should assume positions of importance. Without this radical embrace of the new technologies (so hard for so many intellectuals whose very psyches are, as it were, booked), the pseudotechnological determinism of the current situation will continue and will damage representative democracy and the universal public education that makes that democracy possible. Instead, the new media robber barons—at Microsoft, at Time Warner, at the News Corporation, and at other communication conglomerates—will continue the familiar gobbling up of the electronic means of communication. That is to say, the communication power mongers of post-Fordism will continue to intellectually colonize our citizenry in order to narcotize us into consuming what they so unthinkingly call "information" and "content." In this process, we would all be consumed by the removal of control over the airwaves and the silicon chips. The literacies of Next Rhetoric are positioned in our universities not only to resist this normal capitalist cultural imperialism but to provide radical alternatives to it. Rhetoric and composition studies (and some branches of cultural studies) are now enacting a number of these alternatives.

Let us now turn, in chapter 6, to some strategies against post-Fordist, pseudotechnological determinism to see how the new literacies can wrest power at the alternative sites of the classroom and in the larger public realm as well.

6

Screen Rhetoric: Sophistic Logos Performers and Electric Rhetoric

```
         POWER

ENTER (<)              (>) JUMP

ERASE              CONTROL

        1    2    3

        4    5    6

        7    8    9

             0

MUTE

BACKWARD        FORWARD

        PICTURE
```

Classical paradigms provide ample evidence of the creation of such settings [language-learning environments or schools] in antiquity and of the exclusion of women from the training they provided.... For many women and minorities, for all those who feel deaf and dumb because they are regularly relegated to the peripheral vision of classroom and society, the absence of a port of entry to such modelling and training is a crucial barrier.

C. Jan Swearingen, *Rhetoric and Irony*[1]

Everybody is a teacher.

Spike Lee

It is a bald historical fact that the humanities were born in a rhetorical manger.

James L. Kinneavy, "Restoring the Humanities"[2]

1. Pp. 245–246.
2. In *The Rhetorical Tradition and Modern Writing*, ed. James J. Murphy, p. 20.

Power

The humanities as they have existed for five hundred years—the age of typography—have been drained of so much power that they daily approach an existence as a collection of relics, a feel-good assemblage of positivist object/texts and unexamined assumptions. The humanities' twin exclusions of, first, electric rhetoric (language as a Sophistic *logos* performance that is influenced by, but not wholly dependent on, the electronic forms of communication as I have explored them in the previous five chapters) and, second, of women, minorities, and other marginalized Others from positions of power in U.S. universities makes their continuation questionable. The gradual disempowerment of English in particular as a vital source for the general culture has led to the erosion of *logos* training and from there to a citizenry that cannot speak articulately and that regards writing as a tool divorced from language.

The resonance of the epigraphs by C. Jan Swearingen and Spike Lee derives from one kind of cultural transmission, that of critical pedagogy, the dialectic of student and teacher working toward particular goals. Swearingen focuses on students, while Lee focuses on teachers. Swearingen's compelling understanding of the condition of learning is that if a student has no "port of entry," there can be no modeling. A student who does have a port of entry but who has no modeling cannot learn effectively enough. Look, for example, at the number of African-American English majors in the United States. A strikingly low number of African-American students find this major to be worthwhile outside the Historically Black Colleges and Universities. This is so because there is no point of entry in many departments for African-American students. In fact, explicit barriers exist within the racist writings that continue to be canonized by the design of syllabi, curricula, and major requirements; in addition, the distressingly low number of African-American English professors contributes to this racist construct. As I contended in chapter 4, the rhetorical manger had a construction of race that differed radically from the modernist one that we now take for granted. The rhetoric rehistoricized by Kinneavy offers many ports of entry for marginalized Others as well as for the nonmarginalized.

The cultural/pedagogical status quo continues to change, regardless of the participation of humanists/posthumanists. The consensus of the humanities as they have existed since, say, the murder of Ramus in the sixteenth century has now disintegrated under the weight of the universal/objective/stable subject who is assumed to be autonomous and who is celebrated as an isolated agent. Neither the skills-and-drills aspect of rhetoric and composition studies nor the formalism of New Criticism, both dependent on the autonomous subject and the cult of individualism, can any longer bear the weight of their profound irrelevance in the transitory period of postmodernism and, more important, in whatever will replace postmodernism.

Posthumanists who examine these assumptions in rhetoric and composition studies and in cultural studies have been required to refrain from engaging the general public in a dialogue about these important changes because we remain mired in incessant arguing and strategizing within our own ranks. This rhetorical action is unsound insofar as it transfers dialectical energy from the radical changes being brought about by electric rhetoric and multiculturalism and gender equity and focuses them instead on internecine conflict.[3]

The printed, book-bound word, interacting with various other forces, led to the empowerment of the humanities in the early modern period and now contributes to its precipitous decline in the last two decades. Two hallmarks of the devolution of humanism are the continuing resistance to gendering and racing human subjects and their various positions. This resistance is enacted with a nearly religious fervor. As I have shown here in the case of classical rhetoric and writing practices, it is now intolerable to go on studying and purveying the White male objective, universal subject in a culture that did not construct race as we have in the modern West. When this stance is assumed, the racing and gendering take place anyway. The urgency of this demand compels us to admit the automatic gendering and racing that we all must enact and

3. From another point of view, almost all radical changes involve struggle and profound disagreement among those who see a vision that should be put in place. The U.S. civil rights struggles of the 1950s and 1960s, for example, experienced enormous challenges from the difficulty of maintaining a movement. See, for example, Taylor Branch, *Parting the Waters: America in the King Years, 1954–63*.

to stop hiding behind the strong myth of the neutral subject and the related strong myths of the twin formalisms of the current-traditional paradigm in writing pedagogy and the New Criticism of traditional literary studies.

Electric rhetoric (the consciousness, or mentalité, brought about through 150 years of interaction with the electronic forms of communication) has, perhaps ironically, potentially increased the power of the humanities/posthumanities/literacies. This is so because the screens of computers and televisions have so vividly raced and gendered our world. Even as the wizened, antihuman twin formalisms of the current-traditional paradigm and the New Critical reading daily increase the humanities' irrelevance, with their continuing stranglehold over much of higher education as well as common-school education, the technologies of electric rhetoric have propelled us down a path toward new literacies. So far the posthumanities have merely been playing catch-up to the technowizards of Silicon Valley in the case of computers and to the mind industries of the multinational communication conglomerates in the case of television.[4]

This self-imposed, gradual death was ethically bankrupt before the widespread electronic communication changes in television and computers took place in the 1980s. The mass distribution of the former and the semimass distribution of the latter were not inevitable occurrences. Rather, they were ideological moves driven by corporate interests, including the military and government clients of the multinational corporations. The supposed technological determinism was actually set in motion by corporate interests, but we still have radical change with which the posthumanities must live. My earlier definition of rhetoric— deploying language to critically assess what exists and is in place—can be applied here in useful ways.[5] We are stuck with governmental decisions from, say, 1934 (airwave laws) and 1996 (the Telecommunications Act,

4. The phrase is from Hans Magnus Enzensberger, "The Industrialization of the Mind."

5. Compare the resonance here of this stipulative definition with Plato's definition in *Phaedrus*, Aristotle's in *On Rhetoric*, Kenneth Burke's in *A Rhetoric of Motives*, and Andrea Lunsford and Lisa Ede's in *Singular Texts/Plural Authors*, chapters 1 and 2.

which advances the laissez-faire capitalism that has dominated the United States since the early 1980s).

For all these and other reasons (the semi-inclusion of White women and very few men and women of color and demographic, economic, and governmental factors), higher education finds itself in the middle of a profound restructuring. The electronic technologies have developed without any input from the humanities. (Why would software writers, for example, who devise terms such as "Widows and Orphans Protection," enact this technology differently?) One form of humanities participation is certain, however. Most of these university-trained technology experts were trained in the twin, wizened formalisms of the current-traditional paradigm in writing pedagogy and the New Criticism of traditional literary studies, which featured elite White males with token women (a construction that, of course, excludes most White males). These intelligent people learned that writing is a tool outside an autonomous self.

At this time the humanities/posthumanities/literacies need a radical new identity if we are to reassume institutional and cultural power that brings about positive change, including the paramount issue of regendering and reracing histories of language of all kinds (rhetoric, writing practices, literature, and others) and taking our work outside the enclaves of our disciplines and into the polis. The polis of our time exists on the screens of televisions and computers. Consequently, electric rhetoric as a kind of consciousness partly conditioned by technology but not fully determined by it requires attending to the these screens that are as graphic as they are verbal but whose graphics all remain entrenched in the verbal, as I demonstrated in chapters 4 and 5. One advantage of the verbal-graphic mixture is that the graphic is more obviously gendered and raced than is the purely printed word. However, most humanists, steeped and developed in the beauty and wonderment and fascination of the printed word, want their graphics in the form of art in painting, sculpture, film, and photography, recognized High Art forms. They tend not to want to admit video into their universe of graphics, because it is regarded as déclassé, as I have contended throughout this book.

Dominant U.S. culture remains in dire need of what humanists, posthumanists, and literacy scholar/teachers have to offer. Literacies, including the historicizing of communication technologies, must now not only supplement the humanities, as I try to do in negative and positive ways, but must now forge ahead with those who want to join us. We need the tremendous knowledge base of the Greek and Roman classics, for example, the traditional areas of English studies, the philological tradition, and the rest of the West, including the sophisticated ways of reading that have been developed by theorists in poststructuralism and cultural studies. But we do not need the racism and sexism embedded in much of these areas and in their cultural transmission in educational institutions. In the current reconstructions of higher education, it is imperative to retain the power and brilliance of all these fields and the people who have cultivated them. However, all this knowledge must be theorized, in particular vis-à-vis the faux neutrality of the universal subject and his Cartesian splitting. With this theorizing must come the politics of access. The words and graphics of computer screens and video screens must be made readily available through the rapid training of professors and teachers in the technologies of computers and television. Walt Whitman's vision of democratic vistas is newly alive: the possibility of the grand U.S. experiment remains possible. However, unless the politics of access to human teachers and technology is joined to the training in theories of communication technology, the Whitmanian vision cannot come about.

Indeed, the commitment by moderns to utopian ideas of what machines without humans can do remains a huge obstacle. The idea that the machines can teach with a downsizing of human teachers is so strong in our legislatures and among many of our governors (as well as at the federal level) that plans to mediate teaching and thereby to increase student-teacher ratios are proceeding rapidly. Again, humanists and posthumanists appear to have little input into these far-reaching changes.

Enter

Again, the book is dead; long live the book. The five hundred years of the printed book now draw to a conclusion.[6] This fact, if it is a fact, is so

---

6. The period of five hundred years refers, of course, to Gutenberg's press in 1457 and the widespread use of computers by about 1985. Martha Woodmansee historicizes the period from the eighteenth century with the copyright act to the current time (see "On the Author Effect").

painful for humanists, other intellectuals (including scientists), bibliophiles, and other print-attached people that it is almost intolerable to consider. The psychological metaphor of "imprinting" aptly explains in part the fear and hatred (or just resignation) toward computers and television among many intellectuals today. People who are devoted to the book can be said to have been imprinted by typography. Think of all the intellectuals who, when they are perplexed by a word they have just heard, ask their interlocutors how to spell it; spelling the word, reimprinting the typographic imprint, clears up the confusion as the questioner sees the letters. The radically different communication forms of icons, video, and other screen graphics are thus almost naturally met with resistance by print-imprinted people, which is to say, most members of the academy. Indeed, the culture wars derive in part from this deeply felt and quite legitimate response to the proliferation of screens in which graphics communicate as powerfully as words. Iconography has taken on wholly new meaning as we point and click our computers and zap through our television channels in formerly private living spaces (as a result of Next Rhetoric).

The traditional printed book has not waned because of the tidal waves of graphics that dot our verbal landscapes; instead, it waxes. Printed books proliferate. There is, however, a strong sense that the printed book is or will soon be in decline and that the West will be faced with tremendous loss. One positive outcome of this paradoxical situation has led to a strong field of study in the historicizing of technology in the traditional humanistic periods. For example, scholars in American literature study historical reading practices, as does Cathy N. Davidson in her collection *Reading in America*. Many early modern scholars have been at work on the reading practices of those eras. As this research has grown in each of the traditional areas of English, the term "literacy" has acquired more extensive use and deepened meaning; that is, it has more power than it has had previously. This historicizing remains important and beneficial and provides a bridge between the waning traditional humanities and the waxing literacies.

We must persist with rhetoric/composition studies and cultural studies, both of which resist the isolation that has become typical of the humanities since World War II. These new literacies reject the desiccation of the

twin formalisms of the current-traditional paradigm in rhetoric/compo-
sition and the fetish of New Critical close reading in traditional literary
studies.

The new literacies of electric rhetoric need selected aspects of the traditional humanities, including foreign-language training, as a central concern of scholar/teachers and not as the irrelevance they are so frequently
accorded. Although U.S. English now dominates the Internet, this new
communication technology nevertheless opens us up to the different literacies of acquired languages. Foreign-language training in the United
States has traditionally been less powerful than in most other countries,
both "developed" and not. The xenophobia and backwardness that
characterize those who know only one language, that is, U.S. English,
contribute strongly to the resistance to regendering and reracing the traditional humanities. An understanding of Otherness and its enactment
among rhetorical citizens remain hindered by the segregation of foreign-
language training in most universities.[7]

Citizens who resist foreign-language training and professional humanists who embrace it but cannot articulate why float along in the same

---

7. Of course, important scholarship and teaching continue to take place with
intellectual rigor and commitment in the United States. Nevertheless, in a move
not anticipated by those of us committed to making undergraduate training more
relevant, foreign-language requirements in universities were radically lowered
during the 1970s, a period in which important pedagogical change and openness
took place, progressive change that continues to provide strength in the universities in particular and the general culture at large. When foreign-language
training was tacitly declared to be feeble and expendable, a strong statement
about the humanities was made. Secondary schools, of course, rapidly followed
the lead of the universities' requirements. Most recently, according to statistics
provided by the Modern Language Association, departments of German and the
number of German majors have declined so severely that departments of German
are being downsized by folding them into other departments or maintaining one
tenure line in a different department. At the other end of the spectrum, again
according to the MLA statistics, student demand for Spanish training has grown
tremendously. Surely we should be instituting separate departments of Spanish in
universities that were compelled to fold modern languages into single units as a
result of the 1970s misguided zeal. The current vogue of requiring one and one-
half years of a foreign language is, plainly, ridiculous. After the acquisition of the
language, the student needs to delve deeply into the cultures where the language
is dominant.

boat. Each group has strong tendencies toward not reracing and not regendering the universal White male subject.

It is now time to acknowledge this new world of literacies and to contribute our regendered, reraced Sophistic *logos* performances to it. The change does and will require enormous struggle within universities, which, as with other institutions, remain painfully resistant to change. However, this traditional resistance is not seen by many administrators, who are rapidly moving forward to digitize universities. As with state legislators, but for better reasons, they tend to see the digital present and future. Take a look at any student computer classroom: the students are digitized. The humanities professoriat resists the digital so strongly that we allow technocrats and others to reinvent the university. Exceptions to this group are the field of rhetoric and composition studies, which has been studying computers and composition since 1983, and traditional humanists, many of who have rapidly digitized their fields, as I discussed above.

Jump

The time has now arrived for humanists/posthumanists/literacy experts to acknowledge and jump into the posttypographic age and then to lead it. Science students are already computer literate because their fields require it. Humanities students range from computer nonliteracy coupled with pride in resistance to technology to those with critical computer literacy. For many humanists who came to computers in adulthood, this move will constitute a jump, perhaps even a plunge. The disorientation can be profound and should be acknowledged. For other humanists, however, the move into the digital world will be a tugging as the felt desire for printed books and for the ineffable pleasure they provide the deep reader seems to wane in importance. However, for tremendous numbers of traditional humanists, the dynamic screen of the computer has been embraced with eloquence. Look, for example, at the software Perseus, edited by Gregory Crane.[8] This classical Greek electronic database contains two kinds of archival material: the printed and the graphic. In ad-

8. See chapters 2 and 3, where I deploy research from Perseus 1.0.

dition, it contains links, or visually highlighted words and phrases to which students and scholars can point and click. The classicists who have devised this source have done so in ways that help the Greekless reader as well as the reader with Greek and have explained clear strategies, in pedagogically sound ways, for navigating through this enormous amount of material. This library without walls makes representations of Greek texts and graphics of many kinds available to many who previously have been prevented from accessing this material in research libraries, some of which, of course, are in other nations.[9]

The terms "evolution" and "revolution" are frequently deployed to describe the current and future changes in communication technology. "Evolution" connects emerging technologies with previous ones, while "revolution" connotes a break with the past. However, the binary opposition set up by the terms leads to closure because, as with all the binaries that structure the West, they simply offer too few options. In *Communication at a Distance: The Effects of Print and Sociocultural Organization and Change*, David Kaufer and Kathleen Carley argue persuasively that new technologies reinforce existing ones; there is not a replacement of one technology with another one. In fact, the publication of books has increased in the last twenty years of computer proliferation; print literacy has expanded in electric rhetoric, not contracted. Nonetheless, significant changes in consciousness have taken place as a result of the near-saturation level of television distribution and the substantial distribution of computers.

As I explored in chapter 4, "The Next Rhetoric," the textual shards and fragments of zapping and the new primacy of graphic communication as it entwines with the alphabetic word have intersubjectively reorganized how we think, not just what we think. Many traditional humanists have moved enthusiastically into the world of hypertext, nonlinearity, and graphics.[10] Television itself becomes a kind of hyper-

9. Even casual browsing through the alphabetic and graphic representations of Perseus 1.0 on the Internet or Perseus 2.0 on CD-ROM teaches the browser an enormous amount.

10. The study of art history has acquired a significance that has not been adequately understood. U.S. culture remains in great need of what art historians have to offer in the realm of graphical understanding.

text as decoders attempt, frequently strenuously, to interact through surfing across the water of the channels.[11] Traditional humanists must now come to terms with the changed but not erased dominance of the printed word, not, it must be emphasized, with literacy. They must also come to terms with the fact that writing as an activity and writing pedagogy are not second-order skills-and-drills remediation or romantic expostulations of a self but are in fact primary, performative, Sophistic, gendered, and raced activities.

Erase

Many women, most minorities, and other marginalized Others have been erased in subtle and not so subtle ways from the screens of computers and the screens of television. In the construction of software (for example, Microsoft's Windows 98) and in the construction of channels (for example, the broadcast networks), the mythos of machine neutrality has reigned with little effective expression of opposition. This mythos of the modern period is so entrenched that frequently it is not even questioned outside of the academy, and even there the question tends to be devalued outside film and video studies and some areas of cultural studies. Humanists and posthumanists have so far been unable or unwilling to teach a large audience the nature of the changes in subjectivity and identity, and their rhetorical, technological, and literary histories. In fact, the gutting of the National Endowment of the Humanities occurred with little perceptible protest by humanities scholars; we have been unable to articulate even a low level of persuasion to legislators, who reduce already pathetically small amounts of funding. Beyond handwringing and declarations of the end of Western civilization, humanists and the organizations that represent them have had virtually no influence over the radical reduction in the NEH (recall that the Right includes such humanists and public commentators as William Bennett and Lynn

---

11. One indication of some spectators' deep desire to interact with television is the wearing out of remote control devices. A number of keys on these devices simply wear out, as do the built-in trackball covers of laptop computers. Laptop computers now come with replacement trackball caps to take care of the worn-out knob covers that constitute part of the divided mouse.

Cheney (self-proclaimed humanists each with a humanities Ph.D. and former heads of the NEH). Consequently, it is time for those professors in literacies to take up the challenge.

I offer here one example of the "neutral" technology that electronically and powerfully communicates material for the reinforcement of the status quo. This illustrative narrative begins with the IBM Laptop 755 CE, an advanced machine that partly enabled IBM to recover its steep loss in market share, which had resulted from its failure to see the proliferation of microcomputers. As part of the introductory software preloaded on the machine, IBM offers Photo Gallery, as is typical. The grouping is the typical re-presentation of old technology in a new one (here it resembles a museum display of photographs set within the 10.5-inch computer screen). The photographs in the gallery include a close-up of raspberries, farm buildings, a head-and-shoulders photograph of a Black girl who looks at the camera, baseball hats, a lighthouse, a head-and-shoulders shot of two parrots, a long shot of whitewater rafters (seven White people), a long-shot photograph of a mountain capped with snow, and a long-shot photograph of a seashore. The gallery sequence runs raspberries, farm buildings, Black girl, baseball hats, lighthouse, parrots, White rafters on whitewater, mountain scenery, seashore. The racism of this pictorial juxtaposition, aside from being breathtaking in its insensitivity, communicates volumes about the automatic responses of some anonymous software designers who equate Black girls with beautiful, exotic animals (exoticism) and who present a photograph of a child in a semi-erotic pose as if it were a phenomenon of *physis* (nature) and not of *nomos*, a convention or law or more.[12]

12. Although the individual software designer of this gallery is anonymous, its corporate author, the owner of the intellectual property, is IBM. This representation of the only human in the Photo Gallery reverberates through much of the history of Western painting, as revealed by even a cursory look at Monet, Picasso, and Toulouse-Lautrec, to name only four masters. The woman of color as exoticized, romanticized, and, most of all, eroticized for selective White male spectatorship is still unacknowledged by the dominant culture. The wrapping of Male Master painters in the shredded mantle of the now ethically bankrupt movement of Romanticism enables spectators automatically to decode all these graphic works as "natural."

This representation of a girl in a supposedly new technology has her staring directly into the older technology of the camera with a countenance that seems to be enigmatic. Her presentation intertextually connects some of the salient characteristics of a *National Geographic* issue that features representations of some women who reside in Africa: the girl is objectified into thingness first by the anonymous photographer and then by the IBM anonymous technicians who inserted the Photo Gallery as introductory and purportedly free entertainment for purchasers of this Thinkpad. In other words, this software provided purchasers with free entertainment that displays some of the possibilities of the new computer.

The representation of the girl reveals a number of unintentional messages: that the anonymous person of color is equivalent to a parrot; that the anonymous person of color exists in representational form as an object to be viewed as a representation of a photograph is viewed; that people who are constructed as Black exist representationally to entertain spectators; and that a representation of a girl who is Black is equivalent to pretty animals and lovely landscapes: they are all objects deployed for the visual stimulation of selected decoders.

In other words, the representation of the girl relies on exoticism, a theme now common among many art historians, among others, who have identified the marginalizing of women of color and women constructed as White. In presentation, representation, ideology, and rhetoric, this Photo Gallery then reinforces the status quo that females who are Black are available as commodified objects for the viewing pleasure of those people fortunate enough to work on an IBM Thinkpad.[13]

13. A similar point is made by Harry Edwards, a sociologist of sports, who claims that African-American males are lured into playing high-risk sports such as football and then are used up, injured, not educated, and usually not degreed by the larger institution whose fans previously cheered them on the field of violence. See *Sociology of Sport*. A raced reading of any college or professional team confirms this phenomenon, as does an examination of graduation rates for males who are African-American in high-risk sports. While, fortunately, many African-American, White, and other athletes do in fact graduate and go on to productive careers, it nevertheless remains the case that a substantial number of student athletes are physically injured and intellectually underprepared to work successfully outside the sports arena.

Control

The two largest challenges to understanding electric rhetoric and establishing a new literacy are, first, the analysis of consciousness/mentalité issues and their scholarly/pedagogical implications and, second, the politics of access to the new electronic literacy.

As I have contended throughout this book, the intersubjective human relationships grounded in language have changed in the last 150 years of electronic communication, beginning with telegraphy in the nineteenth century. These relationships have changed the most since 1981 with the widespread use of cable television technology in HUTs. We need people in every area of the humanities/posthumanities to work through the computer-driven problems with intellectual property and citizen/student access to the Internet, issues explored by Andrea Lunsford and others in the Intellectual Property Caucus.[14]

Lunsford et al. make the compelling point that intellectual property exclusions brought about by photocopying limitations recently imposed by federal courts and attempts to charge for Internet access damage pedagogy and will damage it even more if those in the academy who value these sources do not protest.[15]

Why do otherwise reasonable people work to deprive students of access to texts through photocopying and through the Internet? Two strong reasons are (1) money and (2) allegiance to the modernist idea that knowledge is a thing out there in the world, that humans are Cartesian mind/body dualisms, and that knowledge is a commodity— rhetorical issues that I explored in chapters 1, 2, and 4.

14. See Andrea A. Lunsford and Susan West, "Intellectual Property and Composition Studies."

15. A similar technological myopia exists with the wholesale destruction of paper library-card catalogs and the irreplaceable knowledge and histories that they contained from generations of librarians who reinscribed the cards in various telling ways. Compare the destruction of valuable books by the San Francisco Public Library: some librarians allegedly "kidnapped" print books that were slated for destruction. Without the booknapping, these irreplaceable books would have been destroyed, overlooked in the rush to digitize.

The money issue is, perhaps, obvious in this stage of capitalism. However, even in the precapitalist fourth-century-B.C.E. era of Isocrates, the money/intellectual-property issue was strikingly similar. The Sophists were initially attacked because they charged fees for their teaching, for their nearly magical rendering of the upstart, second-class genre of prose, a kind of language that was seen as a threat to the hegemony of poetry. The Sophists Isocrates, Diotima, Gorgias, and others challenged the hegemony of poetry, which provided the book of high culture, the nearly sacred texts of the *Odyssey* and the *Iliad*. This challenge to poetry was nearly heretical. When Gorgias in particular traveled around as an itinerant teacher, he did so partly to raise money for himself. As a foreigner from Leontini, Sophist, teacher of the highly suspect genre of prose (which he was seen to defile daily by deploying poetic language, figures, tropes, and schemes to it), and therefore as a major Other, Gorgias the barbar attached money to the marger of pedagogy, performance, and knowledge making. He transgressed. His transgressions cost him his reputation for 2,300 years, except for brief periods when the Sophists returned to fashion, as they have now done so powerfully, so wonderfully, so magically. And so, as Jean-Pierre Vernant has taught us, it is not only in the period of capitalism that money was a huge problem for pedagogy and the constructions of knowledge in various constructions of consciousness. Money and school have long, intertwined, frequently unhappy, and consistently fascinating histories of their own.

One of these histories, still being enacted, lies in the money-rhetoric connection. It is the galloping merger and acquisition mania of multinational conglomerates that characterizes our laissez-faire historical moment. At the close of the twentieth century, four major companies own and control a very large percentage of material transmitted on television: General Electric, Time Warner, Disney, and the News Corporation. Each of these bulimic companies has an alpha-capitalist leader: Jack Welch, Gerald M. Levin, Michael Eisner, and Rupert Murdock.

The second issue concerning intellectual property and student and scholar/teacher access to the new technologies of the Internet and other machines remains far more serious. Because of a misunderstanding of the nature of rhetoric and the inherent nature of *logos* that constitutes not only thought but how thought occurs, because of the religious zeal associated with modernist ideas of consumption, the dominant culture tends to believe that all knowledge is the same and that the technology that "transmits" it is merely incidental. Modernism as an intellectual movement continues its slow and painful death partly because of the radical transformation of communication technology.

As long as intellectuals and the general public believe that knowledge is a commodity that can be stored in and accessed from the garage, the Internet, a piece of paper, or a television, then the humanities/posthumanities/ literacies cannot flourish. We will remain in the deprivileged binary position of "form," inferior to divine "content." We will remain the wizened, useless pastimes diverted to weekend "arts fairs," where consumers, not citizens, wander around in search of the intellectual/spiritual nourishment that are provided frequently on a subversive basis in our universities.

Mute

In this modernist, wizened, dying but still powerful construction of the trivium, the hegemony of "content," the ideology of knowledge consumption, continues to exert another tremendous negativity as well. This machine neutrality silences women, minorities, and White males who have been constrained by various forces of silence. The silent women of *Women's Ways of Knowing* (Belenky et al.) remain in dire need of the new (and ancient) pedagogies of rhetoric and composition studies. The new communication technologies allow unprecedented access to those who have been silenced through pedagogical wounding (that is, damaging teaching), gender discrimination, racial exclusion, and other deeply flawed, antidemocratic practices that continue to exert enormous control.

Backward

It is undemocratic to deprive our students of the discursive practices of fourth-century-B.C.E. Greece. It is unethical to teach overtly or covertly that writing is a mere tool that resembles, say, a hammer. It is unfair to hide from our students the fact that one's native language constitutes a substantial part of the very essence of thought/existence. This backwardness must be stopped by the recognition of electric rhetoric, the hard-to-describe consciousness or mentality that constitutes who we are as citizens in a representative democracy.

Forward

To reassume legitimate, meaningful, and ethical leadership of the new paradigm of scholar-teachers who merge their research with their pedagogy, we need to consolidate like-minded people in the academy who can put aside their infighting so as to move forward the larger project of seizing the possibilities of Next Rhetoric, the age of new literacies, in which we have Sophistic *logos* performance by the masses. Three strong moves are necessary for this to be accomplished:

• Posthumanists/literacy intellectuals must assume intellectual and ethical leadership over electric rhetoric as a form of consciousness already in place, undergoing change, and susceptible/vulnerable to demagogic legislation. This move requires a retreat from the policies of isolationism that have characterized much of the academy in various historical epochs, most strongly since World War II. In addition, this move requires diverting at least some intellectual/emotional energy away from the three-part division of English departments among rhetoric/composition studies, traditional literary studies, and cultural studies.[16]

• Posthumanists/literacy intellectuals must take to the airwaves, the co-axial cables, and the satellite transmissions to reach citizens in their HUTs. In addition, they must digitize the issues surrounding the humanities. They must also recognize the power inherent in the universal freshman writing requirement and make it, as I suggested in chapter 4, a technology, mind, and articulation course.[17]

16. Of course, many departments of English possess only one part of the three-part English configuration, and that part is the study of traditional Literature with an unproblematic capital "L." Heated disagreement over issues as important as language is to be expected and is, in fact, part of the strife and struggle of pre-Platonic dialectic. However, at this time almost all this energy has gone into intraparty infighting. While some of this must continue, part of this energy needs to be turned to educating the public in what it is we do in the humanities/posthumanities/literacies—the same public, it is useful to recall, who was trained in our classrooms.

17. The universal freshman writing requirement refers to universities and colleges that require all freshman students to take a one- or two-sequence writing course before proceeding to their other studies. See chapter 5.

• In both of the above, posthumanists/literacy intellectuals must return to pedagogy. They must follow the substantial lead of rhetoric and composition studies in English and take pedagogy as seriously as research and publishing. The path has been broken and lies ready to be trod by other fields of the humanities. Nevertheless, as pedagogy becomes ascendant, do not let it eclipse research.

• Posthumanists/literacy intellectuals must remain in the realm of the public to influence legislation that will so forcefully hurt our students and all of our research.[18]

Picture

The humanities/posthumanities/literacies must resist technophobia. Print-imprinted intellectuals, including professors, must relearn the world of the graphic, a word which derives from the Greek *graphe* and refers both to the written and the pictorial. The humanities/posthumanities/literacies must relinquish semiconscious resistance to pictorial communication and its technologies. It is the kairic moment to join with film and video studies and art history to understand the nature of the graphic so that it can be integrated into our research and teaching as something as normal and natural as the all-print book was in the age of typography.

Return to Power

Without a regrounding of ethics and language as central concerns of the humanities/posthumanities/literacies, there is no point in enacting any of these proposals. We remain stuck with the Q Question, Richard Lanham's designation of the old question of whether humanistic study

18. This issue is complicated by the logjam of campaign finance reform. Since so many senators and congresspeople are profoundly influenced by the large sums of money "contributed" by the Mind Industry (the big five telecommunications conglomerates) to all campaigns and their financial offshoots such as foundations, the current legislative situation is heading directly toward further empowering these communication companies. These moves would be a continuation of the ill-conceived 1996 Telecommunications Act, which embraced laissez-faire capitalism with a zeal reminiscent of the Robber Barons of the nineteenth century, whose control over transportation and new machine technology led to many antidemocratic institutions.

(whether digitized or not) will bring about good people. The "Q" refers to the first-century Roman rhetorician/teacher Quintilian, whose dictum "vir bonus dicendi peritus" (a good man who speaks well) drove his powerful ideology (powerful partly because of the extraordinary influence that Quintilian held over the next 2,200 years of education in the West).

Both Lanham and Quintilian answer this stupendously important question in ways they appear never to have thought of. In other words, their unwritten subtexts resonate loudly because each man excludes the category of woman from his visions and each assumes a privileged male subject (White, in Lanham's historical moment). While one can (or cannot) "forgive" Quintilian for excluding women from his "good man who speaks well" construction because he was such a Roman guy, one is less inclined to excuse any post-1980 writer of linguistic exclusion of women.[19] Consequently, Lanham's usage of sexist English in the 'Q' Question resembles his similar exclusion of all female voices in his Works Cited, a list that, with the exception of the second-listed author Lisa Jardine, is all male. Peter Ramus, Richard McKeon, Donald McCloskey (sic), E. D. Hirsch, A. N. Whitehead, Gerald Graff, Allan Bloom, Mark Johnson (no Robin Lakoff), George Steiner, and so on, feature in this important essay. The chorus of women scholars who have contributed to the field of rhetoric, composition, and ethics are silenced by Lanham in his refusal to acknowledge them. A new class of silent women can then be added to Belenky et al.'s different configuration of silent women, this time the silent women scholars who enabled many of these issues to exist in the first place. How can any scholar treat the Q Question, an ethical matter, without addressing and performing the regendering of language that has occurred in the last twenty years?

With the widespread use of television and the computer, literacy, both functional and critical, has changed radically. Next Rhetoric has arrived, and it is imperative for the humanities/posthumanities/literacies to take

---

19. I choose this date because it coincides with the publication of the National Council of Teachers of English pamphlet "Guidelines for Nonsexist Use of Language in NCTE Publications." Anyone alive and reading should be attuned to the demonstrated exclusions of the female half of the world by words such as "mankind," "man," etc.

account of this new Sophistic *logos* performance, which includes the new deployment of the written word and graphic representations. The historicizing of oralism/auralism, including the silencing of women and other marginalized Others, must take its place in this newest revolution of communication technology.

Thus far the humanities/posthumanities have trailed behind policy making for, and the direction of, these new interactions of humans and machines. To continue this inaction is to abrogate our responsibility.

New vistas lie open before us as the world speeds ahead with new technologies and their attendant literacies. If we refrain from theorizing this new era, then other forces will continue to dominate it. Historicized rhetorical theory and writing practices, including the writing of histories of communication technologies, offer us powerful theoretical bases. The adaptability and elasticity of rhetoric reraced and regendered offer us directions for understanding the tidal wave of writing and graphics that now enter not only our HUTs but also our minds/bodies as we inter-subjectively interact with a new *logos* of Next Rhetoric.

Appendix: Excerpt from the *Origin Myth of Acoma and Other Records*

Recorded by Matthew W. Stirling

Origin Myth

In the beginning two female human beings were born. These two children were born underground at a place called Shipapu. As they grew up, they began to be aware of each other. There was no light and they could only feel each other. Being in the dark they grew slowly.

After they had grown considerably, a Spirit whom they afterward called Tsichtinako spoke to them, and they found that it would give them nourishment. After they had grown large enough to think for themselves, they spoke to the Spirit when it had come to them one day and asked it to make itself known to them and to say whether is was male or female, but it replied only that it was not allowed to meet with them. They then asked why they were living in the dark without knowing each other by name, but the Spirit answered that they were nuk'timi (under the earth); but they were to be patient in waiting until everything was ready for them to go up into the light. So they waited a long time, and as they grew they learned their language from Tsichtinako.

When all was ready, they found a present from Tsichtinako, two baskets of seeds and little images of all the different animals (there were to be) in the world. The Spirit said they were sent by their father. They asked who was meant by their father, and Tsichtinako replied that his name was Ūch'tsiti and that he wished them to take their baskets out into the light, when the time came. Tsichtinako instructed them, "You will

From *Origin Myth of Acoma, and Other Records*, recorded by Matthew W. Stirling. Smithsonian Institution, Bureau of American Ethnology, Bulletin, no. 135. Washington: U.S. Government Printing Office, 1942.

find the seeds of four kinds of pine trees, lā'khok, gēi'etsu (dyai'its), wanūka, and lǎ'nye, in your baskets. You are to plant these seeds and will use the trees to get up into the light." They could not see the things in their baskets but feeling each object in turn they asked, "Is this it?" until the seeds were found. They then planted the seeds as Tsichtinako instructed. All of the four seeds sprouted, but in the darkness the trees grew very slowly and the two sisters became very anxious to reach the light as they waited this long time. They slept for many years as they had no use for eyes. Each time they awoke they would feel the trees to see how they were growing. The tree lanye grew faster than the others and after a very long time pushed a hole through the earth for them and let in a very little light. The others stopped growing, at various heights, when this happened.

The hole that the tree lanye made was not large enough for them to pass through, so Tsichtinako advised them to look again in their baskets where they would find the image of an animal called dyu῀pⁱ (badger) and tell it to become alive. They told it to live, and it did so as they spoke, exclaiming, "A'uha! Why have you given me life?" They told it not to be afraid nor to worry about coming to life. "We have brought you to life because you are to be useful." Tsichtinako spoke to them again, instructing them to tell Badger to climb the pine tree, to bore a hole large enough for them to crawl up, cautioning him not to go out into the light, but to return, when the hole was finished. Badger climbed the tree and after he had dug a hole large enough, returned saying that he had done his work. They thanked him and said, "As a reward you will come up with us to the light and thereafter you will live happily. You will always know how to dig and your home will be in the ground where you will be neither too hot nor too cold."

Tsichtinako now spoke again, telling them to look in the basket for Tāwāi'nū (locust), giving it life and asking it to smooth the hole by plastering. It, too was to be cautioned to return. This they did and Locust smoothed the hole but, having finished, went out into the light. When it returned reporting that it had done its work, they asked it if it had gone out. Locust said no, and every time he was asked he replied no, until the fourth time when he admitted that he had gone out. They asked Locust what it was like outside. Locust replied that it was just tsī'ītī (laid out flat). They said, "From now on you will be known as Tsi'k'ă. You will also come up with us, but you will be punished for disobedience by being allowed out only a short time. Your home will be in the ground and you will have to return when the weather is bad. You will soon die but you will be reborn each season."

The hole now let light into the place where the two sisters were, and Tsichtinako spoke to them, "Now is the time you are to go out. You are able to take your baskets with you. In them you will find pollen and sacred corn meal. When you reach the top, you will wait for the sun to come up and that direction will be called ha'nami (east). With the pollen and the sacred corn meal you will pray to the Sun. You will thank the Sun for bringing you to light, ask for a long life and happiness, and for success in the purpose for which you were created." Tsichtinako then taught them the prayers and the creation song, which they were to sing. This took a long while, but finally the sisters followed by Badger and Locust, went out into the light, climbing the pine tree. Badger was very strong and skillful and helped them. On reaching the earth, they set down their baskets and saw for the first time what they had. The earth was soft and spongy under their feet as they walked, and they said, "This is not ripe." They stood waiting for the sun, not knowing where it would appear. Gradually it grew lighter and finally the sun came up. Before they began to pray, Tsichtinako told them they were facing east and that their right side, the side their best aim was on, would be known as kū'ā'mē (south) and the left ti dyami (north) while behind at their backs was the direction pūna'me (west) where the sun would go down. They had already learned while underground the direction nŭk'ŭm' (down) and later, when they asked where their father was, they were told tyunami (four skies above.)

And as they waited to pray to the Sun, the girl on the right moved her best hand and was named Iatiku which meant "bringing to life." Tsichtinako then told her to name her sister, but it took a long time. Finally Tsichtinako noticed that the other had more in her basket, so Tsichtinako told Iatiku to name her thus, and Iatiku called her Nautsiti which meant "more of everything in the basket."

They now prayed to the Sun as they had been taught by Tsichtinako, and sang the creation song. Their eyes hurt for they were not accustomed to the strong light. For the first time they asked Tsichtinako why they were on earth and why they were created. Tsichtinako replied, "I did not make you. Your father, Uchtsiti made you, and it is he who has made the world, the sun which you have seen, the sky, and many other things which you will see. But Uchtsiti says the world is not yet completed, not yet satisfactory, as he wants it. This is the reason he has made you. You will rule and bring to life the rest of the things he has given you in the baskets." The sisters then asked how they themselves had come into being. Tsichtinako answered saying, "Uchtsiti first made the world. He threw a clot of his own blood into space and by his power it grew and grew until it became the earth. Then Uchtsiti planted you in this and by it you were nourished as you developed. Now that you have emerged from within the earth, you will have to provide nourishment for yourselves. I will instruct you in this." They then asked where their father lived and Tsichtinako replied, "You will never see your father, he lives four skies above, and has made you to live in this world. He has made you in the image of himself." So they asked why Tsichtinako did not become visible to them, but Tsichtinako replied, "I don't know how to live like a human being. I have been asked by Uchtsiti to look after you and to teach you. I will always guide you." And they asked again how they were to live, whether they could go down once more under the ground, for they were afraid of the winds and rains and their eyes were hurt by the light. Tsichtinako replied that Uchtsiti would take care of that and would furnish them means to keep warm and change the atmosphere so that they would get used to it.

At the end of the first day, when it became dark they were much frightened, for they had not understood that the sun would set and thought that Tsichtinako had betrayed them. "Tsichtinako! Tsichtinako! You told us we were to come into the light," they cried, "why, then, is it dark?" So Tsichtinako explained, "This is the way it will always be. The sun will go down and the next day come up anew in the east. When it is dark you are to rest and sleep as you slept when all was dark." So they were satisfied and slept. They rose to meet the sun, praying to it as they had been told, and were happy when it came up again, for they were warm and their faith in Tsichtinako was restored.

Tsichtinako next said to them, "Now that you have your names, you will pray with your names and your clan names so that the Sun will know you and recognize you." Tsichtinako asked Nautsiti which clan she wished to belong to. Nautsiti answered, "I wish to see the sun, that is the clan I will be." The spirit told Nautsiti to ask Iatiku what clan she wanted. Iatiku thought for a long time but finally she noticed that she had the seed from which sacred meal was made in her basket and no other kind of seeds. She thought, "With this name I shall be very proud, for it has been chosen for nourishment and it is sacred." So she said, "I will be Corn clan." They then waited for the sun to come up. When it appeared, Tsichtinako once more advised them to sing the first song and to pray, not forgetting their name and their clan name in starting their prayer. After the prayer they were to sing the second song.

When the sun appeared it was too bright for Iatiku and it hurt her eyes. She wondered if Nautsiti's eyes hurt her, too, so she put her head down and sideways, letting her hair fall, and looked at Nautsiti. By doing this the light did not strike her squarely in the face and her hair cast a shade. Tsichtinako said, "Iatiku, the sun has not appeared for you. Look at Nautsiti, see how strongly the light is striking her. Notice how white she looks." And although Iatiku turned to the sun, it did not make her as white as Nautsiti, and Iatiku's mind was slowed up while Nautsiti's mind was made fast. But both of them remembered everything and did everything as they were taught.

When they had completed their prayers to the sun, Tsichtinako said, "You have done everything well and now you are both to take up your baskets and you must look to the north, west, south, and east, for you are now to pray to the Earth to accept the things in the basket and to give them life. First you must pray to the north, at the same time lift up your baskets in that direction. You will then do the same to the west, then to the south and east." They did as they were told and did it well. And Tsichtinako said to them, "From now on you will rule in every direction, north, west, south, and east."

They now questioned Tsichtinako again so that they would understand more clearly why they were given the baskets and their contents, and Tsichtinako replied, "Everything in the baskets is to be created by your word, for you are made in the image of Uchtsiti and your word will be as powerful as his word. He has created you to help him complete the world. You are to plant the seeds of the different plants to be used when anything is needed. I shall always be ready to point out to you the various plants and animals."

The sisters did not realize that they were not taking food and did not understand when Tsichtinako told them they were to plant seeds to give them nourishment. But they were always ready to do as Tsichtinako asked, and she told them to plant first that which would maintain life, grains of corn. "When this plant grows," said Tsichtinako, "it will produce a part which I will point out to you. This will be taken as food." Everything in the basket was in pairs and the sisters planted two of each kind of corn.

The corn grew very slowly so Tsichtinako told them to plant ĭsthĕ (the earliest plant to come up in the spring; gray with a small white flower; dies quickly) and to transmit its power of early ripening to the corn.

They were very interested in the corn and watched it every day as it grew. Tsichtinako showed them where the pollen came out. "That you will call kū'ăch'tīmu," she said, "there the pollen will appear. When the pollen is plentiful, you will gather it, and with it and corn meal you will pray to the rising sun each morning." This they did always, but Nautsiti was sometimes a little lazy.

After some time the corn ripened. Tsichtinako told them to look at it and to gather some. They saw that the corn was hard and they picked four ears. Iatiku took two ears carefully without hurting the plant, but Nautsiti jerked hers off roughly. Iatiku noticed this and cautioned her sister not to ruin the plants. They took the ears of corn to Tsichtinako saying, "We have brought the corn, it is ripe." Tsichtinako agreed and explained that the corn ears when cooked would be their food. They did not understand this and asked what they would cook with. Tsichtinako then told them that Uchtsiti would give them fire. That night as they sat around they saw a red light drop from the sky. After they had seen it, Tsichtinako told them it was fire, and that they were to go over and get some of it. They asked with what, and she told them to get it with a flat rock because it was very hot and they could not take it in their hands. After getting it with a rock, they asked what they were to do with it, and were told they were to make a fire, to go to the pine tree they had planted, to break off some of the branches and put them in the fire. They went to the tree and broke some of the twigs from it. When they got back to the fire, they were told to throw the twigs down. They did so and a large pile of wood appeared there. Tsichtinako told them this wood would last many years till there was time for trees to grow, and showed them how to build a fire. She told them that with the flames from the fire they would keep warm and would cook their food.

Tsichtinako next taught them how to roast the corn. "When it is cooked," she explained, "you are to eat it. This will be the first time you have eaten, for you have been fasting for a long time and Uchtsiti has been nourishing you. You will find salt in your baskets; with this you will season the corn." They began to look for this and Tsichtinako pointed it out to them. As soon as they were told this, Nautsiti grabbed some corn and salt. She was the first to taste them and exclaimed that they were very good, but Iatiku was slower. After Nautsiti had eaten part, she gave it to taste. When both had eaten, Tsichtinako told them that this was the way they were going to live and be nourished. They were very thankful, saying, "You have treated us well." They asked if this would be their only food. Tsichtinako said, "No, you have many other things in your baskets; many seeds and images of animals, all in pairs. Some will be eaten and taken for nourishment by you." After they had used the salt, they were asked by Tsichtinako to give life to this salt by praying to the Earth, first in the North direction, then in the West, then in the South, and then in the East. And when they did so, salt appeared in each of these directions. Tsichtinako then instructed them to take always the husks from the corn carefully and to dry them. They were then instructed to plant hă'mi (tobacco). When the plant matured, they were taught how to roll the leaves in corn husks and to smoke it. (Even now in ceremonies the corn husks must be torn with the fingers and tied in the center with a little strip of corn husk. It may not be cut by artificial means. You smoke in order to make your prayers merge into the minds of the gods to whom prayer is addressed. This will also compel obedience. If a man smokes when a request is made of him, he must obey that request.) They were then told to place the tobacco with the pollen and the corn meal and to remember that these three were always to be together, and to be used in making prayers.

Now they were told that they were to give life to an animal whose flesh they were going to use for food. Tsichtinako named this animal as Ba'shya (kangaroo mouse) and also taught them the first song to be sung to animals. She told them to sing this song in order to make the images alive, and pointed out the images to them in the basket. They did everything as they were taught. They sang the song to the image and with the word, "Come to life, Bashya," it came to life. As it did so it asked, "Why have I come to life?" Tsichtinako told it not to ask any questions because, "It is you that is going to give life to other life." After this was done, Nautsiti and Iatiku told this animal that it was going to live on the ground and said to it, "Go now and increase." After the animal increased, Tsichtinako told the sisters to kill one of the animals. "Now eat the two together, the corn and the field mouse, and also the salt to see how it tastes." She had already told them never to let out the fire which had been given to them. They acted according to Tsichtinako's instructions. They roasted their corn and roasted the flesh of the field mouse with some salt on it. After it was cooked, Tsichtinako told them to pray with the food, not with all of it, but with little pieces from each—corn, flesh, and salt. Each sister did this and prayed to Uchtsiti, the creator of the world, who lives up in the fourth sky. Tsichtinako told them they were to do this always before eating. After this they ate the food. There was not very much of the meat, but it was good. They did not know that there were to be bones but these were not hard and they broke them with their teeth. They liked the flesh so well that they asked Tsichtinako if they might have something larger that would yield more flesh. Tsichtinako answered that they would find other things in their baskets. They went back to them, and Tsichtinako said they would find Tsū'na (rat) and another animal Katsa (mole) and also Nīt^e (prairie dog). "Go, make these images alive," said Tsichtinako, pointing them out according to their names. They were to do this in the same way as with Bashya. Tsichtinako also told them that these animals were to be used as food and that they must tell each of these animals to live in the ground because as yet there was no shade on earth to live in. "But before you give life to them," said Tsichtinako, "it is necessary that you plant seeds of grass which will be the food for them." Tsichtinako pointed out the seeds they were to plant, and they took the seeds of the grasses and scattered them first to the

North, next to the West, then some to the South, and then to the East. And immediately grass covered the ground. They then took the images and prayed to the cardinal points, and, according to the instructions of Tsichtinako, gave life to all of these animals, giving them names as they came to life. Each one as it came to life asked why it had come to life but Tsichtinako told them not to ask questions, that they would give life to other life. As before, the sisters told the animals to increase. After all of this was done, they proceeded to eat the new animals after praying with them, doing just as they did before. The two sisters were now very happy, they had plenty and some to spare. "It is not yet time for the larger animals to be given life," said Tsichtinako, "first the world must have sufficient plants and small animals to feed them."

After a long time, Tsichtinako spoke to them, "What we are going to do now concerns the earth. We are going to make the mountains." She told them to remember the words she was going to say. They were to say, "Kaweshtima kōt^i (North Mountain), appear in the north, and we will always know you to be in that direction." Tsichtinako also pointed out an article in the basket that she named ya'ōni (stone) and instructed them to throw the stone to the North direction as they spoke the words. When they did so, a big mountain appeared in the North. After they had done this, Tsichtinako instructed them to do the same thing in the West, but to name this mountain Tsipīna kot^i, and in the South, naming it Da'ōtyuma kot^i, and in the East, naming it G'ūchana kot^i.

After all this was done, Tsichtinako spoke again and told them, "Now that you have all the mountains around you with plains, mesas, and canyons, you must make the growing things of these places." Tsichtinako told them to go back to the trees which they had planted underground, lakhok, geietsu, wanuka, and lanye. She told them to take the seeds from these trees, and they did so. Following her instructions they spread some to each of the four directions, naming the mountains in each direction, and saying, "Grow in North Mountain, grow in West Mountain, etc." Tsichtinako said to them, "These are going to be tall trees; from them you will get logs. Later you will build houses and will use these." They asked if that was all that was going to grow on the mountains, and Tsichtinako said, "No, there are many other seeds left in your baskets. You have seeds of trees which are going to yield food. You will find dyai'its (piñon tree), sē'isha (kind of cedar), hapani (oak, acorn) and maka'yawi (walnut)." She again instructed them what to do and taught them the prayer to use, which was: "From now on, grow in this mountain and yield fruit which will be used as food. Your places are to be in the mountains. You will grow and be useful." When everything had been done well, Tsichtinako told (them) that there were many smaller seeds left in the baskets and she gave a name to each, telling them to fill the rest of the land. These seeds were planted on every one of the four mountains and in the rest of the world. Tsichtinako spoke to the sisters again and told them, "You still have seeds in your baskets which you will know as scuts'ō¹bewi (wild fruits). These trees you will grow around you and care for." But they mistook the instructions and instead of instructing them to grow nearby, they named the mountains, and that is where they grew. But there were also some that grew close around. It is not known how long they had to wait for these things to happen, but it was a very long time. They noticed that the wild plants grew very fast and produced much fruit, but Tsichtinako had not told them whether or not to eat these, so they left them alone.

They saw that there were still seeds and images in their baskets and asked Tsichtinako how many more kinds there were. Tsichtinako said there were yet many other seeds which would also be important food. They would grow quickly and easily and she named them squash and beans. They were instructed to act with them as with the other seeds, and these also grew into plants. After a time, when they were ripe, Tsichtinako pointed out the parts of the plants which they were to use as food.

Iatiku later asked Tsichtinako, "What remains in my basket?"and she was answered, "You have still many animals; these will be multiplied to populate the mountains." And as the two grew larger, they required more food. Tsichtinako saw this and told them that they were now to bring to life larger animals. She said they would find in their baskets cottontails, jack rabbits, antelope, and water deer. They were told to give life to these animals and to send them into the open plains. Everything was done as before, and when they killed the animals for food they were always careful to pray to their father as before. As they again asked Tsichtinako what remained in their baskets, Tsichtinako said, "You have images of the still bigger game. You will find deer, elk, mountain sheep, and bison." Iatiku asked where these animals were to be told to live and Tsichtinako told them that the elk and deer were to live in the lower mountains and the mountain sheep higher and in the rougher places. The bison, however, were to live on the plains. They followed the instructions and gave life to these animals and told them to go to these places to live and multiply. They again tried all these different animals for food. Their flesh was very good and always they prayed to Uchtsiti before tasting them.

In Nautsiti's basket there were many more things left than in Iatiku's. Nautsiti was selfish and hoarded her images, but Iatiku was ready to let her seeds and images be used. She was more interested in seeing things grow. They again asked what remained, and Tsichtinako replied, "You will find lion, wolf, wildcat and bear. These are strong beasts; they are going to use as food the same game that you also use. There is now game enough for them." When all these had been selected they were brought to life in the same manner as before.

The sisters again asked what was in their baskets, and they were told. "You will find birds which will fly in the air. These birds will also use small game for their food. You will find in the basket the eagles and the hawks (shpi‘ya, ga‘wa, i‘tsa)." Tsichtinako pointed these out to them and they brought them to life. The birds flew up into the high mountains and over the plains. The sisters told the birds to use small game for food, and again Iatiku asked what was in the basket. Tsichtinako pointed out smaller birds which would populate the country, each living in a different kind of region. They were then given life, as the animals before them. The birds were of many and bright colors, some were blue. The wild turkey was among them and they were instructed to tell it not to fly easily like the others. They were told to tell these birds that their food was to be the different seeds on the mountains and the plains. And all these animals were sampled for food after they had been given life. Again Iatiku asked what remained in the baskets, because she found things there that were thorny. Tsichtinako told them their names. They were the various cacti and were said to be very good for food. But Tsichtinako explained that most were intended for animals to eat. All these were planted as before and tried for food, and they found that some tasted good, stī’ăne, īcht, ya’tăp, iteō’on. After they asked again what was left, Tsichtinako pointed out to them that there were still fish, water snakes, and turtles, of which there were many kinds of each. They gave life to them as before and told them all to live in the water as instructed. Tsichtinako pointed out several that were to be used for food. They tried them all for food, and they found that some were good, and others poor, but offered prayers to all and gave thanks to Uchtsiti. So it happened that many animals came alive in the world and they all increased.

References

Ad C. Herennium [*Rhetorica ad Herennium*]. Trans. Harry Caplan. Cambridge: Harvard University Press, 1954.

Alcidamus. "On the Writers of Written Discourses." In *Artium scriptores: Reste der voraristotelischen Rhetorik*, by Ludwig Radermacher. Oesterreiches Akademie der Wissenschaften, Philosophisch-historische Klasse. Sitzungsberichte 227, Band 3. Vienna: in Kommission bei R. M. Rohrer, 1951.

Allen, Robert C. *Channels of Discourse, Reassembled*. Chapel Hill: University of North Carolina Press, 1992.

Anderson, Laurie. "Laurie Anderson Performance Piece with Electronics." Boulder, Colorado, 1 July 1996.

Andrew, Dudley. *Concepts in Film Theory*. New York: Oxford University Press, 1984.

Anson, Christopher N. *Writing and Response: Theory, Practice, and Research*. Urbana, Ill.: National Council of Teachers of English, 1989.

Applebee, Arthur N. *Tradition and Reform in the Teaching of English: A History*. Urbana, Ill.: National Council of Teachers of English, 1974.

Aristotle. *On Rhetoric: A Theory of Civic Discourse*. Trans. George A. Kennedy. New York: Oxford University Press, 1991.

Aristotle. *On Memory*. Trans. Richard Sorabji. Providence: Brown University Press, 1972.

Aristotle. *Poetics*. Trans. W. Hamilton Fyfe. Loeb Classical Library. Cambridge: Harvard University Press, 1960.

Atwill, Janet. "Toward Posthumanist Rhetorics: Aristotle and Productive Knowledge." Paper presented at the Conference on College Composition and Communication. Boston, 1991.

Bailey, Dudley. "A Plea for a Modern Set of Topoi." *College English* 26 (1964): 111–117.

Bain, Alexander. *English Composition and Rhetoric*. Enlarged edition. New York: Appleton, 1887.

Barthes, Roland. "The Death of the Author." In *Image-Music-Text*, by Roland Barthes, pp. 190–215. New York: Farrar, Strauss, Giroux, 1992.

Barthes, Roland. *Image-Music-Text*. Trans. Stephen Heath. New York: Hill and Wang, 1977. Reprint. New York: Farrar, Strauss, Giroux, 1992.

Barthes, Roland. "The Rhetoric of the Image." In *Image-Music-Text*, by Roland Barthes. New York: Farrar, Strauss, Giroux, 1992.

Bartholomae, David. "Inventing the University." In *When a Writer Can't Write: Studies in Writer's Block and Other Composing-Process Problems*, ed. Mike Rose, pp. 134–165. New York: Guilford Press, 1985.

Bartholomae, David, and Anthony R. Petrosky. "Facts, Artifacts, and Counterfacts: A Basic Reading and Writing Course for the College Curriculum." In *Facts, Artifacts, and Counterfacts: Theory and Method for a Reading and Writing Course*, ed. David Bartholomae and Anthony R. Petrosky, pp. 3–43. Upper Montclair, N.J.: Boynton/Cook Publishers, 1986.

Bartholomae, David, and Anthony R. Petrosky, eds. *Facts, Artifacts, and Counterfacts: Theory and Method for a Reading and Writing Course*. Upper Montclair, N.J.: Boynton/Cook Publishers, 1986.

Beck, Frederick A. G. *Album of Greek Education: The Greeks at School and at Play*. Sydney: Cheiron Press, 1975.

Belenky, Mary Field, Blythe McVicker Clinchy, Nancy Rule Goldberger, and Jill Mattuck Tarule. *Women's Ways of Knowing: The Development of Self, Voice, and Mind*. New York: Basic Books, 1986.

Benjamin, Walter. "The Work of Art in the Age of Mechanical Reproduction." In his *Illuminations*, pp. 217–251. Trans. Harry Zohn. New York: Schocken Books, 1969.

Benoit, William L. "Isocrates on Rhetorical Education." *Communication Education* 33 (1984): 109–119.

Berlin, James A. *Rhetoric and Reality: Writing Instruction in American Colleges, 1900–1985*. Carbondale: Southern Illinois University Press, 1987.

Berlin, James A. *Writing Instruction in Nineteenth-Century American Colleges*. Carbondale: Southern Illinois University Press, 1984.

Bernal, Martin. "*Black Athena* and the APA." *Arethusa* 22 (1989): 26–30.

Bernal, Martin. *The Fabrication of Ancient Greece, 1785–1985*. Vol. 1 of *Black Athena: The Afroasiatic Roots of Classical Civilization*. New Brunswick: Rutgers University Press, 1987.

Bernal, Martin. *The Archaeological and Documentary Evidence*. Vol. 2 of *Black Athena: The Afroasiatic Roots of Classical Civilization*. New Brunswick: Rutgers University Press, 1991.

Bernal, Martin. "Exchange with Mary Lefkowitz on *Black Athena*." Internet: Harper Collins Online, http://www. city.com/ascac/news. html, 3 May 1996.

Biesecker, Barbara. "Coming to Terms with Recent Attempts to Write Women into the History of Rhetoric." *Philosophy and Rhetoric* 25, no. 2 (1992): 140–161. Reprinted in *Rethinking the History of Rhetoric: Multidisciplinary Essays on the Rhetorical Tradition*, ed. Takis Poulakos, pp. 153–172. Boulder: Westview Press, 1993.

Bizzell, Patricia. "Arguing about Literacy." *College English* 50, no. 2 (Feb. 1988): 141–153. Reprinted in *The New Rhetorics*, ed. Theresa Enos and Stuart Brown. Also in *Academic Discourse and Critical Consciousness*, by Patricia Bizzell, pp. 238–255. Pittsburgh: University of Pittsburgh Press, 1992.

Bizzell, Patricia, and Bruce Herzberg, eds. *The Rhetorical Tradition*. Boston: St. Martin's Books, 1990.

Bleich, David. *The Double Perspective: Language, Literacy, and Social Relations*. New York: Oxford University Press, 1988.

Bleich, David. *Subjective Criticism*. Baltimore: Johns Hopkins University Press, 1978.

Bollman, Amy K., and Gabriel Rupp. *Sappho: Voices*. Internet: http://www.coe.ou.edu/ ~ akbollman/sappho/sapphoproject.html.

Bolter, Jay David. *Writing Space: The Computer, Hypertext, and the History of Writing*. Hillsdale: Lawrence Erlbaum Publishers, 1991.

Booth, Wayne C. *A Rhetoric of Fiction*. Chicago: University of Chicago Press, 1961.

Bowdon, Melody. "Disappearing Sex: A Rhetoric of Condoms." Paper presented to the Rhetoric Society of America, Pittsburgh, 7 June 1998.

Branch, Taylor. *Parting the Waters: America in the King Years, 1954–63*. New York: Simon and Schuster, 1988.

Brandt, Deborah. *Literacy as Social Involvement: The Acts of Writers, Readers, and Texts*. Carbondale: Southern Illinois University Press, 1990.

Bullock, Richard, and John Trimbur, eds. *The Politics of Writing Instruction: Postsecondary*. Portsmouth, N.H.: Boynton/Cook Publishers, 1991.

Burke, Kenneth. *Counter-Statement*. Berkeley: University of California Press, 1968.

Burke, Kenneth. *A Grammar of Motives*. Berkeley: University of California Press, 1969.

Burke, Kenneth. *A Rhetoric of Motives*. Berkeley: University of California Press, 1969.

Butler, Judith. *Gender Trouble: Feminism and the Subversion of Identity*. New York: Routledge, 1990.

Cahn, Michael. "Reading Rhetoric Rhetorically: Isocrates and the Marketing of Insight." *Rhetorica* 7, no. 2 (Spring 1989): 122–144.

Camargo, Martin. "Rhetoric." In *The Seven Liberal Arts in the Middle Ages*, ed. David. L. Wagner, pp. 96–124. Bloomington: Indiana University Press, 1986.

Carpenter, Rhys. "The Antiquity of the Greek Alphabet." *American Journal of Archaeology* 37 (1933): 8–29.

Carpenter, Rhys. "The Greek Alphabet Again." *American Journal of Archaeology* 42 (1938): 58–69.

Carruthers, Mary. *The Book of Memory: A Study of Memory in Medieval Culture*. Cambridge: Cambridge University Press, 1990.

Chartier, Roger. *Cultural History: Between Practices and Representations*. Trans. Lydia G. Cochrane. Ithaca: Cornell University Press, 1988.

Chartier, Roger. *The Cultural Origins of the French Revolution*. Trans. Lydia G. Cochrane. Durham: Duke University Press, 1991.

Chartier, Roger. *The Cultural Uses of Print in Early Modern France*. Trans. Lydia G. Cochrane. Princeton: Princeton University Press, 1987.

Chartier, Roger, ed. *The Culture of Print: Power and the Uses of Print in Early Modern Europe*. Trans. Lydia G. Cochrane. Princeton: Princeton University Press, 1989.

Chartier, Roger. *Forms and Meanings: Texts, Performances, and Audiences from Codex to Computer*. Philadelphia: University of Pennsylvania Press, 1995.

Cicero. *Brutus*. Loeb Classical Library. Cambridge: Harvard University Press, 1942.

Cicero. *De Oratore*. Trans. E. W. Sutton and H. Rackham. 2 vols. Loeb Classical Library. Cambridge: Harvard University Press, 1942.

Clark, Gregory, and S. Michael Halloran, eds. *Oratorical Culture in Nineteenth-Century America: Transformations in the Theory and Practice of Rhetoric*. Carbondale: Southern Illinois University Press, 1993.

Coles, William E. *Teaching Composing: A Guide to Teaching Writing as a Self-Creating Process*. Rochelle Park, N.J.: Hayden Book Company, 1974.

Comas, James N. "The Presence of Theory/Theorizing the Present." *Research in African Literatures* 21 (1990): 5–31.

"Communication and Institutional Change: Closing the Technology Gap." Roundtable at the Conference on College Composition and Communication, Cincinnati, March 1992.

Connors, Robert J. "Personal Writing Assignments." *College Composition and Communication* 38, no. 2 (May 1987): 166–183.

Connors, Robert J., Lisa S. Ede, and Andrea A. Lunsford. *Essays On Classical Rhetoric and Modern Discourse*. Carbondale, Ill: Southern Illinois University Press, 1984.

Corbett, Edward P. J. *Classical Rhetoric for the Modern Student*. 3rd ed. New York: Oxford University Press, 1990. First published in 1965.

Corbett, Edward P. J. "The *Topoi* Revisited." In Jean Dietz Moss, ed. *Rhetoric and Praxis*, pp. 43–57. Washington, D.C.: Catholic University of America Press, 1986.

Couturier, Maurice. *Textual Communication: A Print-Based Theory of the Novel*. London: Routledge, 1990.

Covino, William A. *The Art of Wondering: A Revisionist Return to the History of Rhetoric*. Portsmouth, N.H.: Boynton/Cook Publishers, 1988.

Covino, William A., and David A. Jolliffe, eds. *Rhetoric: Concepts, Definitions, Boundaries*. Boston: Allyn and Bacon, 1995.

Covino, William A., and David A. Jolliffe. "What Is Rhetoric?" In Covino and Jolliffe, *Rhetoric*, pp. 3–8. Boston: Allyn and Bacon, 1995.

Crowley, Sharon. *The Methodical Memory: Invention in Current-Traditional Rhetoric*. Carbondale: Southern Illinois University Press, 1990.

Crowley, Sharon. "Modern Rhetoric and Memory." In *Rhetorical Memory and Delivery: Classical Concepts for Contemporary Composition and Communication*, ed. John Frederick Reynolds, pp. 31–44. Hillsdale: Lawrence Erlbaum Publishers, 1993.

Crowley, Sharon. "A Plea for the Revival of Sophistry." *Rhetoric Review* 7 (1989): 318–334.

Crowley, Sharon. *A Teacher's Guide to Deconstruction*. Urbana, Ill.: National Council of Teachers of English, 1989.

Czitrom, Daniel J. *Media and the American Mind: From Morse to McLuhan*. Chapel Hill: University of North Carolina Press, 1982.

D'Angelo, Frank J. *A Conceptual Theory of Rhetoric*. Cambridge, Mass.: Winthrop, 1975.

Davidson, Cathy N., ed. *Reading in America: Literature and Social History*. Baltimore: Johns Hopkins University Press, 1989.

De Castell, Suzanne, Allan Luke, and Kieran Egan, eds. *Literacy, Society, and Schooling: A Reader*. Cambridge: Cambridge University Press, 1986.

De Romilly, Jacqueline. *The Great Sophists in Periclean Athens*. Trans. Janet Lloyd. Oxford: Clarendon Press, 1992.

De Romilly, Jacqueline. *Rhetoric and Magic in Ancient Greece*. Cambridge: Harvard University Press, 1975.

Derrida, Jacques. "Plato's Pharmacy." In his *Dissemination*, trans. Barbara Johnson, pp. 63–171. Chicago: University of Chicago Press, 1981.

Doheny-Farina, Stephen. *Rhetoric, Innovation, Technology: Case Studies of Technical Communication in Technology Transfers*. Cambridge: MIT Press, 1992.

DuBois, Page. "Violence and the Rhetoric of Philosophy." In *Rethinking the History of Rhetoric*, ed. Takis Poulakos, pp. 119–134. Boulder, Colo.: Westview Press, 1993.

Dunn, David. *Eigenwelt der Apparate-Welt: Pioneers of Electronic Art*. Linz, Austria: Ars Electronica, 1992.

Eagleton, Terry. *Ideology: An Introduction.* London: Verso, 1991.

Eagleton, Terry. *Literary Theory: An Introduction.* Minneapolis: University of Minnesota Press, 1983.

Eagleton, Terry. *Walter Benjamin, or Towards a Revolutionary Criticism.* London: Verso, 1981.

Eco, Umberto. *Travels in Hyperreality: Essays.* Trans. William Weaver. San Diego: Harcourt Brace Jovanovich, 1976.

Ede, Lisa, and Andrea Lunsford. "Audience Address/Audience Invoked: The Role of Audience in Composition Theory and Pedagogy." *College Composition and Communication* 35 (1984): 155–171.

Edwards, Harry. *Sociology of Sport.* Homewood, Ill.: Dorsey Press, 1973.

Ehninger, Douglas. "On Systems of Rhetoric." *Philosophy and Rhetoric* 1 (1968): 131–144.

Eisenstein, Elizabeth L. *The Printing Press as an Agent of Change: Communications and Cultural Transformations in Early-Modern Europe.* 2 vols. Cambridge: Cambridge University Press, 1979.

Elbow, Peter. *Writing without Teachers.* London: Oxford University Press, 1973.

Eliot, George. *The Mill on the Floss.* Clarendon Press, 1980.

Emerson, Ralph Waldo. "Circles." In *The Complete Writings of Ralph Waldo Emerson,* vol. 1, pp. 216–222. New York: Wise, 1929.

Enders, Jody. *The Medieval Theatre of Cruelty: Rhetoric, Violence, and Representation in France.* Ithaca: Cornell University Press, 1998.

Enders, Jody. "Memory and the Psychology of the Interior Monologue in Chrétien's *Cliges.*" *Rhetorica* 10 (1992): 5–23.

Enders, Jody. "Music, Delivery, and the Rhetoric of Memory in Guillaume de Machaut's *Remède de Fortune.*" *Publications of the Modern Language Association* 107 (1992): 450–464.

Enders, Jody. *Rhetoric and the Origins of Medieval Drama.* Ithaca: Cornell University Press, 1992.

Enos, Richard Leo. "The Epistemology of Gorgias' Rhetoric: A Re-examination." *Southern Speech Communication Journal* 42 (Fall 1976): 35–51.

Enos, Richard Leo. *Greek Rhetoric before Aristotle.* Prospect Heights, Ill.: Waveland Press, 1993.

Enos, Richard Leo. *The Literate Mode of Cicero's Legal Rhetoric.* Carbondale: Southern Illinois University Press, 1988.

Enos, Richard Leo, ed. *Oral and Written Communication: Historical Approaches.* Newbury Park, Calif.: Sage Publications, 1990.

Enos, Richard Leo. "Sophistic Formulae and the Emergence of the Attic-Ionic Grapholect: A Study in Oral and Written Communication." In *Oral and Written*

Communication: Historical Approaches, ed. Richard Leo Enos, pp. 24–31. Newbury Park, Calif.: Sage Publications, 1990.

Enos, Theresa. "A Brand New World: Using Our Professional and Personal Histories of Rhetoric." In *Learning from the Histories of Rhetoric*, ed. Theresa Enos, pp. 3–12. Carbondale: Southern Illinois University Press, 1993.

Enos, Theresa, ed. *The Encyclopedia of Rhetoric and Composition: Communication from Ancient Times to the Information Age*. New York: Garland, 1995.

Enos, Theresa, ed. *Learning from the Histories of Rhetoric*. Carbondale: Southern Illinois University Press, 1993.

Enos, Theresa, and Stuart C. Brown, eds. *Professing the New Rhetorics*. Englewood Cliffs: Prentice-Hall, 1994.

Enzensberger, Hans Magnus. *Critical Essays*. New York: Continuum Publishing, 1982.

Enzensberger, Hans Maguns. "The Industrialization of the Mind." In Enzensberger, *Critical Essays*, pp. 3–14. New York: Continuum Publishing, 1982.

Faigley, Lester. *Fragments of Rationality: Postmodernity and the Subject of Composition*. Pittsburgh: University of Pittsburgh Press, 1992.

Faigley, Lester. "Competing Theories of Process: A Critique and a Proposal." *College English* 48 (1986): 527–542.

Fantham, Elaine. "Translation of Isocrates." Unpublished manuscript.

Febvre, Lucien, and Henri-Jean Martin. *The Coming of the Book: The Impact of Printing, 1450–1800*. Trans. David Gerard. London: Verso, 1984.

Fetterley, Judith. *The Resisting Reader: A Feminist Approach to American Fiction*. Bloomington: Indiana University Press, 1978.

Feuer, Jane. *The Hollywood Musical*. Bloomington: Indiana University Press, 1982.

Finney, Jack. *Invasion of the Body Snatchers*. New Brunswick: Rutgers University Press, 1989.

Firestone, Shulamith. *The Dialectic of Sex: The Case for Feminist Revolution*. New York: Morrow, 1970.

Fish, Stanley. *Is There a Text in This Class? The Authority of Interpretive Communities*. Cambridge: Harvard University Press, 1980.

Fiske, John. *Television Culture*. London: Methuen, 1987.

Fiske, John, and John Hartley. *Reading Television*. London: Methuen, 1978.

Flanigan, Michael C. "Collaborative Revision: Learning and Self-Assessment." In *Literacy, Society, and Schooling: A Reader*, ed. Suzanne de Castell, Allan Luke, and Kieran Egan, pp. 313–321. Cambridge: Cambridge University Press, 1986.

Fogarty, Daniel. *Roots for a New Rhetoric*. New York: Russell and Russell, 1968.

Foley, John Miles. *A Theory of Oral Composition: History and Methodology*. Bloomington: Indiana University Press, 1988.

Foucault, Michel. *The Archaeology of Knowledge and the Discourse on Language*. Trans. A. M. Sheridan Smith. New York: Pantheon, 1972.

Foucault, Michel. "What Is an Author?" In *Textual Strategies*, ed. Josue V. Harari, pp. 141–160. Ithaca: Cornell University Press, 1979.

Fraser, Nancy, and Sandra Lee Bartky, eds. *Revaluing French Feminism: Critical Essays on Difference, Agency, and Culture*. Bloomington: Indiana University Press, 1992.

Freeman, Kenneth John. *Schools of Hellas: An Essay on the Practice and Theory of Ancient Greek Education from 600 to 300 B.C.* London: Macmillan and Co., 1907.

Freire, Paulo. *Pedagogy of the Oppressed*. New York: Seabury Press, 1970.

Gardner, Howard. *Frames of Mind*. New York: Basic Books, 1983.

Gates, Henry Louis, Jr., and Nellie Y. McKay, eds. *The Norton Anthology of African American Literature*. CD-ROM. New York: Norton, 1997.

Gelb, I. J. *A Study of Writing*. Chicago: University of Chicago Press, 1952.

Gilroy, Paul. *The Black Atlantic: Modernity and Double Consciousness*. Cambridge: Harvard University Press, 1993.

Ginsberg, Allen. *Howl and Other Poems*. San Francisco: City Lights Books, 1956.

Glenn, Cheryl. *Rhetoric Retold: Regendering the Tradition from Antiquity through the Renaissance*. Carbondale: Southern Illinois University Press, 1997.

Gless, Daryl J., and Barbara Herrnstein Smith, eds. *The Politics of Liberal Education*. Durham: Duke University Press, 1992.

Gorgias. "Fragments." In *The Older Sophists*, ed. Rosamond Kent Sprague and trans. George A. Kennedy, pp. 42–67. Columbia: University of South Carolina Press, 1972.

Graff, Harvey J. *The Legacies of Literacy: Continuities and Contradictions in Western Culture and Society*. Bloomington: Indiana University Press, 1987.

Grafton, Anthony, and Lisa Jardine. *From Humanism to the Humanities: Education and the Liberal Arts in Fifteenth- and Sixteenth-Century Europe*. Cambridge: Harvard University Press, 1986.

Grimaldi, William J. "The Aristotelian *Topics*." *Traditio* 14 (1958): 1–16. Reprinted in *The Classical Heritage of Rhetoric*, ed. Keith V. Erickson, pp. 176–193. Metuchen, N.J.: Scarecrow Press, 1974.

Grimaldi, William J. *Aristotle's "Rhetoric," Book I: A Commentary*. New York: Fordham University Press, 1980.

Gronbeck, Bruce, Thomas J. Farrell, and Paul A. Soukup, eds. *Media, Consciousness, and Culture: Explorations of Walter Ong's Thought*. Newbury Park, Calif.: Sage Publications, 1991.

Guidelines For Nonsexist Use of Language in NCTE Publications. Urbana, Ill.: National Council of Teachers of English, 1985.

Guillory, John. "Canon." In *Critical Terms for Literary Study*, ed. Frank Lentricchia and Thomas McLaughlin, pp. 233–249. Chicago: University of Chicago Press, 1990.

Gurak, Laura J. *Persuasion and Privacy in Cyberspace: The Online Protests over Lotus Marketplace and Clipper Chip.* New Haven: Yale University Press, 1997.

Guralnick, Elissa S. *Sight Unseen: Beckett, Pinter, Stoppard, and Other Contemporary Dramatists on Radio.* Athens: Ohio University Press, 1996.

Guthrie, W. K. C. *The Sophists.* Vol. 1 of *A History of Greek Philosophy.* Cambridge: Cambridge University Press, 1969.

Harris, William V. *Ancient Literacy.* Cambridge: Harvard University Press, 1989.

Havelock, Eric A. *The Greek Concept of Justice: From Its Shadow in Homer to Its Substance in Plato.* Cambridge: Harvard University Press, 1978.

Havelock, Eric A. *The Literate Revolution in Greece and Its Cultural Consequences.* Princeton: Princeton University Press, 1982.

Havelock, Eric A. *Preface to Plato.* Cambridge: Harvard University Press, 1963.

Hawisher, Gail E., and Paul LeBlanc, eds. *Re-imagining Computers and Composition: Teaching and Research in the Virtual Age.* Portsmouth, N.H.: Boynton/Cook Publishers, 1992.

Heath, Shirley Brice. *Ways with Words: Language, Life, and Work in Communities and Classrooms.* Cambridge: Cambridge University Press, 1983.

Heckel, David. "Ong and Derrida: Orality, Literacy, and the Rhetoric of Deconstruction." Paper presented at the Conference on College Composition and Communication, St. Louis, March 1988.

Heim, Michael. *Electric Language: A Philosophical Study of Word Processing.* New Haven: Yale University Press, 1987.

Heim, Michael. *The Metaphysics of Virtual Reality.* Oxford: Oxford University Press, 1993.

Helton, Edwina. "Diotima of Mantinea." In *The Encyclopedia of Rhetoric and Composition*, pp. 191–192. New York: Garland, 1996.

Hinks, D. A. G. "Tisias and Corax and the Invention of Rhetoric." *Classical Quarterly* 34 (1940): 61–69.

Hobbs, Catherine. "Eighteenth Century Language and Rhetoric: The Death of Rhetoric and the Birth of Rhetoricality." Unpublished manuscript.

Hobbs, Catherine, ed. *Nineteenth-Century Women Learn to Write.* Charlottesville: University Press of Virginia, 1995.

Hogan, Linda. *Everything Has a Spirit.* Directed by Ava Hamilton and Gabriele Dech. Television broadcast. Denver, Colo.: KBDI-TV Channel 12, 1992.

Holdstein, Deborah H., and Cynthia L. Selfe, eds. *Computers and Writing: Theory, Research, Practice.* New York: Modern Language Association, 1990.

Holland, Norman. "A Transactive Account of Transactive Criticism." *Poetics* 7 (1978): 18–189.

Homer. *The Odyssey*. 2 vols. Trans. A. T. Murray. Loeb Classical Library. Cambridge: Harvard University Press, 1919.

Horner, Winifred Bryan. *Nineteenth-Century Scottish Rhetoric*. Carbondale: Southern Illinois University Press, 1993.

Horowitz, Rosalind, and S. Jay Samuels, eds. *Comprehending Oral and Written Language*. San Diego: Academic Press, 1987.

Hunter, Lynette. "Ideology as the Ethos of the Nation State." *Rhetorica* 14 (Spring 1996): 197–229.

Ijsseling, Samuel. *Rhetoric and Philosophy in Conflict: An Historical Survey*. The Hague: Mouton, 1963.

Innis, Harold. *Empire and Communications*. Toronto: University of Toronto Press, 1972.

Invasion of the Body Snatchers. Directed by Philip Kaufman. Performed by Donald Sutherland. United States: Allied Artists, 1978.

Invasion of the Body Snatchers. Directed by Don Siegel. Performed by Kevin McCarthy. United States: Allied Artists, 1956.

Irigaray, Luce. "Sorcerer Love: A Reading of Plato's *Symposium*, Diotima's Speech." Trans. Eleanor H. Kuykendall. In *Revaluing French Feminism*, ed. Nancy Fraser and Sandra Lee Bartky, pp. 64–76. Bloomington: Indiana University Press, 1992.

Irigaray, Luce. *This Sex Which Is Not One*. Trans. Catherine Porter. Ithaca: Cornell University Press, 1985.

Iser, Wolfgang. *The Act of Reading: A Theory of Aesthetic Response*. Baltimore: Johns Hopkins University Press, 1979.

Isocrates. *Against Euthynus*. In *Isocrates*, vol. 3. Cambridge: Harvard University Press, 1945.

Isocrates. *Against Lochites*. In *Isocrates*, vol. 3. Cambridge: Harvard University Press, 1945.

Isocrates. *Against the Sophists*. In *Isocrates*, vol. 2. Cambridge: Harvard University Press, 1929.

Isocrates. *Antidosis*. In *Isocrates*, vol. 2. Cambridge: Harvard University Press, 1929.

Isocrates. *Helen*. In *Isocrates*, vol. 3. Cambridge: Harvard University Press, 1945.

Isocrates. *Isocrates*. Vols. 1 and 2, trans. George Norlin. Vol. 3, trans. Larue Van Hook. Loeb Classical Library. Cambridge: Harvard University Press. Vol. 1, 1928. Vol. 2, 1929. Vol. 3, 1945.

Isocrates. *Isocratis Orationes*. 2 vols. Ed. Friedrich Blass. Leipzig: Teubner, 1913–1937.

Isocrates. *Panathenaicus*. In *Isocrates*, vol. 2. Cambridge: Harvard University Press, 1929.

Jaeger, Werner. *Paideia: The Ideals of Greek Culture*. 3 vols. Trans. Gilbert Highet. New York: Oxford University Press, 1939–1945.

Jameson, Fredric. *The Political Unconscious: Narrative as a Socially Symbolic Act*. Ithaca: Cornell University Press, 1981.

Jamieson, Kathleen Hall. *Eloquence in an Electronic Age: The Transformation of Political Speechmaking*. New York: Oxford University Press, 1988.

Jarratt, Susan C. *Rereading the Sophists: Classical Rhetoric Refigured*. Carbondale: Southern Illinois University Press, 1991.

Jarratt, Susan C., and Rory Ong. "Aspasia: Rhetoric, Gender, and Colonial Ideology." In *Reclaiming Rhetorica*, ed. Andrea A. Lunsford, pp. 9–24. Pittsburgh: University of Pittsburgh Press, 1995.

Jebb, R. C. *The Attic Orators from Antiphon to Isaeos*. 2 vols. London: Macmillan, 1876.

Johnson, Frances. "Ramus and the Current Traditional Paradigm." Unpublished dissertation, University of Oklahoma, 1996.

Johnson, Nan. *Nineteenth-Century Rhetoric in North America*. Carbondale: Southern Illinois University Press, 1991.

Johnson, Nan. "Reader-Response and the Pathos Principle." *Rhetoric Review* 6, no. 2 (Spring 1988): 152–166.

Joyce, James. *Ulysses*. New York: Random House, 1946.

Kairos: A Journal for the Teaching of Writing in Webbed Environments. Ed. Mick Doherty. 1, no. 1 (Spring 1996). Texas Tech University. Internet: http://www.english.ttu.edu/kairos/1.1/, April 1996.

Kaufer, David, and Kathleen Carley. *Communication at a Distance*. Hillsdale: Lawrence Erlbaum Assoc., 1993.

Kennedy, George A. *The Art of Persuasion in Greece*. Princeton: Princeton University Press, 1963.

Kennedy, George A., ed. *The Cambridge History of Literary Criticism*, vol. 1, *Classical Criticism*. Cambridge: Cambridge University Press, 1989.

Kennedy, George A. *Classical Rhetoric and Its Christian and Secular Tradition from Ancient to Modern Times*. Chapel Hill: University of North Carolina Press, 1980.

Kennedy, George A. "Classics and Canons." In *The Politics of the Liberal Arts*, ed. Daryl J. Gless and Barbara Herrnstein Smith, pp. 223–231. Durham, N.C.: Duke University Press, 1992.

Kennedy, George A. "The Evolution of a Theory of Artistic Prose." In *The Cambridge History of Literary Criticism*, vol. 1, *Classical Criticism*, ed. George A. Kennedy, pp. 184–199. Cambridge: Cambridge University Press, 1989.

Kennedy, George A. *A New History of Classical Rhetoric.* An extensive revision and abridgment of *The Art of Persuasion in Greece, The Art of Rhetoric in the Roman World,* and *Greek Rhetoric under Christian Emperors.* Princeton: Princeton University Press, 1994.

Kennedy, William J. *Rhetorical Norms in Renaissance Literature.* New Haven: Yale University Press, 1978.

Kennedy, William J. "Voice as Frame: Longinus, Kant, Ong, and Deconstruction in Literary Studies." In *Media, Consciousness, and Culture,* ed. Bruce Gronbeck, Thomas J. Farrell, and Paul A. Soukup, pp. 77–89. Newbury Park, Calif.: Sage Publications, 1991.

Keohane, Nannerl, Michelle Z. Rosaldo, and Barbara C. Gelpi, eds. *Feminist Theory: A Critique of Ideology.* Chicago: University of Chicago Press, 1982.

Kerferd, G. B. *The Sophistic Movement.* Cambridge: Cambridge University Press, 1981.

Keuls, Eva C. *The Reign of the Phallus: Sexual Politics in Ancient Athens.* Berkeley: University of California Press, 1993. First published in 1985.

Killingsworth, M. Jimmie. *Information in Action: A Guide to Technical Communication.* Boston: Allyn and Bacon, 1996.

Kinneavy, James L. *The Greek Rhetorical Origins of Christian Faith: An Inquiry.* New York: Oxford University Press, 1987.

Kinneavy, James L. "Kairos: A Neglected Concept in Classical Rhetoric." In *Rhetoric and Praxis: The Contribution of Classical Rhetoric to Practical Reasoning,* ed. Jean Dietz Moss, pp. 79–105. Washington, D.C.: Catholic University of America Press, 1986.

Kinneavy, James L. "Restoring the Humanities: The Return of Rhetoric from Exile." In *The Rhetorical Tradition and Modern Writing,* ed. James J. Murphy, pp. 19–28. New York: Modern Language Association, 1982.

Kinneavy, James L. *A Theory of Discourse: The Aims of Discourse.* New York: Norton, 1971.

Kinneavy, James L. "Theory, Theories, No Theories." Paper presented at the Conference on College Composition and Communication, Cincinnati, March 1992.

Knoblauch, C. H., and Lil Brannon. *Rhetorical Traditions and the Teaching of Writing.* Upper Montclair, N.J.: Boynton/Cook Publishers, 1984.

Kristeva, Julia. "The System and the Speaking Subject." In *The Kristeva Reader,* ed. Toril Moi, pp. 24–33. New York: Columbia University Press, 1986.

Kristeva, Julia. "Woman's Time." Trans. Alice Jardine and Harry Blake. In *Feminist Theory: A Critique of Ideology,* ed. Nannerl O. Keohane, Michelle Z. Rosaldo, and Barbara C. Gelpi, pp. 31–53. Chicago: University of Chicago Press, 1982.

LaCapra, Dominick. "Rhetoric and History." In his *History and Criticism,* pp. 15–44. Ithaca: Cornell University Press, 1985.

LaCapra, Dominick. *Soundings in Critical Theory*. Ithaca: Cornell University Press, 1989.

Langer, Susanne K. *Philosophy in a New Key: A Study in the Symbolism of Reason, Rite, and Art*. 3rd ed. Cambridge: Harvard University Press, 1980.

Lanham, Richard A. *The Electronic Word: Democracy, Technology, and the Arts*. Chicago: University of Chicago Press, 1993.

Lather, Patti. *Getting Smart*. New York: Routledge, 1994.

Lauer, Janice M. "Issues in Rhetorical Invention." In *Essays on Classical Rhetoric and Modern Discourse*, ed. Robert J. Connors, Lisa S. Ede, and Andrea A. Lunsford, pp. 127–139. Carbondale, Ill.: Southern Illinois University Press, 1984.

Lefkowitz, Mary R. "Comments on Martin Bernal's Posting, 3 May 1996." In *Black Athena Revisited, Discussion*. Harper Collins Online. Internet: http://www.citycom.com/ascac/news.html, 10 May 1996.

Lefkowitz, Mary R., and Guy MacLean Rogers, eds. *Black Athena Revisited*. Chapel Hill: University of North Carolina Press, 1996.

Lentricchia, Frank, and Thomas McLaughlin, eds. *Critical Terms for Literary Study*. Chicago: University of Chicago Press, 1990.

Lentz, Tony M. *Orality and Literacy in Hellenic Greece*. Carbondale: Southern Illinois University Press, 1989.

Levine, Molly Meyerowitz. "The Challenge of *Black Athena*." *Arethusa* 21 (1989): 7–16.

Liddell, George, and Robert Scott, eds. *A Greek-English Lexicon*. Revised by Henry Stuart Jones et al. Oxford: Clarendon Press, 1968.

Lohr, Steve. "The Great Unplugged Masses Confront the Future." *New York Times*, 21 April 1996, pp. E5, E6.

Loraux, Nicole. *Tragic Ways of Killing a Woman*. Trans. Anthony Foster. Cambridge: Harvard University Press, 1987.

Lord, Albert Bates. *Epic Singers and Oral Tradition*. Ithaca: Cornell University Press, 1991.

Lord, Albert Bates. *The Singer of Tales*. Cambridge: Harvard University Press, 1960.

Lunsford, Andrea A., ed. *Reclaiming Rhetorica: Women in the Rhetorical Tradition*. Pittsburgh: University of Pittsburgh Press, 1995.

Lunsford, Andrea A., and Lisa Ede. "Representing Audience: 'Successful' Discourse and Disciplinary Critique." *College Composition and Communication* 47, no. 2 (May 1996): 167–179.

Lunsford, Andrea A., and Lisa Ede. *Singular Texts/Plural Authors*. Carbondale: Southern Illinois University Press, 1990.

Lunsford, Andrea A., Helene Moglen, and James Slevin, eds. *The Right to Literacy*. New York: Modern Language Association, 1990.

Lunsford, Andrea A., Rebecca Rickly, Michael Salvo, and Susan West. "What Matters Who Writes? What Matters Who Responds? Issues of Ownership in the Writing Classroom." *Kairos: A Journal for the Teaching of Writing in Webbed Environments* 1, no. 1 (Spring 1996). Internet, 18 April 1996.

Lunsford, Andrea, and Susan West. "Intellectual Property and Composition Studies." *College Composition and Communication* 47, no. 4 (1996): 383–411.

MacDonald, Dwight. *Against the American Grain: Essays on the Effects of Mass Culture.* New York: Vintage, 1962.

Madonna. *Express Yourself.* Dir. David Fincher. Perf. Madonna. Music Video. Warner Bros., 1989.

Mahony, Patrick. "Marshall McLuhan in the Light of Classical Rhetoric." *College Composition and Communication* 20 (1969): 12–17.

Mailloux, Steven J. *Interpretive Conventions: The Reader in the Study of American Fiction.* Ithaca: Cornell University Press, 1982.

Mailloux, Steven J. *Rhetorical Power.* Ithaca: Cornell University Press, 1989.

Mailloux, Steven J., ed. *Rhetoric, Sophistry, Pragmatism.* New York: Cambridge University Press, 1995.

Marc, David. *Demographic Vistas: Television in American Culture.* Philadelphia: University of Pennsylvania Press, 1984.

Marchand, Philip. *Marshall McLuhan: The Medium and the Messenger.* New York: Ticknor and Fields, 1989.

Marrou, H. I. *A History of Education in Antiquity.* Trans. George Lamb. Madison: University of Wisconsin Press, 1982.

McKeon, Richard. "Rhetoric in the Middle Ages." *Speculum* 17 (January 1942): 1–32.

McLuhan, Marshall. *The Gutenberg Galaxy: The Making of Typographic Man.* Toronto: University of Toronto Press, 1962.

McLuhan, Marshall. *The Mechanical Bride: Folklore of Industrial Man.* New York: Vanguard Press, 1951.

McLuhan, Marshall. *Understanding Media: The Extensions of Man.* New York: New American Library, 1964.

McQuade, Donald, Robert Atwan, Martha Banta, Justin Kaplan, David Minter, Cecelia Tichi, and Helen Vendler, eds. *Harper American Literature.* New York: Harper and Row, 1987.

Middleton, Joyce Irene. "Confronting the 'Master Narrative': The Privilege of Orality in Toni Morrison's *The Bluest Eye.*" *Cultural Studies* 9, no. 2 (1995): 301–317.

Middleton, Joyce Irene. "The Psychodynamics of Orality in Written Texts." Chapter of "Confronting Lingering Questions in Plato's *Phaedrus*: How Textbook Authors Draw on Historical Speech Strategies to Teach Writing," unpublished Ph.D. diss., University of Maryland, 1988.

Mifflin, Lawrie. "USA Strives for Network, Not Channel." *New York Times*, 30 April 1996, pp. B1, B4.

Miller, Susan. *Assuming the Positions: Cultural Pedagogy and the Politics of Commonplace Writing*. Pittsburgh: University of Pittsburgh Press, 1998.

Miller, Susan. "The Feminization of Composition." In *The Politics of Writing Instruction: Postsecondary*, ed. Richard Bullock and John Trimbur, pp. 39–53. Portsmouth, N.H.: Boynton/Cook Publishers, 1991.

Miller, Susan. *Rescuing the Subject: A Critical Introduction to Rhetoric and Writing*. Carbondale: Southern Illinois University Press, 1989.

Miller, Thomas P. *The Formation of College English: Rhetoric and Belles Lettres in the British Cultural Provinces*. Pittsburgh: University of Pittsburgh Press, 1997.

Miller, Thomas P. "Teaching the Histories of Rhetoric as a Social Praxis." *Rhetoric Review* 12 (Fall 1993): 70–82.

Modleski, Tania. *Loving with a Vengeance: Mass-Produced Fantasies for Women*. Hamden, Conn.: Archon, 1982.

Moffett, James. *Teaching the Universe of Discourse*. Portsmouth, N.H.: Boynton/ Cook Publishers, 1968.

Moi, Toril, ed., *The Kristeva Reader*. New York: Columbia University Press, 1986.

Monk, Meredith. "Book of Days: Concert Version." Dir. Meredith Monk. Perf. Meredith Monk. New York: House Foundation for the Arts, 1985.

Montroy, Trevor. "An Appropriation of Five Keywords in Contemporary Rhetoric." Unpublished diss., University of Oklahoma, 1996.

Morrison, Toni. *Playing in the Dark: Whiteness and the Literary Imagination*. New York: Vintage, 1992.

Moss, Jean Dietz, ed. *Rhetoric and Praxis: The Contribution of Classical Rhetoric to Practical Reasoning*. Washington, D.C.: Catholic University of America Press, 1986.

Mountford, Roxanne. "Qualitative Research and the Politics of Disclosure." Paper presented at the Conference on College Composition and Communication, Chicago, 3 April 1998.

Murphy, James J., ed. *The Rhetorical Tradition and Modern Writing*. New York: Modern Language Association, 1982.

Murphy, James J., ed. *A Short History of Writing Instruction: From Ancient Greece to Twentieth-Century America*. Davis, Calif.: Hermagoras Press, 1990.

Murphy, James J., ed. *A Synoptic History of Classical Rhetoric*. New York: Random House, 1972. 2nd ed.: Davis, Calif.: Hermagoras Press, 1995.

Neel, Jasper. *Aristotle's Voice: Rhetoric, Theory, and Writing in America*. Carbondale: Southern Illinois University Press, 1994.

Neel, Jasper. *Plato, Derrida, and Writing*. Carbondale: Southern Illinois University Press, 1988.

Newcomb, Horace. *Television: The Critical View*. New York: Oxford University Press, 1976.

Norlin, George, trans. and ed. *Isocrates*. Vols. 1 and 2. Loeb Classical Library. Cambridge: Harvard University Press. Vol. 1, 1928. Vol. 2, 1929.

North, Stephen M., *The Making of Knowledge in Composition: Portrait of an Emerging Field*. Portsmouth, N.H.: Boynton/Cook Publishers, 1987.

Ochs, Donovan J. "Cicero's *Topica*: A Process View of Invention." In *Explorations in Rhetoric: Studies in Honor of Douglas Ehninger*, ed. Ray E. McKerrow, pp. 107–118. Glenview, Ill.: Scott, Foresman, 1982.

Ochs, Donovan J. *Consolatory Rhetoric: Grief, Symbol, and Ritual in the Greco-Roman Era*. Columbia: University of South Carolina Press, 1993.

Ohmann, Richard. *English in America: A Radical View of the Profession*. New York: Oxford University Press, 1976. Rev. ed.: Wesleyan University Press, 1995.

Ong, Walter J. *The Barbarian Within*. New York: Macmillan, 1962.

Ong, Walter J. *Fighting for Life: Contest, Sexuality, and Consciousness*. Ithaca: Cornell University Press, 1981.

Ong, Walter J. *Interfaces of the Word*. Ithaca: Cornell University Press, 1977.

Ong, Walter J. *Orality and Literacy: The Technologizing of the Word*. London: Methuen, 1982.

Ong, Walter J. *The Presence of the Word: Some Prolegomena for Cultural and Religious History*. 2nd ed. Minneapolis: University of Minnesota Press, 1981.

Ong, Walter J. *Ramus: Method and the Decay of Dialogue*. Cambridge: Harvard University Press, 1958.

Ong, Walter J. *Ramus and Talon Inventory*. Cambridge: Harvard University Press, 1958.

Ong, Walter J. *Rhetoric, Romance, and Technology: Studies in the Interaction of Expression and Culture*. Ithaca: Cornell University Press, 1971.

Ong, Walter J. "The Writer's Audience Is Always a Fiction." *Publications of the Modern Language Association* 90 (1975): 9–21. Reprinted in his *Interfaces of the Word*, pp. 53–81. Ithaca: Cornell University Press, 1977.

Origin Myth of Acoma and Other Records. Recorded by Matthew W. Stirling. Smithsonian Institution, Bureau of American Ethnology, Bulletin, no. 135. Washington, D.C.: U.S. Government Printing Office, 1942.

Oxford Classical Dictionary. Ed. N. G. L. Hammond and H. H. Scullard. 2nd ed. Oxford: Clarendon Press, 1970.

Parry, Milman. *The Making of Homeric Verse: The Collected Papers of Milman Parry*. Ed. Adam Parry. Oxford: Clarendon Press, 1971.

Penley, Constance, and Andrew Ross, eds. *Technoculture*. Minneapolis: University of Minnesota Press, 1991.

Perelman, Chaim, and L. Olbrechts-Tyteca. *The New Rhetoric: A Treatise on Argumentation*. Trans. John Wilkinson and Purcell Weaver. Notre Dame: University of Notre Dame Press, 1969.

Perfetti, C. A. "Language, Speech, and Print: Some Asymmetries in the Acquisition of Literacy." In Rosalind Horowitz and S. Jay Samuels, eds., *Comprehending Oral and Written Language*, pp. 355–369. San Diego: Academic Press, 1987.

Perseus Project. Perseus 1.0. *Interactive Sources and Studies on Ancient Greek Culture*. New Haven: Yale University Press. Internet: http://www.perseus.tufts.edu/perseusinfo.html, 1992.

Petrucci, Armando. *Writers and Readers in Medieval Italy: Studies in the History of Written Culture*. Trans. Charles M. Radding. New Haven: Yale University Press, 1996.

Plato. *Apology*. In his *Opera*, vol. 1. Oxford: Oxford University Press.

Plato. *Crito*. In his *Opera*, vol. 1. Oxford: Oxford University Press.

Plato. *Euthyphro*. In his *Opera*, vol. 1. Oxford: Oxford University Press.

Plato. *Gorgias*. Trans. W. C. Helmbold. Indianapolis: Bobbs-Merrill, 1976.

Plato. Letter VII. In his *Phaedrus and Letters VII and VIII*, trans. Walter Hamilton, pp. 111–150. Harmondsworth, England: Penguin, 1973.

Plato. *Opera*. 5 Vols. Oxford Classical Texts. Oxford: Oxford University Press. Vol. 1, ed. E. A. Duke, W. F. Hicken, W. S. M. Nicoll, D. B. Robinson, and J. C. G. Strachan, 1994. Vol. 2, ed. J. Burnet, 1915. Vol. 3, ed. J. Burnet, 1903. Vol. 4, ed. J. Burnet, 1905. Vol. 5, ed. J. Burnet, 1908.

Plato. *Phaedrus*. Trans. W. C. Helmbold and W. G. Rabinowitz. Indianapolis: Bobbs-Merrill, 1956.

Plato. *Symposium*. Trans. Alexander Nehamas and Paul Woodruff. Indianapolis: Hackett, 1989.

Porter, James E. *Audience and Rhetoric: An Archaeological Composition of the Discourse Community*. Englewood Cliffs: Prentice-Hall, 1992.

Poulakos, John. *Sophistical Rhetoric in Classical Greece*. Columbia: University of South Carolina Press, 1995.

Poulakos, Takis, ed. *Rethinking the History of Rhetoric*. Boulder, Colo.: Westview Press, 1993.

Poulakos, Takis. *Speaking for the Polis: Isocrates' Rhetorical Education*. Columbia: University of South Carolina Press, 1997.

Poulakos, Takis. "Towards a Cultural Understanding of Classical Epideictic Oratory." *Pre/Text* 9, no. 3 (1988): 147–166.

Quintilian. *Institutio oratoria*. 4 vols. Trans. H. E. Butler. Loeb Classical Library. Cambridge: Harvard University Press, 1920–1922.

Ransom, John Crowe. "Criticism as Pure Speculation." In *The Intent of the Critic*, ed. D. A. Stauffer, pp. 92–124, Princeton: Princeton University Press, 1941.

Rebhorn, Wayne A. *The Emperor of Men's Minds: Literature and the Renaissance Discourse of Rhetoric.* Ithaca: Cornell University Press, 1995.

Reynolds, John Frederick, ed. *Rhetorical Memory and Delivery: Classical Concepts for Contemporary Composition and Communication.* Hillsdale: Lawrence Erlbaum Publishers, 1993.

Rose, Mike, ed. *When a Writer Can't Write: Studies in Writer's Block and Other Composing-Process Problems.* New York: Guilford Press, 1985.

Rosenblatt, Louise. *The Reader, the Text, the Poem: The Transactional Theory of the Literary Work.* Carbondale: Southern Illinois University Press, 1978.

Royster, Jacqueline Jones. "Perspectives on the Intellectual Tradition of Black Women Writers." In *The Right to Literacy*, ed. Andrea A. Lunsford, Helene Moglen, and James Slevin, pp. 103–112. New York: Modern Language Association, 1990.

Said, Edward. *Orientalism.* New York: Vintage, 1979.

Sanjek, David. "Don't Have to DJ No More: Sampling and the 'Autonomous' Creator." *Cardozo Arts and Entertainment Law Journal* 10 (1992): 607–621.

Saussure, Ferdinand de. *Course in General Linguistics.* Ed. Charles Bally and Albert Sechehaye. Trans. Wade Baskin. New York: McGraw-Hill, 1966.

Scaglione, Aldo. *The Classical Theory of Composition from Its Origins to the Present: A Historical Survey.* Chapel Hill: University of North Carolina Press, 1972.

Schatz, Thomas. *The Genius of the System: Hollywood Filmmaking in the Studio Era.* New York: Pantheon, 1988.

Schiappa, Edward. "Isocrates' *Philosophia* and Contemporary Pragmatism." In *Rhetoric, Sophistry, Pragmatism*, ed. Steven J. Mailloux, pp. 33–60. New York: Cambridge University Press, 1995.

Schiappa, Edward. *Protagoras and Logos: A Study in Greek Philosophy and Rhetoric.* Columbia: University of South Carolina Press, 1991.

Schiappa, Edward. "Sophistic Rhetoric: Oasis or Mirage?" *Rhetoric Review* 10 (1991): 5–19.

Schilb, John. *Between the Lines: Relating Composition and Literary Theory.* Portsmouth, N. H.: Boynton/Cook Publishers, 1996.

Schmandt-Bessarat, Denise. "The Envelopes That Bear the First Writing." *Technology and Culture* 21 (1980): 357–385.

Scholes, Robert. *Textual Power.* New Haven: Yale University Press, 1985.

Schultz, Lucille. "Elaborating Our History: A Look at Mid-Nineteenth-Century First Books of Composition." *College Composition and Communication* 45, no. 1 (February 1994): 10–30.

Schuster, Charles I. "Mikhail Bakhtin as Rhetorical Theorist." *College English* 47(1985): 594–607.

Scott, J. Blake. "Constructing Classroom Communities." *Oklahoma English Journal* 7 (Fall 1992): 16–22.

Scott, Joan Wallach. *Gender and the Politics of History*. New York: Columbia University Press, 1988.

Scribner, Sylvia, and Michael Cole. *The Psychology of Literacy*. Cambridge: Harvard University Press, 1981.

Sebeok, Thomas, ed. *The Tell-Tale Sign: A Survey of Semiotics*. Lisse, Netherlands: Ridder, 1975.

Selfe, Cynthia L. *Computer-Assisted Instruction in Composition: Create Your Own*. Urbana, Ill.: National Council of Teachers of English, 1986.

Selfe, Cynthia L. "Computers in English Departments: The Rhetoric of Techno/ Power." *ADE Bulletin* 90 (Fall 1988): 63–67. Reprinted in *Computers and Writing*, ed. Deborah H. Holdstein and Cynthia L. Selfe, pp. 95–103. New York: Modern Language Association, 1990.

Selfe, Cynthia L., and Susan Hilligoss, eds. *Literacy and Computers: The Complications of Teaching and Learning with Technology*. New York: Modern Language Association, 1994.

Shaughnessy, Mina. *Errors and Expectations: A Guide for the Teacher of Basic Writing*. New York: Oxford University Press, 1977.

Shor, Ira. *Critical Teaching and Everyday Life*. Boston: South End Press, 1980.

Shor, Ira. *Freire for the Classroom*. Portsmouth, N.H.: Heinemann, 1988.

Sipiora, Phillip. "Kairos in the Discourse of Isocrates." In *Realms of Rhetoric: Phonic, Graphic, Electronic*, ed. Victor J. Vitanza and Michelle Ballif, pp. 119–135. Arlington, Tex.: Rhetoric Society of America, 1990.

Sklar, Robert. *Movie-Made America: A Cultural History of American Movies*. New York: Vintage Books, 1975.

Smagorinsky, Peter. *Expressions: Multiple Intelligences in the English Class*. Urbana, Ill.: National Council of Teachers of English, 1991.

Smith-Rosenberg, Carroll. *Disorderly Conduct: Visions of Gender in Victorian America*. New York: Knopf, 1985.

Snowden, Frank M. *Before Color Prejudice: The Ancient View of Blacks*. Cambridge: Harvard University Press, 1983.

Snowden, Frank M. *Blacks in Antiquity: Ethiopians in the Greco-Roman Experience*. Cambridge: Harvard University Press, 1970.

Sontag, Susan. *On Photography*. New York: Farrar, Straus, and Giroux. 1977.

Sprague, Rosamond Kent. *The Older Sophists: A Complete Translation by Several Hands of the Fragments in "Die Fragmente der Vorsokratiker," Edited by Diels-Kranz, with a New Edition of Antiphon and of Euthydemus*. Columbia: University of South Carolina Press, 1972.

Stauffer, D. A., ed. *The Intent of the Critic*. Princeton: Princeton University Press, 1941.

Street, Brian V. *Literacy in Theory and Practice.* Cambridge: Cambridge University Press, 1984.

Sussman, Henry S. *High Resolution: Critical Theory and the Problem of Literacy.* New York: Oxford University Press, 1989.

Sutton, Jane. "The Death of Rhetoric and Its Rebirth in Philosophy." *Rhetorica* 4 (1986): 203–226.

Swearingen, C. Jan. "Bloomsday: Doomsday for Literacy?" In *The Right to Literacy,* ed. Andrea A. Lunsford, Helene Moglen, and James Slevin, pp. 215–224. New York: Modern Language Association, 1990.

Swearingen, C. Jan. "Discourse, Difference, and Gender: Walter J. Ong's Contributions to Feminist Language Studies." In *Media, Consciousness, and Culture,* ed. Bruce Gronbeck, Thomas J. Farrell, and Paul A. Soukup, pp. 210–222. Newbury Park, Calif.: Sage Publications, 1991.

Swearingen, C. Jan. "A Lover's Discourse: Diotima, Logos, and Desire." In *Reclaiming Rhetorica,* ed. Andrea A. Lunsford, pp. 25–51. Pittsburgh: University of Pittsburgh Press, 1995.

Swearingen, C. Jan. *Rhetoric and Irony: Western Literacy and Western Lies.* New York: Oxford University Press, 1991.

Thesaurus Linguae Graecae: Canon of Greek Authors and Works. 3rd ed. New York: Oxford University Press, 1990.

Thesaurus Linguae Graecae: Canon of Greek Authors and Works. University of California at Irvine. Internet: http://www.uci.edu/~tlg/, 15 May 1995.

Thomas, Rosalind. *Literacy and Orality in Ancient Greece.* Cambridge: Cambridge University Press, 1992.

Thompson, E. P. *The Making of the English Working Class.* New York: Pantheon, 1977.

Tompkins, Jane P. "An Introduction to Reader-Response Criticism." In *Reader-Response Criticism,* ed. Jane P. Tompkins, pp. ix–xxvi. Baltimore: Johns Hopkins University Press, 1980.

Tompkins, Jane P. "The Reader in History." In *Reader-Response Criticism,* ed. Jane P. Tompkins. Baltimore: Johns Hopkins University Press, 1980.

Tompkins, Jane P., ed. *Reader-Response Criticism: From Formalism to Poststructuralism.* Baltimore: Johns Hopkins University Press, 1980.

Too, Yun Lee. *The Rhetoric of Identity in Isocrates: Text, Power, and Pedagogy.* Cambridge: Cambridge University Press, 1995.

Trimbur, John. "Literacy and the Discourse of Crisis." In *The Politics of Writing Instruction,* ed. Richard Bullock and John Trimbur, pp. 277–295. Portsmouth, N.H.: Boynton/Cook Publishers, 1991.

Trimmer, Joseph, and Tillie Warnock, eds. *Understanding Others: Cultural and Cross-Cultural Studies and the Teaching of English.* Urbana, Ill.: National Council of Teachers of English, 1992.

Tuman, Myron C., ed. *Literacy Online: The Promise (and Peril) of Reading and Writing with Computers.* Pittsburgh: University of Pittsburgh Press, 1992.

Tuman, Myron C. *Word Perfect: Literacy in the Computer Age.* Pittsburgh: University of Pittsburgh Press, 1992.

Turkle, Sherry. *Life on the Screen: Identity in the Age of the Internet.* New York: Simon and Schuster, 1995.

Ulman, H. Lewis. *Things, Thoughts, Words, and Actions: The Problem of Language in Late Eighteenth-Century British Rhetorical Theory.* Carbondale: Southern Illinois University Press, 1994.

Ulmer, Gregory. *Teletheory: Grammatology in the Age of Video.* New York: Routledge, 1989.

The United States of Poetry. Video. Public Broadcasting System, 1996.

Untersteiner, Mario. *The Sophists.* Trans. Kathleen Freeman. Oxford: Basil Blackwell, 1954.

Van Hook, Larue, trans. *Isocrates.* Vol. 3. Loeb Classical Library. Cambridge: Harvard University Press, 1945.

Vasulka, Steina, and Woody Vasulka. *Machine Media.* San Francisco: Museum of Modern Art, 1996.

Vasulka, Steina, and Woody Vasulka. *Technology.* Video-art installation. San Francisco Museum of Modern Art, Feb. 1996.

Vernant, Jean-Pierre. *Myth and Society in Ancient Greece.* New York: Zone Books, 1988.

Vernant, Jean-Pierre. *Origins of Greek Thought.* Ithaca: Cornell University Press, 1982.

Vitanza, Victor J. *Negation, Subjectivity, and the History of Rhetoric.* Albany: State University of New York Press, 1997.

Vitanza, Victor J. " 'Notes' Towards Historiographies of Rhetorics; or, Rhetorics of the Histories of Rhetorics: Traditional, Revisionary, and Sub/versive." *Pre/Text* 8, (1987): 63–125.

Vitanza, Victor J., ed. *Writing Histories of Rhetoric.* Carbondale: Southern Illinois University Press, 1992.

Vitanza, Victor J., and Michelle Ballif, eds. *Realms of Rhetoric: Phonic, Graphic, Electronic.* Arlington, Tex.: Rhetoric Society of America, 1990.

Vygotsky, Lev. "The Genetic Roots of Thought and Speech." In Lev Vygotsky, *Thought and Language,* trans. Eugenia Hanfmann and Gertrude Vakar, pp. 33–51. Cambridge: MIT Press, 1962.

Vygotsky, Lev. *Mind in Society: The Development of Higher Psychological Processes.* Cambridge: Haravard University Press, 1978.

Vygotsky, Lev. *Thought and Language.* Ed. and trans. Eugenia Hanfmann and Gertrude Vakar. Cambridge: MIT Press, 1962. Rev. ed. edited by Alex Kozulin. Cambridge: MIT Press, 1986.

Wagner, David, ed. *The Seven Liberal Arts in the Middle Ages.* Bloomington: Indiana University Press, 1986.

Waithe, Mary Ellen, ed. *A History of Women Philosophers*, vol. 1: *Ancient Women Philosophers, 600 B.C.–500 A.D.* Dordrecht, Netherlands: Kluwer Academic Publishers, 1987.

Walker, Alice. *The Color Purple.* New York: Harcourt Brace Jovanovich, 1982.

Warnick, Barbara. *The Sixth Canon: Belletristic Rhetorical Theory and Its French Antecedents.* Columbia: University of South Carolina Press, 1995.

Watt, Ian. *The Rise of the Novel: Studies in Defoe, Richardson, and Fielding.* London: Chatto and Windus, 1957.

Welch, Kathleen E. "Autobiography and Advanced College Writing." ERIC (Educational Resources Information Center, U.S. Department of Education), ED 281 229 (1987), pp. 1–12.

Welch, Kathleen E. *The Contemporary Reception of Classical Rhetoric.* Hillsdale: Lawrence Erlbaum Publishers, 1990.

Welch, Kathleen E. "Ideology and Freshman Textbook Production: The Place of Theory in Writing Pedagogy." *College Composition and Communication* 38 (October 1987): 269–282.

Welch, Kathleen E. "Interpreting the Silent 'Aryan Model' of Histories of Classical Rhetoric: Martin Bernal, Terry Eagleton, and the Politics of Rhetoric and Composition Studies." In *Writing Histories of Rhetoric*, ed. Victor J. Vitanza, pp. 38–48. Carbondale: Southern Illinois University Press, 1992.

Welch, Kathleen E. "A Manifesto: The Art of Rhetoric." *Rhetoric Society Quarterly* 16, no. 3 (1986): 169–179.

Welch, Kathleen E. "The *Pisteis* and Composition Theory: *Ethos* in Mary McCarthy's *Memories of a Catholic Girlhood*." Unpublished essay.

Welch, Kathleen E. "Writing Instruction in Ancient Athens after 450 B.C." In *A Short History of Writing Instruction: From Ancient Greece to Twentieth-Century America*, ed. James J. Murphy, pp. 1–17. Davis, Calif.: Hermagoras Press, 1990.

Welch, Kathleen E., Cheryl Glenn, and Andrea A. Lunsford. "Histories of Feminist Rhetorics and Writing Practices." Internet: http://rossby.ou.edu/ ~femrhets, 1997.

Welch, Kathleen E., Cheryl Glenn, and Andrea A. Lunsford. "Histories of Rhetorics and Writing Practices." Paper presented to the Rhetoric Society of America, Pittsburgh, 5 June 1998.

Wells, Ida B. *Southern Horrors and Other Writings: The Anti-lynching Campaign of Ida B. Wells, 1892–1900.* Ed. Jacqueline Jones Royster. Boston: Bedford Books, 1997.

Williams, Raymond. *Keywords: A Vocabulary of Culture and Society.* 2nd ed. New York: Oxford University Press, 1983.

Williams, Raymond. *Television: Technology and Cultural Form.* New York: Schocken, 1975.

Winterowd, W. Ross. "Composition Textbooks: Publisher-Author Relationships." *College Composition and Communication* 40 (May 1989): 139–151.

Womack, Craig. "A Creek National Literature." Unpublished dissertation, University of Oklahoma, 1995.

Woodmansee, Martha. "On the Author Effect: Recovering Collectivity." In *The Construction of Authorship: Textual Appropriation in Law and Literature*, ed. Martha Woodmansee and Peter Jaszi, pp. 15–28. Durham, N.C.: Duke University Press, 1994.

Woodmansee, Martha, and Peter Jaszi, eds. *The Construction of Authorship: Textual Appropriation in Law and Literature*. Durham, N.C.: Duke University Press, 1994.

Woods, Marjorie Curry. "What Isocrates Taught/How We Teach Him. Part I." Paper presented at the Speech Communication Association, Chicago, November 1990.

Woolfe, Virginia. *Mrs. Dalloway*. New York: Harcourt, Brace, 1925.

Yates, Frances A. *The Art of Memory*. Chicago: University of Chicago Press, 1966.

Zuckert, Catherine H. *Postmodern Platos: Nietzsche, Heidegger, Gadamer, Strauss, Derrida*. Chicago: University of Chicago Press, 1996.

Zumthor, Paul. *Oral Poetry*. Minneapolis: University of Minnesota Press, 1990.

Index

African-Americans. *See* Others
Alcidamus, 36, 42
Antidosis, 110
 antidosial form of, 80 (n. 9), 87
 as apology, 56, 80
 and aptitude, 76
 dancing-bears episode of, 79
 dominant themes of, 82 (*see also*
  Isocratic *logos*; Isocratic *paideia*;
  Isocratic *philosophia*)
 epideictic features of, 48
 logos within (*see* Isocratic *logos*)
 sampling within, 37–38, 89 (n. 35)
 Sophistic identification within, 53
Arete, 4
Aristotelian rhetoric, 17–18, 113–114.
 See also Koinoi topoi, Artistotelian
 as anti-Sophistic, 56
 logic-dominant tradition of, 12, 68,
  71–72, 185
 receptions of, 33
Aristotle
 Poetics, 12 (n. 16)
 Rhetoric, 68, 114, 116
Art
 history of, 139, 201 (n. 10), 208
 reproducibility of, 111
Articulation, 70, 147, 153. *See also*
 Oralism/auralism; Thought/
 articulation binary; Writing
 as action, 22–23, 97 (*see also*
 Delivery [canon of])
 and technology, 105, 132

Aspasia, 14 (n. 19), 52, 71–72, 74, 83,
 161
Audience-response theory. *See* Reader-
 response theory

Barthes, Roland, 16
Belenky et al., *Women's Ways of
 Knowing*, 206, 209
Benjamin, Walter, *The Work of Art
 in the Age of Mechanical Reproduction*, 111
Benoit, William L., 83
Berlin, James A., 33, 40
Bernal, Martin
 and analysis of the Arnolds, 121–122
 and ancient and Aryan models, 120–
  122, 124, 128
 and *Black Athena*, 118
 receptions of, 125–127
Binary constructions, 74, 76. *See also*
 Content/form binary; Thought/
 articulation binary
 consumption versus production of
  discourse, 23, 31, 43 (n. 31), 49, 71,
  96
 high art versus low art, 27, 62, 66, 196
 literacy versus orality, 59–65, 103–
  104, 187
 public versus private, 36, 68, 71–72
 writing men versus speaking women,
  130
Bizzell, Patricia, 60, 65–66
Black Athena, 118

Black Athena Revisited, 125–126

Black English Vernacular, 48

Black Petitions for Freedom, 118. *See also* Oralism/auralism, and erasures of race

Bleich, David, 65

Bolter, Jay David, 4
  Writing Space, 108

Brandt, Deborah, 60–61, 64, 66

Burke, Kenneth, 16
  Burkean identification, 96
  Burkean parlor, 13, 139 (n. 5)
  Counter-Statement, 110, 171

Canons. *See* Classical rhetoric; Five canons of rhetoric; Literary studies

Carpenter, Rhys, 57

Carruthers, Mary, 152

Cartesian ideology, 38, 52, 69, 205. *See also* Binary constructions

CD-ROMs, 151–152, 156

Chartier, Roger, 187

Cicero, 17, 78

Classical rhetoric. *See also* Historicized rhetoric; History, feminist interventions in; Rhetoric and composition studies
  canonicity of, 19, 52, 124 (*see also* Formalism, and Heritage School)
  as comprehensive discourse theory, 44–45 (n. 33)
  exclusions of Others in, 49, 52, 77, 83–84, 91, 96, 98, 129
  five canons of, 107 (n. 21), 143–144, 149–150, 152–153
  literacy and, 13, 26, 64, 198
  reconstruction of, 32, 67, 105–106, 118
  Sophistic redeployment in, 12–13, 30–31, 72, 97, 161

Classic Hollywood Cinema, 169, 171

Classics, 20, 30–31 (n. 4), 41, 75, 81. *See also* Philology
  and racism, 124
  and resistance to current theory, 125–126

Comas, James N., 126

Commonplaces. *See Koinoi topoi*

Communication studies, 5 (n. 1), 12, 30, 75, 81

Composition studies. *See* Rhetoric and composition studies

Computers. *See also* Internet; *Koinoi topoi*, digital; Literacy, types of, computer
  and composition (*see* Writing, computer-assisted)
  and democracy, 23, 108 (n. 22)
  and digital texts, 179 (*see also* Decoding, computer images/texts)
  as narcotic, 184 (*see also* Television, as narcotic)
  user class and gender distictions of, 179

Computer software, 200
  and erasures of Others, 201, 202–203

Conference on College Composition and Communication (CCCC), 154–155, 161

Consciousness/mentalité, 14, 26
  defined, 67
  denial of, 21
  and electronic *logos*/rhetoric, 101, 104
  introduced, 8–9, 23

Content/form binary
  and bilingualism, 105
  and Isocratic receptions, 40–44, 81–82
  versus oralism/auralism, 103, 105, 107, 110, 134, 158
  and racism/sexism, 153, 206
  and *topoi*, 114
  and truncated canons, 145

Copyright law, 151–152, 204–205

Covino, William A., and David Jolliffe, "What Is Rhetoric?" 94

Critical *logos* performance. *See under* Households using television (HUTs); Isocratic *paideia*; Isocratic *philosophia*

Crowley, Sharon, 15 (n. 23), 16, 34
The Methodical Memory, 152–153
Cultural studies, 6, 155, 193, 198
Current-traditional paradigm, 15–16,
34, 71, 85, 115, 145–146, 150–151,
194, 195

Davidson, Cathy N., *Reading in
America*, 197
Decoding. *See also* Discourse
communities; Reader-response
theory
computer images/texts, 182–183,
197, 201, 208
static translations, 17
televisual, 134, 143, 157, 162, 182,
201 (*see also Koinoi topoi*,
televisual)
universalized reader, 15, 95
Deconstruction, 65
Delivery (canon of)
as action, 22
disappearance of, from canon, 144–
146, 149–150
as medium, 153–154, 158
and oralism/auralism, 143
Derrida, Jaques, 11 (n. 12), 76, 184
Diotima, 12, 52, 71–72, 74, 83, 161
erasures of, 17
receptions and repositioning of, 93–
95
as teacher of Socrates, 92
Discourse communities, 69, 95, 96,
103, 110
and language, 105, 107
and little histories, 49–50, 70, 82–83
televisual, 157–158 (*see also*
Decoding, televisual; *Koinoi topoi*,
televisual)
Doheny-Farina, Stephen, 4
Dominant culture, 16, 69–70, 151
and notion of humanities, 153–154,
206
DuBois, Page, 29

Eagleton, Terry, 45 (n. 33)

Education
colleges of, 14 (n. 19)
critique of, 51, 59
Ehninger, Douglas, 35, 53
Electric rhetoric, 10, 56, 106, 108. *See
also Koinoi topoi*, for electric
rhetoric; Next Rhetoric
defined, 104
Diotimic/Isocratic/Sophistic features
of, 75, 106, 108, 136, 187
as extension of literacy, 143, 157, 194
pedagogy for, 139–140, 160–161,
206–207
English departments, 12. *See also*
Cultural studies; Literary studies;
Rhetoric and composition studies
internal divisions of, 207
literary hegemony of, 20–21
and racist barriers, 192–193
and resistance to video, 5–6
WASPness of, 182 (n. 56)
Enos, Richard Leo, 12, 72

Feminist theory. *See* History, feminist
interventions in; Others
Femrhets (website), 177, 181, 182. *See
also* Histories of Feminist Rhetorics
and Writing Practices (university
course)
oral features of, 184–186
Film studies. *See* Television, and video
studies
First-year writing programs. *See*
Freshman writing programs
Five canons of rhetoric, 107 (n. 21),
143–144, 149–150. *See also*
Delivery (canon of); Memory (canon
of); *NBC Nightly News with Tom
Brokaw*, arrangement of; Style
(canon of)
including memory and delivery, 152–
153
Fogarty, Daniel, 15
Foley, John Miles, 113
The Theory of Oral Composition,
110

Formalism, 17, 21, 41, 71, 131. *See also* Current-traditional paradigm
aesthetic, 66
and Heritage School, 17, 24, 123, 125
New Critical, 28, 56, 84–85, 88, 96, 115, 194, 195
and resistance to oralism, 88–89
and strong-text interpretation, 60–64, 66, 68
Foucault, Michel, 16, 77
Freshman writing programs, 20, 54, 134
advancing digital literacy in, 139–140
and freshman writing requirement, 207

Gender constructions. *See* Others
Glenn, Cheryl, 13, 72, 131, 177–178
Rhetoric Retold, 94
Goody, Jack, 60, 104, 187
Gorgias
Encomium of Helen, 101, 137–138
and *logos* as drug, 167, 184
as outsider, 36 (n. 16), 205
receptions of, 52, 78
Great-divide theory. *See also* Binary constructions, literacy versus orality; Isocratic receptions, in great-divide theory; Ongian receptions, in great-divide theory

Havelock, Eric A., 47, 55, 57–58, 60, 129, 187
Heath, Shirley Brice, 60
Heckel, David, 66
Heim, Michael, 61
Electric Language, 108
Historicized rhetoric, 14 (n. 20), 24, 73
avoidance of, 4, 53–54
racist constructions in, 117–119, 128
Histories of Feminist Rhetorics and Writing Practices (university course). *See also* Femrhets (website); Others
course aims, 178, 181–182
course listserve, 186

History, feminist interventions in. *See also* Femrhets (website); Others
and oralism/auralism, 130–131
regendering classical rhetoric, 83, 92, 93–98
History studies (Anglo-American), as objectivist, 77, 84 (n. 20), 91, 118, 128 (n. 56)
Homeric epics, 48, 57, 86, 89, 113, 142, 175, 176. *See also* Poetry, hegemony of
Households using television (HUTs), 104, 110, 204. *See also* Decoding, televisual; Discourse communities, televisual; Television
critical *logos* performance within, 136, 161–162
introduced, 101
Humanities, 5. *See also* Posthumanities/postliteracies
marginality/decline of, 15 (n. 23), 23, 109, 188, 191–192, 193
revival of, 27, 54, 135, 153, 196
right-wing attacks on, 16

Ijsseling, Samuel, 42, 68
Intellectual property. *See* Copyright law
Internet, 186. *See also* Computers; Libraries, without walls; Listserves
features of, 147, 151, 185
features of surfing, 180–181, 183
multi-user domain (MUD), 156
Irigaray, Luce, 16, 94
Isocrates, 9–10
Against Euthynus, 44
Against the Sophists, 38, 50, 53
Antidosis (*see Antidosis*)
Panathenaicus, 44
Isocratic *logos*
central in Isocrates' work, 45–46, 81
and inner speech, 35, 162
versus Platonic and Artistotelian logic, 11, 24, 32–33, 103
reductions of, 40
in writing, 49

Isocratic *paideia*
aptitude within, 51–52
and critical *logos* performance, 71–72
defined, 10, 12, 47
five-part system of, 51, 79
in fourth-century B.C.E. Greece, 36–37
and healthy culture, 91
versus Plato's *paideia*, 31–32
Isocratic *philosophia*
and critical *logos* performance, 70, 103, 106
as development of judgment, 38–40, 43–44
versus Plato's philosophy, 31–32
Isocratic receptions
in consciousness theory, 66–68
in formalist theory, 40–41, 50 (n. 42), 56, 68, 88–89
in fourth-century B.C.E. Greece, 87, 90
Isocrates as developer of general education, 40, 69
Isocrates as educationist, 73
Isocrates as "father" of liberal arts, 40, 42–43, 90
in great-divide theory, 64–66
philological, 39–40, 46–47, 50, 77–79, 82–83, 91
Sophistic, 10, 31, 47–48
Isocratic rhetoric
and commonplaces, 102 (*see also* *Koinoi topoi*)
against instrumentalism of language, 41–42, 51
oral features of, 37–38, 48, 64–65, 80, 85–86, 88–89 (*see also* Oral-formulaic theory)
and prose development, 9, 31, 37–38, 90–91, 177

Jaeger, Werner, 56, 68, 77–78, 82–83
Jameson, Fredric, 66
Jamieson, Kathleen Hall, 140–141
Jarratt, Susan C., 12, 30, 69, 72

Jebb, R. C., 39, 50, 68, 70, 79
Johnson, Nan, 95

Kaufer, David, and Kathleen Carley, *Communication at a Distance*, 200
Kennedy, George A.
The Art of Persuasion in Greece, 40
Classical Rhetoric, 41, 46 (n. 35), 50 (n. 42), 82
translation of Aristotle's *On Rhetoric*, 39 (n. 22)
Keuls, Eva C., 92
Keyword(s), 39 (n. 22), 45 (n. 33), 77
"consciousness" as, 67
"literacy" as, 14
"*logos*" as, 45–46
"*paideia*" as, 47
"*topos*" as, 114–115
"transformation" as, 106 (n. 15)
Kinneavy, James L., 72, 191
Knoblauch, C. H., and Lil Brannon, 35
Rhetorical Traditions and the Teaching of Writing, 123
Koinoi topoi. *See also* Isocratic rhetoric, and commonplaces; *NBC Nightly News with Tom Brokaw*, *koinos topos* analysis of
Aristotelian, 113–114, 116
digital, 179–183
for electric rhetoric, 115–116
and oral/aural features, 112–113, 116–117
televisual, 132–133, 139, 163–169, 173–175

Langer, Susanne K., 16, 68
Lanham, Richard A., 4, 208–209
The Electronic Word, 108
Lee, Spike, 191, 192
Legislation of media issues, 72–73. *See also* Telecommunications Act (1996)
copyright law, 151–152, 204–205
Lentz, Tony M., 62
Liberal arts, 127. *See also* Techno-liberal-arts
reform of, 23, 55, 70, 72–73, 119

Libraries
   democratic function of, 152
   without walls, 152, 161, 200
Listserves, 156. *See also* Histories of
   Feminist Rhetorics and Writing
   Practices (university course), course
   listserve; Internet
Literacy
   and consciousness/mentalité, 14,
      154
   definitions of, 7–8, 14, 25, 67
   history of, 57–59, 89
   and intersubjectivity, 8, 71
   and Isocratic oralism, 75
   and Next/electric rhetoric, 53, 157–
      158, 161
   and rhetoric studies, 13, 26, 64, 198
   strong-text view of, 60–61
   and technology, 7, 14–15, 30, 67,
      72
Literacy, types of
   alphabetic, 113
   anthropological, 60
   computer, 139, 154–155, 197, 199
   craft, 89
   cultural, 68
   functional, 8, 26
   print, 21, 102, 107–108, 117, 131
   school, 23, 27
   screen (television and computer), 3–
      4, 14, 72, 101–102
   televisual, 160–161
Literary studies, 19–20
   of American literature, 63
   Arnoldian stance of, 121, 127
   canonicity of, 17, 62, 68, 145 (*see
      also* Formalism)
   critique of, 96
   Romanticism of, 28, 32, 54, 69 (*see
      also* Writing, pseudoromantic
      perceptions of)
Logos. See under Aristotelian rhetoric;
   Isocratic *logos*; Isocratic
   philosophia; Platonic rhetoric
Lord, Albert Bates, 59–60
Lunsford, Andrea A., 16, 177, 204

McLuhan, Marshall, 37 (n. 18), 101–
   102 (n. 4)
Memory (canon of), 86, 107–108
   disappearance of, from canon, 144–
      146, 149–150
   new interpretations of, 152–153
   and repeatability, 110, 134
Middleton, Joyce Irene, 66
Miller, Susan, 16
Modernism, 20
   critique of, 62
   and technology, 206
Morrison, Toni, 63–64
Murphy, James J., 33, 40

National Council of Teachers of
   English (NCTE), *Guidelines for
   Nonsexist Use of Language*, 209
National Endowment of the
   Humanities (NEH), 201–202
Native North Americans, 22, 57, 63
   (n. 64), 147, 186. *See also Origin
   Myth of Acoma*
   and oralism/auralism, 141–142
NBC Nightly News with Tom Brokaw
   arrangement of, 171
   encoders of, 165–166
   ethos of, 165–166, 170, 172
   koinos topos analysis of, 163–167
   narrative line of, 168–169
   and oral-formulaic theory, 169–170,
      172–173, 175–177
   racist elements of, 173–175
   Sophistic features of, 166–167
Neel, Jasper, 141
New Criticism, 28, 56, 84–85, 88, 96,
   115, 194, 195
Next Rhetoric
   features of, 134
   humanities reformed by, 54–55, 207
   introduced, 53–55
   reraced/regendered, 119, 129
Nietzsche, Friedrich, 31
Nomos/physis constructions, 21
   defined, 127 (n. 55)
   and historicizing, 119, 139 (n. 5)

and marginalization of Others, 51–52, 82–83, 93–94, 127–128, 202
Nonsexist language, 39 (n. 22). *See also* National Council of Teachers of English (NCTE), *Guidelines for Nonsexist Use of Language*
Norlin, George, 39–40, 46–47, 50, 68, 70, 77–78, 80 (n. 9), 82–83
North, Stephen M., 123

Olson, David R., 60, 187
Ong, Walter J.
  and gender issues, 55, 129 (n. 58)
  and language acquisition, 130
  Orality and Literacy, 29, 37 (n. 18), 55, 59, 65
  Presence of the Word, 59
  and primary orality, 57–59, 65
  Ramus, Method, and the Decay of Dialogue, 55
  Rhetoric, Romance, and Technology, 59
  and secondary orality, 25, 55, 58–59, 65
Ongian receptions
  in consciousness theory, 61–64
  in great-divide theory, 60–61
Oral-formulaic theory, 58, 66, 110–112, 155–156, 169–170, 172–173, 175–177
Oralism/auralism, 48, 107
  defined, 25
  and erasures of race, 117–118
  and erasures of women, 84, 97
  as intersubjective activity, 49, 70
Origin Myth of Acoma, 59, 86, 110. *See also* Native North Americans
  oral/aural features of, 142, 147, 175–176, 187
Others. *See also* Aspasia; Bernal, Martin; Diotima; Gorgias; Native North Americans
  and Black English Vernacular, 48
  and classical rhetoric, 83, 92, 93–98
  and classics, 124
  and computers, 179

and content/form binary, 153, 206
in English departments, 182 (n. 56), 192–193
exclusions of, in classical rhetoric, 49, 52, 77, 83–84, 91, 96, 98, 129
and historicism, 117–119, 128
and Next Rhetoric, 119, 129
and *nomos/physis* constructions, 51–52, 82–83, 93–94, 127–128, 202
and oralism/auralism, 84, 97, 117–118, 130–131
and posthumanities/postliteracies, 195
representations of, in software, 201, 202–203
and Walter J. Ong, 55, 129 (n. 58)
and writing men versus speaking women binary, 130

Perseus (software), 200
Philology, 20, 77, 91, 118. *See also* Classics; Isocratic receptions, philological
Philosophy (Anglo-American), 11–12, 72, 75
  Platonic origins of, 35 (n. 12), 38–39
Pisteis, entechnic, 52, 173
Plato
  Apology, 35 (n. 12)
  Phaedrus, 71, 81, 94
  Symposium, 92, 94–95
Platonic rhetoric
  as anti-Sophistic, 56
  hegemony of, 7, 11, 39, 68
  paradoxical relationship of, to writing, 86
  receptions of, 35 (n. 12), 90
Poetry, hegemony of, 11, 48, 79, 177, 205. *See also* Homeric epics
Porter, James E., 97
Posthumanities/postliteracies, 6, 9, 154, 207. *See also* Techno-liberal-arts
  and foreign-language training, 198–199
  goals of, 207–210
  reracing and regendering disciplines in, 195

Postmodernism, 6, 136
  and video, 162–163
Poulakos, John, 12, 47
Poulakos, Takis, 12, 69
Print, 159, 188, 197
  in electric rhetoric, 200–201
  hegemony of, 152, 160, 188
  literacy, 21, 102, 107–108, 117,
  131
Prosopopoeia, 84 (n. 20), 138
Protagoras, 36 (n. 16), 52, 71, 167

Quadrivium, 41 (n. 27), 72
Quintilian, 14 (n. 19), 91, 130, 209

Racism. *See* Others
Ramus, Petrus, 14 (n. 19), 21 (n. 34),
  53–54, 81, 149–150, 193
Ransom, John Crowe, 56
Reader-response theory, 45 (n. 33)
  applied to classical rhetoric, 95–98
  and households using televisions
  (HUTs), 110
  problems with, 97
Representation (mimesis), 4, 8
Rhetoric. *See also* Aristotelian rhetoric;
  Classical rhetoric; Electric rhetoric;
  Historicized rhetoric; Isocratic
  rhetoric; Next Rhetoric; Platonic
  rhetoric; Sophistic rhetoric
  canons of, 107 (n. 21), 143–144,
  149–150, 152–153
  as decoration, 21 (n. 34), 82
  defined, 109, 194
  eighteenth- and nineteenth-century,
  30 (n. 3)
  origins of, 112 (n. 31)
  pejorative use of term, 150 (n. 24)
Rhetoric and composition studies, 5
  (n. 1), 14 (n. 19), 27 (n. 46), 117,
  193. *See also* Writing
  agenda of, 50, 73, 135, 154, 198
  central to humanities, 23, 188
  graduate programs in, 20
  pedagogical commitment of, 14
  (n. 19), 26, 73, 208

Rhetoric of television. *See* Electric
  rhetoric; Television, rhetoricity of
Rosenblatt, Louise, 95

Said, Edward, 126
Sappho, 14 (n. 19), 52
Schiappa, Edward, 12
Schilb, John, 19
Selfe, Cynthia L., 4
  *Computer-Assisted Instruction in
  Composition*, 108
Semiotics, 36, 65, 85
Snowden, Frank M., *Before Color
  Prejudice*, 128
Socrates, 71, 74
  as construction of Plato, 84 (n. 20),
  94
Sophistic rhetoric. *See Antidosis*,
  Sophistic identification within;
  Classical rhetoric, Sophistic
  redeployment in; Electric rhetoric,
  Diotimic/Isocratic/Sophistic features
  of; Isocratic receptions, Sophistic;
  *NBC Nightly News with Tom
  Brokaw*, Sophistic features of
Sophists. *See* Alcidamus; Aspasia;
  Diotima; Gorgias; Isocrates;
  Protagoras
Status quo. *See* Dominant culture
Street, Brian V., 104, 135 (n. 70)
Style (canon of), 163
  divorced from ideology, 81–82, 149–
  150
Sussman, Henry S., 61–66, 68, 86, 135
  High Resolution, 141, 157
Swearingen, C. Jan, 12, 68, 72, 93,
  192
  "A Lover's Discourse," 94
  Rhetoric and Irony, 191

Techno-liberal-arts, 54, 73. *See also*
  Posthumanities/postliteracies
  pedagogy for, 134
Telecommunications Act (1996), 158–
  159 (n. 30), 195, 208 (n. 18). *See
  also* Legislation of media issues

Telecommunications conglomerates, 188–189, 194–195, 205, 208 (n. 18)
Television. *See also* Decoding, televisual; Discourse communities, televisual; Households using television (HUTs); *Koinoi topoi*, televisual
 and allegory, 133
 as kitsch/déclassé, 62–63, 104, 112, 135, 157, 196
 as narcotic, 167
 and oral-formulaic theory, 111–112, 169–170
 and oralism/auralism, 25, 101, 102, 109, 132
 pedagogy for, 5 (n. 1), 134, 196
 research of, 5 (n. 1)
 rhetoricity of, 13, 104 (n. 12), 139 (*see also* Electric rhetoric)
 and sight bites, 163–164, 170
 and sound bites, 101–102, 170
 texts (content) of, 158, 164, 166
 and video studies, 5–6, 26, 139, 208
Textbooks. *See* Writing textbooks
Thought/articulation binary
 and classical-rhetoric receptions, 17–18, 45
 and formalism, 27, 41
 and Isocrates, 34–35, 51
 versus language production, 22–23
 and Vygotsky, 67
 and writing programs, 70, 114
Tompkins, Jane P., 19, 45 (n. 33)
 The Reader in History, 96
Trivium, 41, 72
Truth, Sojourner, 181
Tuman, Myron C., 4
 Word Perfect, 109
Turkle, Sherry, 183
 Life on the Screen, 137

Ulmer, Gregory, *Teletheory*, 107–108

Van Hook, Larue, 39, 46–47
Vernant, Jean-Pierre, 205
Video

and repeatability, 110
 studies (*see* Television, and video studies)
 and transformation of literacy, 10, 109
Vitanza, Victor J., 12, 121
Vygotsky, Lev, 49, 67, 103 (n. 8)
 Genetic Roots of Thought and Speech, 22
 and language acquisition, 130

Waithe, Mary Ellen, 93–95, 97
Welch, Kathleen E., *The Contemporary Reception of Classical Rhetoric*, 16
Wells, Ida B., 181–182
Williams, Raymond, *Television, Technology, and Cultural Form*, 138–139
Women. *See* Others
Woods, Marjorie Curry, 73
World Wide Web. *See* Internet
Writing
 abstraction (disembodiment) of, 38, 57
 bromides of, 54
 computer-assisted, 108–109, 161
 and expressivism, 36 (n. 14), 90, 136
 hegemony of, 84, 86
 pseudoromantic perceptions of, 54, 69
 as secondary activity, 16, 20–21, 115, 149 (*see also* Thought/articulation binary)
 student, 5, 97–98, 112 (n. 30), 134, 141 (n. 9), 159 (*see also* Freshman writing programs)
Writing textbooks
 for electric rhetoric, 150–152, 154
 and forms of electronic discourse, 158–160
 production and consumption of, 147–149
 on the Internet, 151–152

Yates, Frances A., *The Art of Memory*, 152